Sven Ludvig Lovén

On Pourtalesia

A genus of Echinoidea

Sven Ludvig Lovén

On Pourtalesia
A genus of Echinoidea

ISBN/EAN: 9783337345082

Printed in Europe, USA, Canada, Australia, Japan

Cover: Foto ©Andreas Hilbeck / pixelio.de

More available books at **www.hansebooks.com**

ON
POURTALESIA
A GENUS OF ECHINOIDEA

BY

SVEN LOVÉN.

WITH TWENTY ONE PLATES.

COMMUNICATED TO THE R. SWEDISH ACADEMY OF SCIENCES JUNE 11 1879 AND JUNE 7 1882.

STOCKHOLM, 1883.
KONGL. BOKTRYCKERIET.
P. A. NORSTEDT & SÖNER.

When Alexander Agassiz made known the results obtained from the dredgings in deep water executed in the year 1868 between Cuba and the Florida Reef by the late Count Louis-François de Pourtalès,[1]) there was, among numbers of Echinoidea then for the first time brought to light, none that excited more wonder and curiosity than the very singular animal described under the doubly appropriate name of Pourtalesia miranda Al. Ag. Nor was the interest its strange and abnormal aspect awakened in any way lessened, when the same author, in his great work on the Echinoidea,[2]) gave a description, accompanied with figures drawn by himself, and the late Sir Charles Wyville Thomson, shortly afterwards, added two new species, Pourtalesia Jeffreysi and P. phiale, and at the same time threw fresh light upon several important points in the structure of the former of these.[3])

Alexander Agassiz had the extraordinary kindness to lend me, for inspection and study, his unique specimen of Pourtalesia miranda. Such is, however, the excessive thinness and fragility of this species, that I did not feel warranted to do more than subject it to repeated, but superficial examination, confirming the general accuracy of the original description and figures, and to speculate, during the long time it was allowed to remain with me, upon the presumable morphological relations existing between the parts composing its skeleton and the corresponding parts in the other Echinoidea, which had then for several years been to me a subject of some study.

In the mean time my Norwegian friends, in the course of their well-planned and highly successful survey, on board the Steamer »Vöringen», of the Hydrography and Biology of the North Atlantic, had the good fortune to fall in with a habitat of Pourtalesia Jeffreysi, and, with a liberality I cannot too amply acknowledge, through one of their staff, Dr D. C. Danielsen of Bergen, placed at my disposal several more or less uninjured specimens as well as some fragments of that species, and thus afforded me the long wished for opportunity of examining, fully and at leisure, the most extraordinary Echinoid hitherto known.

I have also to express my deep obligations to the late Sir Wyville Thomson, who most kindly came to my aid with a few specimens of Pourtalesiæ collected

---

[1]) Preliminary Report on the Echini and Starfishes dredged in deep water between Cuba and the Florida Reef, by L. F. de Pourtalès, Assist. U. S. Coast Survey; prepared by Alexander Agassiz. Bulletin of the Museum of Comparative Zoology, Cambridge, I, N:o 9, Oct. 1869, p. 272.
[2]) Illustrated Catalogue of the Museum of Comparative Zoology at Harvard College. N:o VII. Revision of the Echini by Alexander Agassiz, p. 344, Pl. XVIII.
[3]) Wyville Thomson, the Depths of the Sea, p. 108, fig. 12. — On the Echinoidea of the »Porcupine» Deep-sea Dredging Expeditions. Phil. Trans. Roy. Soc. London, Vol. 164, pt. 2, p. 747, pl. LXX, LXXI.

by the Challenger Expedition, and described by ALEXANDER AGASSIZ.[1]) When they arrived, the description of P. Jeffreysi was long finished and the five first plates engraved. Although the specimens were in a very fragmentary condition, they permitted me to add some facts of importance.

In the following pages I have laid down the results of my studies on the materials thus afforded, and also some observations, old and new, on certain particulars in the structure of other Echinoidea that have not hitherto met with the attention they deserve, and the knowledge of which is necessary in order fully to appreciate the remarkable characteristics of the Pourtalesiae.

I. GENERAL FORM OF THE SKELETON.

The skeleton of the Echinoidea, its terminology, bilateral symmetry, antero-posterior axis, and peristomal formula. The skeleton of Pourtalesia.

In the whole of the Echinoidea the skeleton is a hollow sack inclosing the visceral cavity, and constituted by the three distinct systems: the perisomatic or interradial, the ambulacral, and the calycinal or apical, all simultaneously present in the adult animal, and in view outwardly. Each of these systems is composed of a number of more or less flattened ossicles of definite outline, contiguous and arranged in regular order, rarely imbricated, and consisting in most cases of a calcified, reticular and rigid tissue, continually in a state of resorption and renewal, and extending between the dermal tegument with its dependencies, and the subjacent connective tissue with the peripheral nerves, on the outside, and the peritoneal lining of the visceral cavity, on the inside.

For the sake of brevity I shall here, as in my former work,[2]) designate by numbers the divisions of each of these systems. Thus among the five ambulacra the one which is anterior and frontal will be marked III, the two on its right II and I, and the two on its left IV and V. The interradial areas will be denoted by the numbers 1 to 5, counting from the lateral right hand one, 1, to the posterior odd one, 5. Within the calycinal system the ossicles contiguous to the ambulacra will bear the corresponding numbers of these: I ... V, while those adjoining the interradia will be numbered accordingly, 1 ... 5. It is of course altogether indifferent how these numbers are applied from the first, provided only the order once chosen be adhered to. It seemed convenient to make the recognised frontal ambulacrum of the Exocyclic number III, from its having a medial position relatively to each of the two pairs, II and IV, I and V, and from III being the mean of I + V as of II + IV.

[1]) Proc. Amer. Acad., XIV, 1879, p. 265. — Report on the Echinoidea of the Voy. of the Challenger, p. 124.
[2]) Études sur les Echinoidées. K. Sv. Vetenskaps-Akademiens Handlingar. Vol. XI, N:o 7. With 53 plates. Stockholm 1874.

As far as the skeleton of the Echinoidea has been subjected to a somewhat accurate and detailed investigation, it has invariably come to light that it is in no wise to be regarded as a radiate structure in the sense of the Cuvierian System, but that its constituent elements are, in reality and fundamentally, arranged bilaterally and symmetrically on the two sides of a mesial plane indicated by its antero-posterior axis. The completely bilateral structure of the larva is in reality never totally discarded in the adult, though profoundly obscured. With the bilateral conformation in the adult we have long been familiar, manifest as it is in the later forms of the Archaeonomous[1]) type, for instance in the Clypeastridae, of Cenozoic origin, and in the whole of the Neonomous[2]) type, as in the Spatangidae, known to us from the Cretaceous period and onward, and in the other forms called Irregular, that come into view during the Mesozoic time. But when we trace back the Echinoidean type into still older periods, those manifestly symmetrical forms are lost, and the class is represented solely by the Cidaridae and others, in which the perfectly circular ambitus of the test and the apparent similarity of all the five ambulacra as also of the interradial areas of the perisome to one another, are such as seemingly to exclude any idea of their skeletal elements being subject to bilateral symmetry. Nevertheless, and whatever may have been the case with their predecessors, the little known Perischo-echinidae, a closer inspection reveals in the antique Cidaridae and their allies a bilateral mode of conformation concealed beneath the deceptive appearance of radiate disposition, exactly identical with that plainly in force in all the rest of the Echinoidea, recent as well as fossil, at present known.[3]) This is another instance of the validity of one of the laws more than once ascertained to underlie evolution, namely that structures which are to be gradually, but forcibly worked out during the course of geological ages into specialised and highly characteristic features, are virtually present within the fabric of the earlier forms, though dormant and, as it were, lying in abeyance, and to be detected only by a close scrutiny. Such is the case with the antero-posterior axis of the Echinoidean skeleton. In the Exocyclic it manifestly divides lengthwise one of the five ambulacra and the opposite interradial area, and the stomo-proctic axis lies in its plane. In most of these forms the ambulacrum which thus becomes the frontal one, III, at its aboral, that is dorsal termination has on its right the one among the ossicles of the calycinal system which in the adult is permeated by the madreporic apparatus, or through which, in the young, this begins to break out from the interior. Now in the Endocyclic forms, of antique origin, which have the stomo-proctic axis vertical and ending dorsally with piercing in its middle or sideways the dismembered central ossicle, the madreporal filter is invariably and permanently restricted to one of the calycine ossicles alone. To any one believing in the consistency of nature's ways, there is no reason whatever for doubting that this ossicle is strictly homologous to the one which, in the Exocyclic, harbours the madreporite. Acting upon this legitimate supposition Desor and Cotteau in their important works, differing in this point from Johannes Müller, and from Louis Agassiz, invariably adjusted conformably to it all the forms

---

[1]) Ἀρχαιόνομος, old-fashioned. [2]) Νέος, new, νόμος, custom, law. [3]) Études, p. 11–46.

described, regular and irregular. And that such and such alone is the true and normal position necessarily to be maintained in every case, and to be neglected only at the risk of creating confusion, is proved beyond the possibility of a doubt by the circumstance, that the peristomal formulæ:

$$I\ a,\ II\ a,\ III\ b,\ IV\ a,\ V\ b,$$
$$I\ b,\ II\ b,\ III\ a,\ IV\ b,\ V\ a,$$

in the third and fifth members of which a is changed into b and, invertedly, b into a, and which are of universal validity in the irregular forms, hold good with equal consistency in the Endocyclic, but solely and exclusively on that one of the ambulacra which has the madreporite on its right, being recognised as the front ambulacrum, III, and placed foremost, and in no other position whatever [1]). Then the five ambulacra, similar to one another as they apparently are, separate into the trivium, II, III, IV, and the bivium, I, V, while the peristome, traversed potentially by the antero-posterior axis, though in most genera it remains strictly circular or pentagonal, in others, for instance in Heterocentrus and Colobocentrus, is seen to deviate slightly from the regular form, and that precisely in the direction of this same axis, so as to present a distinctly deeper incurvation between the two ambulacra of the bivium, without regard to the direction of the longitudinal axis [2]).

All this will now be perfectly clear, and it may perhaps seem little worth mentioning that if any two different forms of Echinoids are compared together with regard to their peristomal formulæ, the sequence of the terms of these will invariably be the same in both, provided that the counting is begun at homologous points. If, on the contrary, while in the Exocyclic Echinoid the undisputed frontal is maintained as III, in the Endocyclic any other ambulacrum except that which has the madreporite on its right is tried, the formulæ will disagree all around, until that ambulacrum becomes the frontal, III. Then the two formulæ, the Endocyclic and the Exocyclic, will at once coincide, thereby proving the adjustment to be true. All this is self-evident, and in no way affects the significance of the formulæ relatively to the determination of the antero-posterior axis.

The normal form of the single plates that compose the perisomatic and ambulacral systems is the hexagonal, which regularly manifests itself, whenever the growth of the plate is not affected in consequence of its being appropriated to some special use or by pressure from other plates of its own system or from contiguous plates of other systems.

In regard to these general features: the distinctness of the three systems, their bilateral disposition, the division of the ambulacral in a bivium and a trivium, the normally hexagonal form of the plates, Pourtalesia Jeffreysi and its allies accord with the other Echinoidean types and approach the Spatangidæ.

In its general form, *Pl. 1*, Pourtalesia Jeffreysi is very unlike any other Echinoid hitherto met with. When placed with the oral end foremost and so as to be seen in its dorsal, *fig. 1*, or ventral aspect, *fig. 2*, its skeleton presents an outline which

[1]) Études, p. 19, 20, 27, 29, 36. [2]) Ib., p. 26, pl. XVIII, f. 157, 158.

has been well compared to that of an inverted short-necked bottle, while in the side view, *fig. 3*, the front line appears bluntly truncated, and the dorsal line, slightly more convex than the ventral, is separated from it behind by a deep depression, beyond which the test is ventrally produced in a short, contracted, depressed, and truncated caudal prolongation. The back, in nearly its anterior half, is uniformly vaulted from side to side, in its posterior half rather more convex, and raised along the middle-line into a distinct keel, which is continued and somewhat more prominent on the caudal prolongation. The ventral surface is slightly tumid a little before and again a little behind the middle. All around the front the test is suddenly bent inward and backward, *fig. 2*, so as to form a deep ovoidal recess projecting into the peritoneal cavity, *Pl. III, fig. 10, 12; IV, 18, 19*; and, as this incurvation takes place on the ventral side farther back than on the dorsal, or at about one sixth of the entire length and a little behind the stoma, the ventral margin of the recess lies at the hindmost part of a parabolic depression or sinus, the depth of which seems to vary somewhat. At its bottom and close within the ventral margin is the oesophageal opening of the alimentary canal, *Pl. III, fig. 12; IV, 18, 19, 20*.

The excretory opening is at the bottom of the hinder depression, *Pl. 1, fig. 4; III, 13*, and the stomo-proctic axis makes an acute angle with the antero-posterior and longitudinal axis.

The whole of this anomalous configuration appears, as though it were the result of the dorsal portion of the body having moved forward beyond the normal measure, and so as to leave behind the subanal part of the ventral portion, and as though its forepart, produced into a rostrum projecting ventrally and compressed from both sides, had been drawn in, by invagination, into the peritoneal cavity, its bridge thereby having become the highest part of the hollow thus formed.

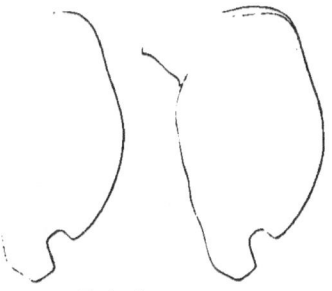

The imaginary rostrum
invaginated   protruding.

The vertical transverse section of the test, a little behind its middle, is somewhat elliptic and slightly higher than broad, the dimensions of the whole being

	Specimen 1.	Sp. 2.	Sp. 3.	Wyv. Thomsons sp.
Length	36 mm.	34 mm.	31 mm.	45 mm.
Breadth	18 »	18 »	15,5 »	28 »
Height	19 »	19 »	16 »	20 »

The greatest breadth lies a little higher up than the longitudinal axis, and the greater half of the section therefore belongs to the ventral surface.

The lengthened body and its nearly circular section distantly recall the cylindroid form of the Holothuriæ. Among the Echinoids the Spatangi alone offer anything like it, although the resemblance at last turns out slight enough. Nor is it to their oldest forms that we have to go in search of it. On their first appearance, as the Cretaceous period dawns upon us, the Spatangidæ, universally Adete or Prymnadete, that is: devoid of fascioles or provided with a peripetalous or lateral one only, but never with a subanal fasciole, were of a short and high, or globose form, as though not very far removed from a pristine spheroidal type still unseen by us. Genera such as Hemiaster Desor, powerfully developed and abundant in species, prevailed in the Cretacean seas; in all of them the vertical dimension was considerable relatively to the transverse, even so as to exceed it, andt he longitudinal dimension did not very largely surpass the transverse. The dorsal and ventral halves of the test were generally conformable in outline, the ventral being even more or less convex, the front ambulacrum was rarely deep, the periproct sub-dorsal, and the stomo-proctic axis made with the longitudinal a not very acute angle. The thickset form of these antique Spatangi strongly contrasts with the elongated build of Pourtalesia Jeffreysi. Nor is it that the contrast becomes less striking, when in a few genera of the middle Cretaceous time the calycinal part of the test is strongly raised, and at the same time drawn forward so as to make the front almost vertical, as is the case in certain species of Cardiaster and the closely allied Infulaster Hagenow. Of this remarkable form I have been able, through the kindness of Dr C. A. Dohrn of Stettin, to compare a cast [1]. At the first glance there seems to be some little resemblance to Pourtalesia, in the convexity of the ventral surface, in the vertically raised forepart with its slightly sunk ambulacral groove and in the caudal part projecting a little beyond the anal region, a feature shared in a higher degree by some Cassidulidæ. But with these really unessential features the resemblance ceases, and, as will be seen hereafter, Pourtalesia in characteristics of primary importance departs very far from those Cretaceous types. Nor is this dissimilarity diminished in any respect when in the course of geological time great changes are seen going on in the structure and general conformation of the Spatangean type, and other forms are introduced, Prymnadete as well as Prymnodesmic, thoroughly different from their predecessors, in the calycinal system opening posteriorly [2] for the reception of the restored central piece and costal 5, and in the test discarding the high and thickset build, and assuming more and more the lengthened and depressed form with a flattened ventral surface, prevalent among the Tertiary, and still more among the existing species. But in the whole number of forms, in which this change has been brought about, there is not one that comes near Pourtalesia in the cylindroid build of its skeleton, and the shortness of its frontal part as defined by the paired ambulacra of the trivium, compared to the lengthening of its hinder and by far greater portion.

It is also in vain looking among the older Spatangidæ for anything that may be said to resemble that most striking feature, the bending in upon itself of the test, by which the deep infra-frontal recess is produced, with the oesophageal opening at its bottom. Among those forms that first come in sight, in the oldest Cretacean beds, Anancites [3] has the five ambulacra all nearly uniform, the front ambulacrum differing

[1] The collections once made by Fr. v. Hagenow (b. 1797, d. 1865), who was blind during the last eight years of his life, at present form part of the Pomeranian Museum at Stettin. Dr C. A. Dohrn and his son Dr H. Dohrn were good enough to search it for the original specimen of Infulaster, but without success. Casts in plaster of Paris were however found, evidently taken from it.
[2] Études p. 12, 83. [3] Ib., pl. XXIV. fig. 181.

very slightly from the four paired ones. In the other Adetes sharing with Anancites the want of a compact sternum, the front ambulacrum is already distinct in outline and in structure; thus in Hemipneustes, Holaster [1]), Cardiaster. Then Prymnadete genera make their appearance, in which the paired ambulacra in their dorsal petaloid portions, subservient to respiration, are more or less deeply sunk, thus setting forth the bilateral structure of the body, while the forepart, which heads its movements, assumes a form of its own, allowing the front ambulacrum, with its more or less specialised, often highly extensible pedicels, to sink more or less deep between the interradia 2 and 3. It was at the close of the Cretaceous time, and in the beginning of the Tertiary period, that this peculiar independence in form of the front ambulacrum was freely developed, and the older times have little comparable to the excess it attains in the species of Schizaster [2]), Tertiary and recent, and in the strangely resembling deep-sea form, Aceste bellidifera Wyv. Thoms [3]). In these a more or less considerable portion of the front ambulacrum is deeply sunk, so as to protrude inwardly into the peritoneal cavity. But this depression begins near the calycinal system, hanging down from the roof, and, bulging in its middle part, continues decreasing towards the vicinity of the mouth. In Pourtalesia, on the contrary, it is the ventral portion, from behind the mouth and onwards, that is inverted so as to rise from the floor of the general cavity, carrying along with it the peristome and the lip, and raising them into a vertical position, so as to make nearly a right angle with the antero-posterior axis.

It is from the skeleton of Pourtalesia Jeffreysi that this description is taken. In its principal terms it applies also to the other species of the group, to the somewhat slenderer P. miranda; the more elongated P. phiale Wyv. Thoms, with its widely gaping infra-frontal recess; the broad P. hispida Al. Ag.; the more tumid P. lagunculla Al. Ag. and P. carinata Al. Ag., and even to the stout P. ceratopyga Al. Ag. with its strongly expanded forepart. The two other members of the group, both apparently Adete, the ovoid Spatagocystis Challengeri Al. Ag. with but a short caudal prolongation, and the triangular gibbous Echinocrepis cuneata Al. Ag. with the broad forepart and the subventral periproct, are linked to Pourtalesia by more than one characteristic, but mainly by that most singular one, the deep infra-frontal recess.

Thus with regard to the general form of the skeleton there is not one among all the known genera of Spatangidæ, and still less among the other groups of Echinoidea, to which the Pourtalesiæ bear any closer relation. In that respect, as in most others, they stand alone at present.

---

[1]) Études, pl. XXV, fig. 182.
[2]) Comp. Schizaster antiquus Cotteau, Bull. Soc. Géol., VI, 567.
[3]) Voyage of the Challenger, I, 376. — Al. Agassiz. Rep. Chall Echinoidea, 197. pl. XXXII, fig. 7 11, XXXIII a fig. 1—7, etc.

II. THE PERISOMATIC SYSTEM.

The perisomatic system in the Cystoidea and in the Echinoidea. The anomalous disposition of its elements in the Pourtalesiadæ approaching to annulose differentiation; the heteronomy of 1 and 4 maintained; the periproct, its position in Pourtalesia similar to its position in the Cassidulidæ. The fasciola. The spines.

The perisome is the general envelope, and the interradia — the »areæ» of Linnæan terminology — are the portions of it that are exposed to view between the ambulacra and outside the calycinal system. It alone makes up the whole skeletal sack of some Cystoidea. In Callocystites it is easily seen to be continuous under the ambulacra, which are attached solely by their first adoral plates, but otherwise free. Its sutures are clearly observable running under them, and its surface is marked with impressions

Callocystites Jewetti HALL.
Restored; showing the marks left on the perisome by the slightly raised ambulacra.   Ambulacrum broken away to show the marks.

caused by their backs, when at rest and reclining against it. The independent nature of the two systems cannot be more clearly indicated. Supposed then, as seems at present quite lawful, that those movable members, which in the Cystoidea bear the oral grooves issuing from the corners of the mouth, are homologous to the ambulacra — the fettered limbs — of the Echinoidea, the question arises whether it may not be possible some day by skilful manipulation to demonstrate, in some species or other, the uninterrupted continuation, under the ambulacra, of the interradia, as a very thin membrane. But this is only one of the many questions to be taken up by a thorough investigation of the histology of Echinodermata. Another is that concerning the relation of the perisomatic system to the calycinal. In the Cystoidea, — in which every trace of a calyx is wanting, at least in the adult — the basal part of the skeleton is formed by the perisome alone. It is this that has led me to inquire whether in Endocyclic Gnathostomes, where the primitive dorso-central ossicle is broken up in consequence of the eruption of the excretory opening, or, as in the case of Salenia, where a periproct is formed more or less outside that ossicle, the anal membrane which is substituted for the removed parts, may not belong to the perisomatic system, continuous under the calycinal as well as under the ambulacral system, and thus forming by itself the whole of the skeletal sack.

Being thus the principal constituent of the exterior of the Echinoidean skeleton, the perisome has a tendency to assert its supremacy, so to speak, by intervening between the two other, or even infringing upon them. I have shown how largely this takes place among the Star-fishes.[1]) In the young of Asterias glacialis the calycinal system, originally compact and complete in all its parts: central ossicle, five costals and five radials, is broken up owing to the predominant development of the perisome, by dint of which the central ossicle is replaced by an anal membrane, the five costals severed from one another almost past recovery, and the five radials moved far off to the tips of the rays. And among the Echinoidea, when in the Collyrites the ambulacra of the bivium are seen diverging from their normal position, the space left open is found to be filled by expanded interradials. Wherever there is a question of thoroughly making out the relations of the three systems combined in the Echinodermal skeleton, it is of primary importance to keep in view this ascendency of the perisomatic system, in virtue of which it is seen in more than one way, and often in a delusory manner, to mix itself with the other systems, and obscure their relations.

The Perischo-echinida are characterised by the presence in each interradium, at the ambitus, of more than two series of perisomatic plates, out of which the adambulacral alone attain to the peristome and the calycinal system. It was believed that this mode of structure was limited to the Palæozoic era, and that with the single exception of the genus Tetracidaris COTTEAU, of the Cretacean era, all the Mesozoic, Tertiary and existing Echinoidea had only two series of plates in each interradium. To this another exception has lately been added. During the latter part of the Triassic period the sea that covered Southern Tyrol was inhabited by a fauna, preserved at S:t Cassian,[2]) in which survivors from the Palæozoic era, such as Spirigera, Cyrtina, Retzia and Murchisonia, were coeval with numerous Mesozoic and modern types, then, as far as we know, appearing for the first time, and species of Orthoceras lingered among the earliest Ammonites, of an antique aspect. In this assemblage of old and new the Echinoidea were represented by numerous forms referable to Cidaris and a single Hypodiadema, and along with these by the very singular little Tiarechinus princeps (LAUBE) lately described by NEUMAYR.[3]) I am indebted to D:r FRANZ V. HAUER, and D:r DIONYS STUR, of Vienna, for the opportunity kindly offered to exa-

---

[1]) Études, p. 86, pl. LIII, fig. 256—260.
[2]) LAUBE, die Fauna der Schichten von S:t Cassian, Wiener Denkschriften, XXIV, XXV, XXVIII, XXX, 1868.
[3]) Sitzungs-Berichte d. K. Akad. d. Wiss. Wien, Abth. I, LXXXIV, Juni 1881.

mine carefully the original specimens of this species, and thus fully to confirm the description given by NEUMAYR, even on points that to him seemed dubious; *Pl. XIII, fig. 150—162*. The ambitus of the test is more or less oval, the relation between length and breadth being as 53 : 50, 48 : 48, 39 : 38. The dorsal face, almost entirely constituted by the calycinal system, is high and hemispherical, the basis flat, even concave. The antero-posterior axis, which coincides with the longitudinal, is determined by two of the ambulacra, those of the bivium, I and V, being notably closer together, almost adjoining one another, while those of the trivium are more widely separated, and by equal distances. The stoma is large, conformable to the general ambitus, and the peristoma, made up of ambulacral and interradial plates, shows no trace of notches. The ambulacra, all alike and equal, are expanded at the peristome, and, as it were, connected there by a narrow somewhat raised margin, then a little contracted, slightly expanding again, while ascending the flanks, and terminating a little above half the total height. Their zones of pores, diverging near the peristome, are simple, the plates being all primary, each bearing near the outer margin a geminous pedicellar pore, placed obliquely, the inner perforation being nearer to the adoral margin. Inside the pore there is a hemispherical tubercle, smaller and perhaps wanting near the peristome; the middle part of the ambulacrum is finely granulated.

Regarding the interradia NEUMAYR thought he observed, in each of them, a single peristomal plate, followed by three plates separated by vertical sutures. This I have verified, *fig. 152, 154*, the exceedingly fine sutures having been made to come forth distinctly, in all the five interradia of the best specimen, by keeping it immersed in a mixture of spirits and glycerine, a medium that at times is effectual on refractory specimens. The first peristomal plates are single, those of 1, 2, 3, 4 equal in breadth to the ambulacra, that of 5 considerably smaller, all of the same shape, hexagonal. The single peristomal plate is everywhere followed by three very high, laterally contiguous plates, extending to the termination of the ambulacra. Of these the middle one adorally almost equals the two lateral, and narrows upwards, while these expand. The first plate is smooth, and bears a single, central, large tubercle; the three second plates, smooth in their flattened basal portion, are each provided with a tubercle somewhat larger than that of the first, the three tubercles making a transverse row, and being connected by a distinct rounded ridge, which limits the basal surface from the ascending flanks. All the four tubercles consist of a hemispherical imperforate mamelon surrounded by a narrow, not very distinct areola. Laterally, and from a little above the tubercles, the whole dorsal face is thickly covered with oval or roundish granules, which in the interradials partly assume the appearance of vertical rows.

This disposition of the plates of the interradia is completely foreign to the Endocyclic Echinoids. A single peristomal is a characteristic proper to the Neomomous, — the Echinonei excepted —; but the triple row following it is without a parallel in the whole class. The peculiar form of the middle plate recalls, in a distant manner it is true, what is seen in certain Cystoideans, in which however it is barely possible to find out any attempt at order in the disposition of the plates of the perisome.

When from this eminently archaic form we turn at once to Pourtalesia Jeffreysi, so profoundly contrasting in every particular of its build, the five interradia are found to conform to the rule prevailing in the Neonomous Echinoids, of Mesozoic and later origin; they all consist of a double series of plates, Pl. II, fig. 9. The two anterior, 2 and 3, considerably smaller than the lateral ones, 1 and 4, are, as usual, enclosed between the frontal ambulacrum, III, and the paired ambulacra II and IV. Occupying the corners of the front, with their inner series of plates drawn in into the infrafrontal recess along with the ambulacrum III, they rise on either side, and terminate dorsally within the angles formed by the trivious ambulacra and the calycinal system. Their plates are, upon the whole, smaller than any other in the whole test. They enter the peristome each with a single plate 2 b 1, 3 a 1, Pl. II, fig. 9; III, 12; IV, 18, 19, belonging to their inner series, a long, rather narrow and flexuous plate, joining anteriorly the a 1 and b 1 of the ambulacrum III, extending along the nearly vertical sides of the stoma, and meeting ventrally and posteriorly the minute labrum marked 5, Pl. II, fig. 9; IV, 16, thus excluding from the peristome the ambulacra II and IV, 1 and V. In the same series 2 b and 3 a, this first plate is followed by a large second plate, joining its entire aboral margin, and preceding a series of ten or eleven sub-hexagonal oblong plates, soon diminished in size, and ending at the calycinal system with a small squarish or sub-pentagonal plate, Pl. II, fig. 9; V, 25, 26, 27, 28. The outer series, 2 a and 3 b, Pl. II, fig. 9; III, 12; IV, 18, 19, of ten plates, commences with a middle-sized plate, 2 a 1 and 3 b 1, having its hinder extremity inclosed between the ambulacrals II b 1, 2, 3, and IV a, 1, 2, 3, and the interradials 2 b, 1, 2, 3, and 3 a, 1, 2, 3, and thereby excluded from the peristome. It is followed by nine hexagonal plates, somewhat larger than those of 2 b and 3 a, increasing up to the fourth or fifth, then diminishing, and joining the calicynal system with an irregularly squarish terminal plate, Pl. V, fig. 25, 26, 27, 28.

The lateral interradia 1 and 4 are much more expanded, as generally in the Spatangidæ, and especially in the Prymnodesmic genera. They constitute the flanks of the body. On the dorsal surface their plates are the largest of all, and on the ventral inferior to the sternum, 5, 2, alone. By an arrangement hitherto without parallel, they commence, not, as by rule they ought, in the peristome and separately, but apart from it and jointly, in the middle of the ventral surface, Pl. I, fig. 2; II, 9; III, 10. As in most Spatangidæ, Prymnadete and Prymnodesmic, the first plate of these interradia, though properly belonging in common to both series 1 b and 1 a, 4 b and 4 a, still seems to appertain more especially to the anterior of them, 1 b and 4 a,[1]) so also in Pourtalesia Jeffreysi it is the first plates of the anterior series that alone are reciprocally contiguous, and this along the entire inner margins of their first plates, 1 7, 4 1, thus separating from one another the first and second plates of the ambulacra I and V. In the specimens from which the figures Pl. I, fig. 2, 8; II, 9; III, 10, were taken, the first plate of the interradium 4 is twice the size of 1, 1, and alone in contact with the ambulacrals I, 1 and V, 1. But in this respect there may be some variation. These

---

[1]) Etudes, pl. XXVIII—XXXVIII, XL—XLIII.

two first plates of 4 and 1 are followed in the anterior series on either side by ten or nine large oblong hexagonal, finally irregularly pentagonal or squarish plates.

The hinder series, beginning outside the seconds of the ambulacra I and V, contain each seven separate hexagonal plates, 2—8, among which the 1 *a* 3 and 4 *b* 3 are lengthened, the following slightly diminishing, and rather squarish.

But, after all, strangely displaced and brought out of their normal position in the peristome as are the lateral interradia 1 and 4 in Pourtalesia Jeffreysi, they still retain a peculiarity eminently characteristic of the Spatangidæ. In my former memoir on Echinoidea [1]) I called attention to the singular deviation invariably met with in the structure of their interradium 1, the one on the right side of the animal. In all the known genera of Prymnodesmic Spatangidæ, from the extinct Micraster of the Chalk to Lovenia,[2]) this heteronomy is so strikingly displayed as not to be overlooked. It is brought about by the constant combination of the plates 1 *a* 2 and 1 *a* 3 into one single compound plate 1 *a* 2 + 3. It is no less apparent, and effected in a similar manner in most of known Prymnadete genera, in Hemiaster, Abatus, Agassizia, Schizaster, Moira,[3]) and, among the Adete forms, in Echinospatagus.[4]) In Palæostoma[5]), exceptional in other respects also, the plates 1 *a* 2, 1 *b* 2, and 1 *b* 3 are all united into one, while Faorina and Desoria[6]) have the plates 1 *a* 2 and 1 *b* 2 compounded into one single binary plate. This same disposition holds good also in the almost extinct group of Adetes, such as Ananeites,[7]), Holaster,[8]) Cardiaster, Offaster, characterised by the plates of the interradium 5 following the labrum not being united into a shield-like double sternum, but separate, transversely pentagonal and wedge-like. In times farther back yet, among the Collyrites, there seems to have been no trace of the heteronomy.

This striking feature presents itself under a new form in Pourtalesia Jeffreysi, *Pl. I, fig. 2; II, 9; III, 10*. If in this species the plates of 4 *a* and 1 *b* are counted, there are ten in the former, and only nine in the latter. This may depend on one plate being wanting in the 1 *b* series, or on two plates having been united into one. That this latter is really the case is seen plainly enough. The two hinder series, 1 *a* and 4 *b*, consist each of eight plates, the first, marked 1, *l* and 4, *l*, belonging in common to the two series 1 *a* and 1 *b*, 4 *a* and 4 *b*. When the plates are compared one by one from side to side, as their numbers correspond, they are found symmetrically conformable and evident counterparts, from 4 *b* 8 and 1 *a* 8 to 4 *b* 3 and 1 *a* 3. But 4 *b* 2 is not conformable to 1 *a* 2, the former being distinctly hexagonal, the latter as evidently pentagonal. This is so because the former, 4 *b* 2, has to face adorally the three plates 2, 3, 4 of the series 4 *a*, while the 1 *a* 2 has to front two plates only. But the plate 4 *a* 4 evidently answers to the third in order in 1 *b*, so this latter must be marked 1 *b* 4 and the plate between it and the plate 1, *l* set down as 1 *b* 2+3. Pourtalesia laguncula AL. AG., *Pl. VI, fig. 37*, presents exactly the same heteronomous disposition of the identical plates, 1 *b: 1. 2+3. 4 = 4 a: l. 2. 3. 4.* and presumably it will be found to pervade the whole group. It seems strange that the plate 1 *b* 2+3.

[1]) Études, p. 19—52. [2]) Ib. pl. XXXII—XLIII. [3]) Ib. pl. XXVI, XXIX, XXX, XXXI. [4]) Ib. p. 58.
[5]) Ib. p. 50, pl. XXXII, fig 197. [6]) Ib. pl. XXVII, XXVIII. [7]) Ib. pl. V. fig. 51; pl. XXIV, fig. 181.
[8]) Ib. pl. XXV, fig. 182—184.

containing the matter of two plates, is so out of proportion to the plates 4 *a* 2 and 4 *a* 3 taken together, which it represents, but this is often the case also in the Spatangidæ, and, as in these so in Pourtalesia Jeffreysi, one or two among the following plates in 1 *b* to some extent compensate for the defect. And finally the position of the heteronomy in these very same plates clearly testifies, that the two remaining innermost plates of the series are really the 1, *1* and 4, *1*, and that thus these interradia, though displaced, are complete and normally constituted.

The formulæ of the heteronomy in the different groups are:

Adetes: Anancitidæ .... 1 *a* 2 + *b* 2 : 4 *a* 2 : 4 *b* 2.
Prymnadetes: Desoria, Faorina .... 1 *a* 2 + *b* 2 = 4 *a* 2 : 4 *b* 2.
    »   Heminster — Moira .... 1 *a* 2 + *a* 3 · 1 *b* 2 : 4 *b* 3.
Prymnodesmians: all the genera .... 1 *a* 2 + *a* 3 · 4 *b* 2 : 4 *b* 3.
Pourtalesia: two species .... 1 *b* 2 + *b* 3 = 4 *a* 2 : 4 *a* 3.

The union, in 1, of two plates into one, which in the great majority of the Spatangidæ takes place within the *a* series, and in the Adetes and a few Prymnadetes within both series, *a* and *b*, in the Pourtalesiæ is transferred, entirely, to the *b* series, a deviation corresponding with their remoteness in other respects. Everywhere the heteronomy is, on the right, confined to the interradium 1. Evidently connected with the obliquity represented by the axis *αω*, it is derived from some point in the larval development not yet understood, a mark, perhaps, recording the heterologous position of the young Echinus in the interior of its Pluteus.[1]

In ascending the tumid flanks of the body, the interradia 1 and 4 in Pourtalesia Jeffreysi slightly incline forward, and terminate in joining again from either side on the back, nearly at the anterior third of the entire length. *Pl. I, fig. 1; III, 11; V, 25—28*. There they end, without attaining their proper position, as by rule they ought, in contact with the calycinal system, being kept apart from it by the intervenience of the terminal plates of the odd interradium 5. Thus, while ventrally they do not, as in all other Echinoidea, take their origin separately, in the peristome, between the ambulacra I and II on the right, and IV and V on the left, so dorsally they do not terminate, as conformable to rule, isolated from one another, and at the calycinal system, but at a distance from it and uniting reciprocally. Below, they break through the bivious ambulacra; above, they disjoin the posterior odd interradium and take up among them its detached plates, and all through the space thus opened, they describe a broad perisomal belt continuously encircling the body around its middle.

Unlike the paired interradia just described, the odd posterior interradium is represented, conformably to the general rule, in the peristome of Pourtalesia Jeffreysi, by a true, though very minute labrum, 5, *Pl. II, fig. 9; IV, 16*. Its position is entirely within the incurved forepart of the test, and there it is wedged in between the first plates of the interradia 2 and 3 and the first of the ambulacra II, IV, and I, V. By the interposition of all these plates the labrum is widely separated from the seconds of 5, which here, as in the Spatangidæ, are formed into a sternum, 5, *a b* 2, *Pl. I.*

---

[1] See Études, p. 37—39, pl. XVII, fig. 140.

fig. 2; II, 9; III, 10. But in Pourtalesia this essential constituent of the ventral surface is not composed of two collateral, lengthwise suturally united plates, but compact, all of one single piece, shield-like, slightly bulging, pentagonal, widening a little anteriorly, and having its front margin faintly arcuated. Although, if taken as a whole, surpassing in size all the other plates, it is considerably smaller, relatively to the entire ventral surface, than the sternum of the Spatangidæ, but notwithstanding this and its backward position, it is at once recognised by its mesial position and its numerous crowded spines. It is followed by a pair of well defined and fairly sized episternals, somewhat lengthened, but else not unlike those of Meoma and Brissus[1]), crossed, as they ought to be, by the ventral portion of the subanal fasciola, and contracted a little posteriorly so as to form on either side, with the first pair of abdominals, *5 a 4, 5 b 4*, an open but distinct episternal angle into which are received the bivious ambulacrals I *a 4* and V *b 4*. *Pl. II, fig. 9*. By curving upward rather abruptly, *Pl. I, fig. 3*, this first pair of abdominals and of pre-anals constitute the hindermost blunted end of the test, and cause the second and third pre-anals, *5, 5* and *5, 6*, to form the dorsal, flat or even slightly concave surface of the caudal prolongation. Of these the first-named, *5, 5*, is traversed by the fasciola, *Pl. I, fig. 1, 3; II, 9*. Then come three pairs of anal plates, *5, 7, 5, 8, 5, 9, Pl. I. fig. 4*, diverging sideways to give room to the excretory opening, and having their inner margins cut out for the periproct, the two first-named forming its inward sloping sides, *Pl. I, fig. 4; III, 13*. The third, *5, 9*, turns abruptly over on the back, and is there followed by a forwards directed series of seven pairs of dorsal plates, *5,10* to *5,16* which gradually contract, *Pl. I, fig. 1; III, 11*. They are at first transverse, then somewhat squarish, at last longitudinal, all irregularly hexagonal, having one of their sides lengthened, and another hinder one very short, thus giving rise to an almost straight-looking middle suture. It is this part of the back which is raised into a distinct mesial ridge subsiding into the simple convexity of the pairs *5, 15* and *5, 16*. In these two pairs the *a* plate becomes distinctly smaller than the *b* plate, in a manner analogous to the checked growth of the corresponding plates observable in certain Spatangidæ [2]). Situated within the anterior third part of the dorsal surface, and separating from one another the terminals of the bivious ambulacra, the dorsals *16* of the interradium 5 are there met by the two lateral interradia 1 and 4, *Pl. I, fig. 1; III, 11*, joining one another from either side, and intervening with their large plates between them and the calycinal system. But it is only at the first collision that the dorsals give way. Taking advantage, as it were, of the intersecting point of the sutures of the four terminal plates of 1 and 4, the odd interradium 5 there reappears as *5, 17*, rather out of shape, and with the *a* plate still more reduced, *Pl. I. fig. 1; II, 9*, or altogether lost in the conflict, *Pl. III, fig. 11*. And when, on the further side of 1 *b 10* and 4 *a 10*, it comes forth again, its two plates, *5, 18*, have resumed their proper size and due proportions, and at the same time have attained their legitimate position in close contact with the calycinal system. Thus, in Pourtalesia Jeffreysi, the sequence of these dorsal plates of the interradium 5 is broken. From

---

[1]) Études, pl. XXXIV, XXXV. [2]) Ib., p. 60.

analogy it seems probable that the continuous series of much reduced plates which in the Collyrites connects the periproctal area with the dismembered calycinal system, and keeps asunder the interradia 1 and 4, may be found to consist of true interradials belonging to the odd posterior interradium 5.

It is important to know whether the highly anomalous disposition of the perisomatic system in Pourtalesia Jeffreysi is a peculiarity more or less characteristic of that species alone, or, like the frontal recess, a feature common to all the different forms of the group. In Pourtalesia laguncula AL. AG.[1]), *Pl. VI, fig. 37—40*, the labrum, 5, *l*, much larger than in P. Jeffreysi, excluded from the peristome, expands posteriorly, drives asunder the first plates of 1 and V, and attains the adoral ends of 1 *b l* and 1 *b 2+3*, 4 *a l* and 4 *a 2*, herein very strongly differing from the labrum of that species. But the interradia 1 and 4, expanded as in P. Jeffreysi, exhibit exactly the same disposition by uniting mesially, and forming a continual broad ring passing round the middle of the body, and where they meet dorsally from either side, their junction is completed by the interposition of detached plates of the posterior odd interradium 5, *Pl. VII, fig. 52*.

According to the figures given by AL. AGASSIZ[2]) of Spatagocystis Challengeri, its interradia 1 and 4 unite ventrally as well as dorsally, and by their interposition, and that of the ambulacra I and V, the labrum is separated from the sternum, which is very minute and narrow. Dorsally a row of plates of the interradium 5 separates them from the calycinal system.

These three forms, therefore, Pourtalesia Jeffreysi, P. laguncula and Spatagocystis Challengeri, all agree in the annular disposition of the middle region of the perisome formed by the lateral interradials 1 and 4; — but they seem to be extreme cases.

For, as far as the fragmentary condition of the specimens available has permitted me to ascertain these points, Pourtalesia carinata AL. AG.[3]) and P. ceratopyga AL. AG.[4]) as well as Echinocrepis cuneata AL. AG.[5]) differ from them in a marked manner. Like P. laguncula they all have the labrum, 5, *l*, expanding aborally. In P. carinata, *Pl. VI, fig. 42, 43, 45, 46*, as in that species, but unlike what is seen in P. Jeffreysi, the ambulacrals I, *l* and V, *l* are bi-seriate, *a* and *b*, but aborally they are not, as in P. laguncula, separated from 1 *a* and *b 2*, V *b* and *a 2*, but contiguous to them. Consequently the interradials 1 and 4 do not join one another on the mesial line, but are wholly lateral, as they ought to be. They do not, however, form part of the peristome, being excluded from it by the close contiguity of the ambulacra I and II, V and IV, but are to be seen, narrow, deformed and isolated, squeezed in between the 1 *b l* and II *a l* on the right, and the V *a l* and IV *b l* on the left, as if forced out of their proper places in the peristome. The fragment examined permits me to observe how the V and IV unite behind the 4, *l*, and how the 4, *2* makes its appearance outside the union of V *a 2* and IV *b 2*, *fig. 42, 46, 45*. On the right side, where the 1, *l* is

---

[1]) Chall. Rep. p. 137, pl. XXII *a*, fig. 7—15; XXXI, fig. 1—11. [2]) Ib. p. 141, pl. XXVI. XXVI *a*.
[3]) Ib. p. 133, pl. XXVIII *a*   [4]) Ib. p. 134. pl. XXVIII, XXXV *b*, fig. 17.   [5]) Ib. p. 143, pl. XXXII, XXXV *a*, fig. 9—13.

considerably larger, the broken test shows only the junction, behind it, of 1 *b* and II *a*. The labrum, like that of P. lagunculla, is very narrow aborally, *fig. 42—44*, — it is hard to say whether it reaches the peristome or not, *fig. 46*, — and enlarges aborally, till it meets a pair of plates that occupy exactly the place between the ambulacra I and V, regularly allotted to the sternum, 5 *a b 2*. According to AL. AGASSIZ they seem to carry spines bigger than others, on closely packed tubercles. From all this it follows that in P. carinata the interradials 1 and 4 do not join ventrally in the middle, and consequently do not form a continuous ring. Dorsally they are very much the same as those of P. laguncula.

In Pourtalesia ceratopyga, *Pl. VII, fig. 48, 49, 50*, with its bi-seriate ambulacrals I and V, there also appears between them and II and IV, on either side, a wedge-shaped interradial 1, *I* and 4, *I*, excluded from the peristome, but on the left side, 4, *I*, not very far from being admitted to its legitimate position in it. Dorsally, *fig. 51*, the interradials 1 and 4 unite, broadly separating the last plates of 5, out of which a few are pushed forward so as to infringe upon the calycinal system.

Echinocrepis cuneata AL. AG.[1]) ventrally seems to present the same disposition *Pl. VII, fig. 53*. The first plates of 1 and 4, excluded from the peristome, occupy the same places as in the two preceding species, and probably are contiguous to their respective interradia. The labrum, 5, perhaps without reaching the peristome, is produced aborally, and according to the figure given by AL. AGASSIZ, seems to reach the ambulacrals I *a b 2* and V *b a 2*, which separate it widely from the sternum, 5, *2*. Dorsally, *fig. 54*, the 1 and 4 laterally touch the calycinal system, while posteriorly the ambulacra I and V intervene between it and the last plates of 5.

Thus, within the definite and narrow limits of the little group of the Pourtalesiadae, consisting at present of only ten species distributed into three genera, and held firmly together by a few essential and constant characteristics, there exists in the perisomatic system a movement at once forcible and anomalous, tending to transform its most important elements into something unlike every precedent. Ventrally the change may be supposed to begin with the withdrawal of the 4, *I* and 1, *I* from the peristome, and their secluded reception between I *b* and II *a*, V *a* and IV *b*, as in Pourtalesia carinata, P. ceratopyga and Echinocrepis cuneata, while these same ambulacrals are left in legitimate contiguity to the respective I *a b 2* and V *a b 2*; — and to end, in Pourtalesia Jeffreysi, P. laguncula and, apparently, in Spatagocystis Challengeri, with the entire removal of 1 and 4 from their old places between I and II, V and IV, to a new position, on the mesial line of the skeleton, where they interrupt the succession of plates in the ambulacra I and V and the interradium 5. Dorsally, while in Echinocrepis the 1 and 4 can hardly be said to join one another, they in all the other species examined unite freely and largely, with the intervenience of plates from the interradium 5. And thus in these three species at least, the interradia 1 and 4 combine to form a continuous ring all around the middle of the body. Once before, early in Mesozoic time, for a while and not unlike a trial soon given up, a structure resembling

---
[1]) Chall. Rep. p, 143, pl. XXXV *a*, fig. 10.

this was seen, in the Collyritidæ, but imperfect, the ring being open ventrally and closed dorsally only. In these Pourtalesiæ it is complete above as below. This is a feature hitherto unseen among Echinoidea. With it the appearance of a radiate disposition of the skeletal elements, still kept up, to no small extent, in the Spatangidæ, is destroyed in an essential degree, and a tendency betrays itself towards an annulose differentiation of the bilaterally symmetrical constituents of the cylindroid skeleton. When reflecting on the great difference between Tiarechinus and Cidaris on the one hand, represented already in the earliest of Mesozoic times, and Pourtalesia on the other, nowhere recognised among extinct forms, and on the general character of the succession of varying forms separating their epochs, the idea presents itself that, while one branch of the Echinoidea, the Archæonomous, has tenaciously persisted in maintaining its original features, the other, the Neonomous, has been striving all the time to lay aside the radiate sameness of the ancient structure, and gradually to approach a higher standard of organisation endowed with superior appliances for ministering to the varied activities of life; and that something like such a stage of its evolution is on the eve of being touched, among the Pourtalesiadæ, by means of this primitive attempt at an annulose differentiation of some of the skeletal elements.

Each of the different groups of Exocyclic Echinoids, Dentiferous as well as Edentate, on its first appearance, has the excretory opening placed at or near the calycinal system, and from thence, in the course of time, it gradually recedes farther and farther back. Thus, among the Echinoconidæ [1]), in Pygaster, the oldest of them, it is dorsal and still partly calycinal, as though it had just broken through the circle of costals; in Pileus, of the Middle Oolite, it is dorsal, sub-marginal; in the Oolitic species of Holectypus it is marginal or ventral, in the Cretaceous ventral and farther removed; in Discoidea, of Cretaceous origin, it is ventral, in Echinoconus and Anorthopygus posterior, sub-ventral. In this group therefore, the excretory opening is seen early to have broken through the calycinal circle, and, when out of it, to retrograde farther and farther back. But this branchlet of the Dentiferous type was not strong enough to endure all through the Tertiary period and up to the present era — its sole survivor, the Pygaster relictus of the Caribbean sea, is of very diminutive dimensions —, it is upon the main branch, the Endocyclic, that it has devolved to people the seas of successive geological ages, and at its side the Dentiferous Exocyclics are actually represented by the Clypeastridæ, of all but Tertiary origin. In these the periproct is far removed from the calyx, and they present many a feature foreign to the primary types.

Long before their appearance the other great branch of the Echinoidea, the Edentate, not upon record from Palæozoic time, already formed a conspicuous part of one of the earliest among Mesozoic faunas as yet recognised. From whatever point of the common trunk it may have once originated, whatever may have been its phases of existence previous to its appearance, and still unknown to science, it gives evidence enough of having undergone profound modification, and, in assuming new distinctive features, of having done away with structural formulas deeply characteristic of its elder

[1]) Études, p. 79.

sister-branch. And in the whole course of its development it continues to deviate more and more.

It begins with the Echinoneidae. Galeropygus and Hyboclypeus, the oldest known, from the Liassic and Oolitic periods, with a rounded ambitus, have the excretory opening close to the calyx; in Galeroclypeus, Pachyclypeus, Desorella, from the Middle Oolite, it is posterior, even marginal. In the Oolitic species of Pyrina it is near the calyx, or at the middle between it and the posterior margin; in the Cretaceous species it is marginal, and it becomes ventral in Echinoneus, Tertiary and recent.

Among the Cassidulidae the Oolitic genera, Clypeus and Pseudodesorella, have the periproct not far removed from the calyx, and the gap is often filled by a prolongation of the radials I and V. Out of twenty Oolitic species of Echinobrissus nine belong to the older division, and five of these have the periproct sub-calycinal, one not far behind, and three at half the distance between the calyx and the posterior margin; seven species are Middle Oolitic, and it is sub-calycinal in one of these, at one fourth, one third, or one half of the distance in five, behind the middle in one. In the Upper Oolite, of four species, one alone has the vent sub-calycinal, three posteriorly in the middle, and the three Cretaceous species, as also E. recens, of a lengthened general form, all have it posterior, at the middle, or even behind. In all the numerous genera of the Cretaceous and Tertiary periods the periproct is from supra-marginal to infra-marginal, and in those of Tertiary origin ventral, even sub-oral. In general, and with the sole exception of Pygurus, in which, in Oolitic time, it remained marginal or was even infra-marginal, the site of the periproct in the oldest known forms of Edentates was in close vicinity to the calycinal system, and from this point it retrograded farther and farther during the Cretaceous and Tertiary periods, even so as at last to become ventral.

In the Collyrites, of Oolitic existence, the periproct is posterior, and so it is in the Holasteridae. Among the earlier forms of the Spatangidae its site is more or less dorsal, in those of later appearance it recedes, according as the abdomen lengthens. Like other features permanent in earlier forms, transitory in the more recent, this progressive modification is exhibited in the course of the individual development of recent forms.

Philippi, when describing the antarctic Spatangi [2]) for which Troschel afterwards created the genus Abatus, relates that he found, within their deepened petals, some very minute specimens which he suspected to be their young, and this discovery has since been confirmed and extended by Al. Agassiz [3]), who examined specimens collected at the Kerguelen Islands, as well as by Sir Ch. Wyville Thomson [4]) and by Studer [5]), who both at that same locality had frequent opportunities of seeing live specimens. I am indebted to the well-known liberality of the late Professor W. Peters for a present, which cannot be too highly appreciated, of three young ones taken out of the marsupial petals of the unique specimen bearing such, in the Berlin Museum.

---

[1]) Études. p. 81. [2]) Wiegm. Arch. XI, 1845, p. 347. [3]) Proc. Amer. Acad., XI, 1876, p. 231. — Rep. Echin. Chall., p. 177, pl. XX a. [4]) Journ. Linn. Soc., XIII, p. 67. — Voy. Chall., II, p. 229. [5]) Mon. Ber. Berl. Akad., 1876, p. 457 — Ib. 1880, p. 881. — Zool. Anzeiger, 1880, p. 343.

Only one among them was entire, but taken all together they afforded materials enough for observing some details not noticed before, *Pl. XIV, fig. 163—171*. Although apparently not far from leaving the nursery, they are still without oesophageal and excretory openings. In length they measure 2,3 mm., in breadth 1,9 mm. The general form of their test is very much that of the parent, as is also the dark brown colour. The whole body, spines and all, are tightly enveloped by a thick membraneous covering, the larval covering, closed at every point, and devoid of any opening for the alimentary organs, the animal still subsisting solely on the nutritious matter in store from the previous state of its development. In this stage now, the last one of its evolutional life, a stage of external rest passed through alike by the Cidaridæ and the Echinidæ, and by the Spatangidæ, the future skeleton is being built up, while internally the different organs receive their final structure as demanded by the mode of life of the adult. Under the thick envelope of the young Abatus cavernosus the spines, straight, conic, erect and bristling, look strong like those of an Archæonomons Echinoid, while the calcified plates of the ambulacral and interradial systems are already distinctly visible, and can be followed all the way up to the calycinal system, *fig. 165, 166, 167*. The skeleton, thus laid out in its principal parts, presents two clear spaces, both however overspread by the general covering and both unpierced, the one on the ventral side, not much before the middle, being the pentagonal stoma, *fig. 163, 165*, the other, on the dorsal side, a little behind the middle, being the central part over which the calycinal system is forming. *fig. 164, 164 A*. When the test is cut open horizontally, the intestinal tract is seen to be thick in its middle part, contracted in its oesophageal and rectal parts. Both portions end cæcally, and their closed extremities are seen to touch the wall of the visceral cavity, to which they are attached by the peritoneal lining descending upon them: the oesophageal extremity at the centre of the stoma, *fig. 165, 167*, the excretory at the centre of the clear space of the back, *fig. 166, 168*. Thus, at this stage, while directing its oral end towards a point slightly in front of the middle of the ventral surface, and its excretorial end to the central part of the calycinal region, only a little behind the middle of the back, the intestinal tract for a while has an ortho-proctic position, and recalls its Endocyclic termination in the ancient types. But this is here only a transitory condition, the centre of the calycinal system remains unpierced, and the excretory end of the intestinal tube, still blind, retrogrades, and opens only when beyond the limits of the calycinal system, — a movement, analogous to that known to have taken place, during past geological periods, through a long succession of Exocyclic species. The two large plates of the interradium 5, *fig. 166*, that approach nearest to the calycinal system, are those of the sixth pair, the labrum counting as the first. And, because in the adult the periproct is surrounded by the fifth, sixth and partly the seventh pairs, and, as I have shown in the case of Brissopsis lyrifera [1]), the periproctal plates remain the same in the adult as in a specimen not very much older than this young one of Abatus, it may be presumed that, in consequence of the forward movement of the apical part of the test, and

---

[1]) Études p. 60, pl. XXXVII, fig. 218.

the backward growth of the abdomen, combined with the tendency of the alimentary canal towards an antero-posterior direction, its excretory end, after having opened — which, as far as I have been able to observe, is done simultaneously with the opening of the oesophageal end — is drawn back towards the plates of the sixth pair, and that subsequently the seventh and following subanal plates are added, increasing its distance from the calyx. A young specimen of Echinocardium flavescens O. F. M., 1.7 mm. in length, Pl. XV, fig. 173, has the opened periproct high up on the back, near the calyx, from which it is separated by only two interradial plates. It is large, widely elliptic, and the calcified laminæ of the anal membrane are disposed in two rings, surrounding five converging triangular scales. Thus here also the stomatoproctic axis is not very far from vertical.

The manner in which the periproct is formed in Pourtalesia will probably never be known. In the adult of Pourtalesia Jeffreysi it is placed as far back perhaps as in any other species of the Neonomous forms, Pl. I, fig. 3, 4; II, 9; III, 13, over the caudal prolongation, in the deep depression between the interradials 5 a and b, 5 to 9, and the ambulacrals I a and V b, 5 to 7. It is transverse, cut out in the interradial plates 7, 8, 9 of 5 a and b, that form, with 5 and 6, the circum-anal region, which is expanded and received on either side into the sinus made by I a and V b, plates 5—7. The anal membrane is divided into two portions, an upper and overhanging one, between the interradials 8 and 9, and an under and rising one, between 8 and 7. The upper is broader and covered with smaller laminæ; it is the site of the excretory opening, a narrow transverse slit; the under portion, semi-circular, has larger scales. This structure agrees with what is seen in the Cassidulidæ. In this group the periproct, transverse and reniform, is likewise placed in a depression above the slight caudal prolongation, and the posterior under portion of the anal membrane, filling nearly the whole, is covered with a few large scales, while the upper, with the transverse excretory opening, is very small and drawn up close under the margin of the somewhat projecting post-anal plates. In the Spatangidæ, on the other hand, the membrane is of one piece, with its scales arranged concentrically all around, and the excretory opening, roundish and sub-central, closed by converging laminæ, as in the young of Echinocardium flavescens described above, Pl. XV, fig. 173, or in Palæostoma mirabile Gray, Pl. XVI, fig. 184, 186, 191 [1]).

In Pourtalesia Jeffreysi and its congeners only one fasciola is present, a well-marked subanal fasciola encircling the caudal prolongation, Pl. I, fig. 1, 2, 3; II, 9. Like the corresponding fasciola of the Spatangidæ, it crosses the third and the fifth plate of the interradium 5, but, contrary to what is the universal rule in that group, it traverses, not the sixth and certain following plates of the rows I a and V b, but the fourth plate alone, which by itself fills the episternal angle. It thus marks off, not the fifth, but the third plate of both rows as the hindmost of the ventrals. In Pourtalesia laguncula, Pl. VI, fig. 38, it has the same position, which it probably

---

[1]) Études, pl. XIII, fig. 113, 118; XXIX, 190; XXX, 193; XXXI, 196; XXXII, 199; XXXIV, 204; XXXV, 207; XXXVI, 212; XXXVII, 217; XXXVIII, 221; XXXIX, 226; XLII, 231; XLIII, 234.

maintains in the other species. According to AL. AGASSIZ it is indistinct in Spatagocystis, and absent in Echinocrepis.[1]) Upon the nature of the fasciola no fresh light is thrown from its mode of existence in the Pourtalesia; it remains as obscure as ever. The young of Abatus cavernosus, of 2,3 mm., *Pl. XIV, fig. 164*, already possesses the peripetalous fasciola, minute knobs rather irregularly scattered conformably to the elliptical outline of the test, and traversing the interradia and the trivium, but not the bivium. In the young of Echinocardium flavescens, of 1,7 mm., *Pl. XV, fig. 173*, the star-like heads of the rods of the spinules of both fasciolæ are very apparent, sparse and easily counted, the peripetalous crossing the calycinal system, but not touching the bivium, the ends of which it will traverse in the adult, causing, as it seems, branchial leaflets to be replaced by simple tubular pedicels. Thus the fasciola begins, along the greater part of its future course, with the development of solitary spinules, which however are soon to become densely crowded and equal, like the nap of a velvet. In the course of its growth its position relatively to the underlying parts is altered. In both the young specimens it does not cross the bivium, and in that of Echinocardium flavescens it traverses even the calycinal system. I have elsewhere shown, after a careful comparison between a young, of 4,6 mm., and an adult Brissopsis lyrifera,[2]) that in both the fasciolæ traverse corresponding plates, and that the movement becomes manifest solely from differences in the tracks of the former relatively to the figure and dimension of the plate. Upon the whole therefore the fasciola may be said to become, at an early age, all but stationary, but not absolutely so, as there seems to remain a small amount of reciprocal mobility. I once ventured to show that the fasciola is a structural element independent of the skeletal systems, belonging neither to the ambulacra nor to the interradial areas, but on the contrary, so to speak, dominating them in some manner. No trace of it is to be seen on the inner surface of the plates, and nowhere does it occupy their interstices. It is entirely external to them, forming by itself a layer outside that of the spines, growing amidst these, amidst pedicellariæ and pedicels, removing as much of them as lies in its way, and depositing in its stead its own band, incrusted with minute tubercles bearing the densely packed club-shaped spinules. Sometimes it allows the markings it thus covers to remain discernible through its substance, as in a specimen of Agassizia scrobiculata,[3]) in which the fasciola, intact and entire, like some gauzy tissue, lets clearly perceive the underlying tubercles, which are perfectly recognisable as to place and form and relation to the free tubercles contiguous to its margin, and parts of which it even covers. It is as though the fasciola, having caused the spine to drop, had grown over its tubercle. Sometimes also, as in specimens of Plagionotus pectoralis and Brissus Scillæ,[4]) the fasciola has split, and the underlying tubercles stand forth in the crevice, as though their spines had succeeded in resisting its subversive agression, and in keeping the crevice open, in the one case aided no doubt by the presence of a pedicel, which from its great muscular power was still more competent to check the advance of the spinules.

[1]) Rep. Chall. p. 141.   [2]) Etudes, p. 62, pl. XXXVII, fig. 213, 218.   [3]) Ib., p. 62, pl. XIII, fig. 121.
[4]) Ib., pl. XIII, fig. 122, 123.

The spines of Pourtalesia Jeffreysi are generally slender and sparse, but stronger and crowded on the sternum and more particularly on the palatal vault of the buccal recess, Pl. I, fig. 2; IV, 24. Within the scrobicular circle of the tubercle, Pl. V, fig. 31, rises the perforated mamelon surrounded by a »milled ring». The perforated condyle of the spine, fig. 30, is encircled by an undulated ring answering to the milled ring of the tubercle, and the whole surrounded by a wide, radiately waved brim, all these parts being of a dense and glossy, partly homogeneous calcareous substance. Above the brim, fig. 32, an apparently confused mass of compact meshy texture begins to rise obconically, forming the thick basal part which ends above in »the collar». There the slender calcareous fibrils of the meshes are seen, bending centrally, to unite, fig. 32, 33, into the regular string-like pillars that constitute the shaft, fig. 36; Pl. XIV, fig. 171, joining one another all along by giving off, on either side and inwardly, fig. 32, 34, 35, at regular intervals, the connecting processes that produce the well-known radiated texture seen in transverse sections. This is, in general terms, the structure of the spines in the Spatangidæ, and, in the main, of all the Echinoidea. In the following it will be seen that an analogous disposition of the constituent parts is met with in the rods which strengthen the filaments of the phyllodean, subanal and sometimes the frontal pedicels, Pl. VIII, fig. 55, 56, 57, 60, 61, 62 and 64; Pl. XI, fig. 121, 129, the basal circlet answering to »the collar», with the protruding nave below, its meshes uniting above, to form the shaft which sometimes shows signs of being composed of two or more string-like pillars rudely joined.

Like the fasciolæ the spines stand in no constant and fixed relation, with regard to their growth and position, to the underlying ambulacral plates. In my former work, a series of figures is consecrated to the development of the frontal ambulacrum, III, of Toxopneustes droebachensis [1]). In a specimen of 3 mm., the first primary tubercle in III *a* covers the suture of the primary plates *2* and *3*, in III *b* those of plates *2*, *3*, *4*, and so it continues in somewhat larger specimens, gradually reduced, till in a specimen of 11 mm., and before that size, it aborts or is shed in III *a*, as later in III *b*. And in the same specimen the primary tubercle is seen to cover more or less completely the sutures of each group of plates: *4—6*, *7—10*, *11—14* (*15*), of III *a*, and *5—7*, *8—11*, *12—16*, of III *b*. In a Meoma ventricosa [2]), they are seen to expand across the mesial suture of the interradia, in an Hemiaster expergitus [3]) the upper spines of the interradia 2 and 3 not only extend their bases partly over the terminals of the ambulacra II and III, but even invade the calycinal system. Nothing, in fact, is more easily observed than this independence of the radiolar system. Covered itself by the fasciolar stratum, it overlies the ambulacra as well as the perisome. Its genesis, the order and mode of appearance of its spines, their growth and decay, and their slow change of position, are inviting subjects of research.

The pedicellariæ, which now begin to be properly studied, are in these respects as little known as the spines. On those of Pourtalesia I have nothing to add to the descriptions given by Wyville Thomson and Al. Agassiz.

[1]) Études pl. XVII, fig. 140–147. [2]) Ib., pl. XII, fig. 106. [3]) Ib. pl. XI, fig. 93.

III. THE AMBULACRAL SYSTEM.

The peristome and the œsophageal opening in the young of Echini and Spatangi. The peculiar structure of these parts in Pourtalesia. The infra-frontal recess an incipient buccal cavity. The bivium and its abnormal structure. The spherids; their ventral position in Pourtalesia. The pedicels; their various forms in the Spatangidæ; the evolution of the phyllodean pedicels; the pores; peripodia. Pourtalesia homœopodous; its pedicels simple.

Like one and another of his predecessors LINNÆUS in some Spatangi overlooked the front ambulacrum, and thus came to attribute to them only four ambulacra, an error that was repeated by LAMARCK, CUVIER, BLAINVILLE and others. In all Echinoids there are five ambulacra, or radii, the frontal one in many irregular forms differing more or less from the rest, and sometimes being but faintly marked.

The young Echinoid, when on the point of assuming its final form, enveloped in the larval membranous covering, which is closed all around and destitute of any opening, oral or anal, for a while floats beneath the surface of the sea, until, having begun to take food, it sinks, and commences the mode of life of the adult. A minute Echinus[1], *Pl. XIX, fig. 232, 233*, genus unknown, 0,6 mm. in diameter, astomous and aproctic, presents a spheroidal form and a smooth, unbroken, richly pigmented surface above as below, with the spines standing on their tubercles, and, on the ventral side, the primary pedicels over their pores. Within the envelope the final skeleton is forming, ten paired calcified laminæ, the rudiments of the five ambulacra, each giving passage, through a simple pore, to the circulatory apparatus on its way into the tubes of the pedicels. Outward of these ten laminæ five others are seen, answering to the interstices between their pairs, and thus apparently representing the future interradia. The five primary ambulacra here alone constitute the peristome, and the open space enclosed within them is the future circular stoma. With this stage JOHANNES MÜLLER first made us acquainted many years ago[2]. The act of opening outward of the extremities of the intestinal tube still remains to be observed.

In Abatus cavernosus, as in many cases where the young are abnormally reared by the parent or kept within the maternal body, or else under exceptional conditions, the development is abridged[3]), and those phases are left out, in which, as in the great majority of the Echinoidea, the young has to lead a free oceanic life, and to evolve its future permanent structure under the protection of peculiar, transitory, perhaps mimically diverting larval forms. As described above, the development of Abatus ends with a stage analogous to that well-known in the Echinidæ, a resting stage, astomous

---

[1]) Études p. 27, pl. XVII, fig. 149. [2]) JOHANNES MUELLER, Metamorphose der Echinodermen: I, Berl. Abhandl. 1846, sep. p. 22, pl. VII; IV, ib. 1852, sep. p. 22, pl. IX, fig. 3, 4; VII, ib. 1855, sep. p. 22, pl. VIII, fig. 9—11. — KROHN, Müllers Archiv, 1851, p. 351. — AL. AGASSIZ, Embryology of Echinoderms, Mem. Amer. Academy, IX, 1864, p. 1; Revision Echin., p. 709, pl. IX, fig. 1; pl. X. — BROOKS Handbook of Invertebrate Zoology, Boston, 1882, p. 99—129, fig. 43—77. [3]) Compare WYVILLE THOMSON, Voyage of the Challenger, II, p. 229.

and aproctic, Pl. XIV, fig. 163—171. The stoma, inside the general envelope, is covered over by the pentagonal buccal membrane, fig. 165, in which a few crooked and branching spicules indicate the future calcified laminae, and this membrane, like the whole of the envelope, is entire, the œsophageal end of the alimentary canal, still closed, touching it on the inside, but not piercing it, fig. 167. This, however, is soon to be done. Another young specimen of the same species, which I owe to the kindness of Mr JOHN MURRAY of the Challenger Expedition, a little larger than that just described and slightly more advanced, — the phyllodean pedicels just begin to develop their filaments, and the spines to bend and faintly to indicate the partings so characteristic of the adult, — has the membrane of the stoma pierced in its very centre by the œsophageal opening just formed, the pressure from within causing it to protrude a little, while the calcareous spicules, somewhat more numerous, tend to collect in a circle all around. In both of these young specimens of Abatus the peristome is already constituted by five pairs of ambulacral plates and five single interradials.

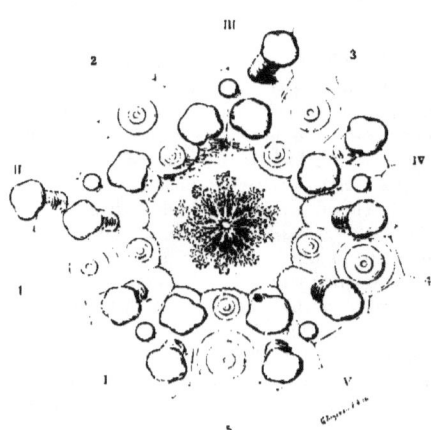

Peristome of a young specimen of Abatus cavernosus PHIL.

The same is seen in the young of Echinocardium flavescens O. F. M., 1.5 mm. in length, having just acquired the final shape, Pl. XV, fig. 172—183. Although smaller than the young of Abatus cavernosus, it is more developed, the alimentary canal being opened at both its extremities. The test presents a pentagonal outline. The stoma is placed somewhat before the middle, fig. 172, at the two fifths of the entire length, the periproct, fig. 173, at the three fifths of the same. The pentagonal peristome[1]) is composed of the five still narrow ambulacra, forming its angles, and of the five broader interradia, constituting its sides. The meshy tissue of the test is still rather transparent, and that of the ambulacral system more dense and compact, its meshes being markedly smaller and less open than those of the interradial system. It may also be seen, that each plate of the first pair of ambulacrals, close within the peristome and on its internal surface, sends out from its lateral margin on either side, across the adjoining interradium, a somewhat tapering lamina of compact texture. Viewed from the outside by transparency, fig. 174, these laminae seem to form five narrow uninterrupted ridges running across the interradial areas parallel to the peristome, but seen from the inner side, fig. 183, they are lost midways under a thick mass of calcareous meshes. These streng-

[1]) Compare Études p. 14, pl. III, fig. 32. 33 35; pl. V, fig. 46, 47.

thening ridges are no longer observed in specimens but little larger, in which the peristome has begun to change form, and are not to be recognised in mature specimens. The nearly circular orifice of the alimentary canal has just opened in the centre of the buccal membrane. In this there are deposited a number of calcified laminæ, in three concentric series, the outermost consisting of by far the largest, ten in number, placed two and two against the interradia, while the median, sub-pentagonal series is composed of about fifteen much smaller laminæ, and the innermost, encircling the opening, is a chain of numerous minute particles of reticular tissue. This calcified incrustation may possibly be found to pertain to the interradial system.

Thus, it is seen, in the true Echinids as in the Spatangi, at a very early age, and at the time when the skeleton assumes its final form, the five ambulacra one and all are constituent parts of the peristome, each by both the two plates of its first pair. And in the adult this is the general rule, found to hold good everywhere in the whole of hitherto known Echinoidea, without exception. Normally the first ambulacrals alternate with the first interradials, which reach the peristome with two plates or with a single compound plate. But between the Dentiferous and the Edentate forms, these last as far, at least, as we know them at present, there is this difference that, in the former, the peristome, central and perfectly circular from the beginning, and divided equally among the five ambulacra as likewise among the five interradia, remains so with very little change during life, whereas in nearly all the Edentates it is at first sub-central and pentagonal, but during growth is drawn forward, and becomes transverse and more or less labiate. In the Spatangidæ these changes are accompanied with very unequal alterations in the constituent parts, by the enlargement of the trivious peristomals, in a few cases to the exclusion of the interradials 1 and 4, or even 2 and 3, the bivious ambulacrals retaining more or less their wedge-shaped outline; by the first interradial, 5, 1, advancing and arching, so as to form a prominent labrum; and by the œsophageal opening becoming, from an almost circular aperture, a transverse fissure.[1])

From this a single form alone among the Spatangidæ is an exception, the Palæostoma mirabile (GRAY, *Pl. XVI, fig. 184—196.*[2]). In all essential points it is a true Prymnadete Spatangean, with an oviform body, inflate posteriorly, the back being raised behind the middle. The peristome is somewhat anterior, at the four fifths of the entire length, rather small, slightly sunk, regularly pentagonal and clabiate even in the adult, being composed of five broad interradials of similar form, constituting its sides, and five equal pairs of ambulacrals at its angles. On the inside, *fig. 188*, it is strengthened by a pentangular ridge running parallel to the margin, and corresponding to that described above in the young of Echinocardium flavescens O. F. M., but here observable, at least, in the half-grown animal. The pentangular stoma is filled, not with a pliant membrane incrusted with calcified laminæ, but with five flat, equal, triangular and contiguous valves, meeting together centrally, each of them composed of an external basal part articulating with the corresponding interradial side of the

---

[1]) Etudes, p. 11, pl. III, fig. 32, 33—37; V, fig. 16, 47; VII, fig. 61, 67.
[2]) Ib. p. 16, 50; pl. XXXII, fig. 197—199.

peristome, and made up of a thicker calcified tissue of coarser meshes, and two narrow, more finely reticular, lateral, perhaps slightly movable pieces.[1])

When any of these various characteristics of the Echinoidean peristome is looked for in Pourtalesia Jeffreysi, it at once becomes obvious, that the exceptional case of Palæostoma no less than whatever there is in the others of conformity to a general law, is set aside in the disposition of the corresponding parts of its skeleton. Its peristome is altogether of a peculiar construction, Pl. II, fig. 9; III. 12; IV, 15—19. Out of the five ambulacra one alone, the front ambulacrum, III, with its greater part sharing in the singular incurvation of the whole region, partakes of its formation, the other four are all excluded from it, and, while the front ambulacrum and the two lateral ones, II and IV, each begin with a pair of plates, the two bivious ambulacra each commence with a single plate only. Now it is known that, while in the Archæonomous Echinoidea the peristomal plates generally maintain their entire breadth,[2]) in the Neonomous, and more particularly in the Spatangidæ[3]) they are more or less contracted adorally, especially in the bivium, and more so in the young than in the adult. In Pourtalesia Jeffreysi this feature is carried to an extreme. The front ambulacrum, III, enters the peristome with its entire breadth, while the peristomal plates of the bivium and those of the two paired ambulacra of the trivium, II and IV, are all diminished, cuneiform, narrowing adorally almost to a point. The two pairs that belong to II and IV are very small, half the size of the single ones of the bivious ambulacra, I and V, and all these six plates together have their adoral contracted portions bent over abruptly, at an acute angle, into the hollow of the infra-frontal niche, at the bottom of its ventral sinus, thus forming there a keen edge, strengthened inside by strong partitions, fig. 17, reminding of the trabeculæ of the Clypeastridæ. In consequence of this incurvation, while the greater part of their surfaces is visible in the ventral aspect, fig. 2, 15, their adoral terminations are not visible, unless their portion of the test be cut out, and placed with its inside toward the observer, fig. 16. Then it may be seen, although not without some difficulty, that the narrowing terminations of the two single first plates of the two bivious ambulacra, I and V, as well as the plates II a 1 and IV b 1, of the two paired trivious ambulacra, do not reach the margin of the peristome, but are excluded from it by a single mesial subtriangular plate, 5, which is the labrum, and, as such, belongs to the interradial system, while the terminations of II b 1 and IV a 1 are not even visible in that position, being situated on the curvature itself and thereby concealed. Thus, in this extraordinary Echinoid, the front ambulacrum, III,

---

[1]) See S. Lovén: Om Leskia mirabilis Gray, Öfversigt af K. Vetenskaps-Akademiens Förhandlingar, 1867, p. 431. In that paper I regarded the five-valved covering of the stoma of Palæostoma as homologous to the »pyramid« of Echinosphæra and Sphæronis. I soon afterwards perceived that this was an error, as Lütken clearly set forth in his memoir: Endnu ett par ord om de gamle Söliliers »Snabel« og Mund, Videnskablige Meddelelser fra den Naturhistoriske Forening i Kjöbenhavn, 1869, 160; Geological Magazine, V, 179; Canadian Naturalist, new series, III, 437.

[2]) Etudes, pl. X, fig. 84, 86, 89, 91; pl. XVII, fig. 140—148; pl. XVIII, fig. 153—158; pl. XIX, fig. 165; pl. XX, fig. 166.

[3]) Etudes, pl. III, fig. 32—35, 39; pl. IV, fig. 41—43; pl. V, fig. 46-48, 51, 54; pl. VI, fig. 55, 58—60; pl. VII, fig. 61-64, 66, 67; pl. XXII—XLIII.

alone maintains its normal share in the composition of the peristome, while the two paired trivious ambulacra, diminished in size, and the bivious ambulacra, reduced to single plates only, are all excluded from it, and so closely pressed together on its under side, as to occupy, all taken together, considerably less space than the front ambulacrum alone on the upper. The space intervening between the minute interradial 5, *1*, and the large ambulacrals III *a 1* and III *b 1*, is filled by the interradials 2 *b 1* and 3 *a 1*, Pl. II, fig. 9; III, 12; IV, 18, 19, and, as these last are very high, the stoma assumes an elliptical form, unseen among the rest of the Echinoidea. For, if in Ananchites and its allies the labrum is but slightly developed, and even less so in Collyrites whose stoma is longitudinally sub-elliptical, the constituents of the peristoma are nevertheless normal everywhere. In Pourtalesia Jeffreysi, on the contrary, it has been seen that they are: ambulacrum III, interradials 2 *b 1* and 3 *a 1*, and interradial 5, while the ambulacrals I, II, IV, V, interradials 2 *a 1* and 3 *b 1*, and interradials 1 and 4 are excluded. The plane of the peristoma thus composed is nearly vertical, and perpendicular to that of the longitudinal axis of the body, or somewhat overhanging into the peritoneal cavity; it is not, as in the Spatangidæ in general, all but coincident with the stomato-proctic axis, but, as in the Endocyclic forms, though in an opposite manner, perpendicular to that also. In one of the specimens the two plates *1* of the ambulacrum III, and the interradials 2 *b 1* and 3 *a 1*, in a part of their margins are dissolved into an assemblage of minute rounded laminæ, fig. 19, 20, but in two other specimens they are entire.

The buccal membrane, Pl. IV, fig. 20, is destitute of calcified deposits. In its middle is seen the œsophageal opening, an oblong slit, with naked, rather tumid and coarsely wrinkled margins. Its direction is that of the vertical longitudinal plane of the body, perpendicular to the direction of the transverse fissure in the great majority of the Spatangidæ.

This description of the peristome and adjoining parts in Pourtalesia Jeffreysi applies upon the whole equally to the same parts in the other species of the group; the differences presented by the ambulacra I, V, II, IV, will be taken up hereafter. The species all agree in the important points resulting in that most striking feature, the deep anterior recess. There can be no doubt that the elliptical frame surrounding the stoma in the Pourtalesiadæ, widely different though it be in its composition, is strictly homologous to the peristome in all the other Echinoidea, and, no less so, that the vertically placed membrane with its longitudinal slit is homologous to the horizontally stretched membrane in the Dentifera and Edentata, with the rounded or transverse orifice of the alimentary canal. But the peculiar structure of these parts in the Pourtalesiadæ is such as to call forth the idea, that what is going on here may be looked upon as the first move, so to speak, towards forming a rudimental mouth, a *cavum oris*, the invaginated parts of which, if they were flexible and provided with muscles, might be protruded like a proboscis, which, owing to the great size of the frontal ambulacrals and interradials, would be directed downwards and backwards. As it is, its rigid and motionless lips are indicated by the line of incurvation all around its entrance, its palate, *sit venia verbo*, Pl. III, fig. 10, 12; IV, 18, 19; VI, 45, is made up of the large and unreduced bi-seriate plates of

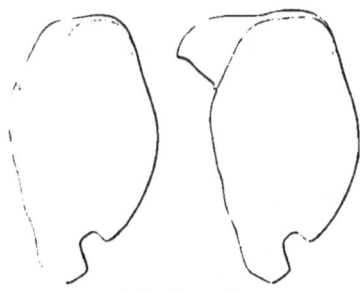

The imaginary rostrum invaginated   protruding.

the ambulacrum III, while its sides are constituted by the interradia 2 and 3, inferiorly meeting to the right and left of the shortened and compressed intra-labial space, and its innermost portion, together with the elliptical membrane, Pl. III, fig. 12; IV, 18, 19, 20, may represent a pharynx, the slit being the œsophageal opening. The vaulted palate is armed with spines, stronger and more closely packed than anywhere, Pl. IV, fig. 24, and the site, no doubt, of a powerful ciliary activity, and outside the under lip are seen the spherids in pairs or in clusters, Pl. IV, fig. 15; VI, fig. 40, 41, 44; VII, fig. 47, 48, 49, 50. Just as in another part of the skeleton of certain Pourtalesiadæ, as has been suggested above, a movement is introduced in the perisomatic system, directed towards an annulose conformation of the body, thus here also, in the peristome and surroundings, a tendency seems to be exhibited towards a vermiform constitution. This tendency, to be generally surmised already, in the Tertiary and recent Spatangidæ, from the increasing length and flatness of their test, the stomato-proctic axis approaching to horizontality, from the reclining direction of the slender spines, and the forward movement of the peristome, appears heightened, in another and peculiar manner, in the Pourtalesiadæ by the anterior part of the body being definitely marked out by the terminal mouth-like recess, and by a more strongly displayed differentiation of the upper dorsal side of the skeleton from the under, ventral side. In the Spatangidæ the frontal phyllode is still in part ventral, and touches the ground in which the animal is living; in the Pourtalesiadæ it is elevated on the tops of the erect interradials 2 and 3, and thus brought to roof dorsally the rudimentary mouth, therein strongly contrasting with the other four phyllodes, which all of them are ventral, and employed in forming its ground-floor and lower external surface.

In all the known forms of the Echinoidea, Archæonomous and Neonomous, each ambulacrum, from its beginning in the peristome to its termination, is bi-seriate, that is presents an uninterrupted succession of plates, almost invariably arranged throughout in two alternate rows. When the ambulacra of Pourtalesia Jeffreysi are examined in this respect, they are found to differ more widely than those of any other Echinoid, even the most specialised among Prymnodesmiic Spatangidæ.

The front ambulacrum, III, normal in its peristomal origin, continues so throughout to its termination, Pl. II, fig. 9. It is shorter than any of the other four ambulacra. It consists of thirteen to fifteen pairs of plates, out of which the second is somewhat broader than the first, and the following eight or nine slowly diminish in breadth, the terminal three to five suddenly becoming very minute. The first five pairs form the roof of the frontal niche, or buccal cavity, Pl. III, fig. 10, 12, the sixth, seventh, eighth and ninth curve upwards, and constitute with the last five or six the mesial, moderately impressed part of the blunted front, the small terminal plates closing with the calycinal system just on reaching the dorsal surface.

The two paired ambulacra of the trivium, II and IV, Pl. II, fig. 9; I, 1, 2, 3; III, 10, 11, are somewhat larger than the front one. They are slightly curving forward symmetrically, broad in the middle and suddenly contracted at their summits. In the described specimen the number of plates is about fourteen in each. The first two are, as above stated, small and wedge-shaped, the second pairs suddenly expand, and still more so the following pairs, each ambulacrum attaining its greatest breadth before reaching half the height of the test, after which it slowly decreases, the plates of the posterior row in each, the II a and IV b, surpassing throughout those of the anterior, and both nearly preserving the hexagonal form. The thirteenth and fourteenth pairs suddenly contract, and become very minute, when joining the calycinal system.

Thus the trivious ambulacra, from their beginnings in or near the peristome, conformably to the general rule, present throughout their whole length a continuous double row of plates, and their summits attain the calycinal system. In the bivium all this is different.

As above stated, the ventral surface, Pl. I, fig. 2, 8; II, 9; IV, 15, presents anteriorly two contiguous elongated plates, I, 1. V, 1, one on each side of the mesial line, having the terminal portions of their gradually narrowing adoral halves bent over into the infra-frontal niche. Pl. IV, fig. 16. Their anomalous form and their contiguity to the first plates of II a and IV b combine to make it more than uncertain how to distribute correctly, to their respective ambulacra, all these six closely joining plates, from external inspection alone. But their relations at once become obvious, when they are examined from the peritoneal cavity, after the test has been cut open longitudinally, Pl. III, fig. 10, 11; IV, 18, 19. In the whole of the Echinoidea the neural collar, at each of its five angles, sends off a cord that follows the mesial line of each ambulacrum on its inner surface, and gives off alternate branches which enter the pedicellar pores, and come out again on the outside of the test, there to distribute themselves among the different external organs,[1]). The neural collar and the main nerve-cords are closely accompanied by the circular vessel and the great trunks of the aquiferous system, outside emerging along with them from out of the pores, and entering the tubes of the pedicels. When the test of Pourtalesia Jeffreysi is laid open, and the recess is examined on its peritoneal surface, Pl. III, fig. 10, 11; IV, 18, 19, it is seen that here also the neural collar and the circular aquiferous vessel respectively send out their five main branches, one for each ambulacrum. Of these an odd one runs along the mesial suture of the vaulted front ambulacrum, III, on the top of its roof, and ascends to the calycinal system, giving off, on every plate, a branch to its pore, but two on the plate III b 1, fig. 10, 18, 19. The two paired ambulacra II and IV also each receive two main trunks, one neural, one aquiferous, giving off branches to the

---

[1]) Etudes, p. 8, pl. II, fig. 28—31.

pores of the plates II *a 1*, II *a 2*, etc. and II *b 1*, II *b 2*, etc., on the right side, as also, on the left, to those of the plates IV *b 1*, IV *b 2*, IV *b 3*, etc., and IV *a 1*, IV *a 2* etc. And from these beginnings the main trunks are seen to emit regularly alternate branches to the ambulacral pores, Pl. III, fig. 10, 11. It follows from this that these plates were rightly referred, from the outside aspect, to the ambulacra II and IV, as true peristomal plates, although excluded from their legitimate position.

Lastly, the neural collar and the circular vessel each give off two main branches directed backward and slowly diverging, Pl. II*, fig. 18, 19; III, 10. Just on their leaving the collar, a first branchlet descends from each of them to the pedicellar pore of one of the two single contiguous plates V and I, fig. 18, V, 1, 1, 1; fig. 19, V, 1, thereby rendering it manifest that these plates are in reality what they were pronounced to be from without, the reduced and displaced peristomal plates of the bivium, V, 1 and I, 1. But when the further continuation from thence of the bivious ambulacra is looked for from without, Pl. I, fig. 2, the sequence of their plates is found to be broken by the interposition of four longitudinal plates of considerable size evidently not ambulacral, the less so, as none of them presents any trace of a pedicellar pore. They belong, as shown above, to the perisome, being the 1 *b 1*, 1 *b 2+3* and 4 *a 1*, 4 *a 2*, of the interradial system. Viewed from the peritoneal cavity, Pl. III, fig. 10, these same plates are seen to be spanned by the two trunks which, after their first branchlets, do not give off a second till reaching, on the farther side, two pairs of plates, contiguous in the mesial line, 1 *a 2*, 1 *b 2*, V *b 2*, V *a 2*. There again a branchlet is seen to proceed from each trunk, the first for the inner of the two plates: 1 *a 2*, V *b 2*, the second for the outer ones: 1 *b 2*, V *a 2*, and so on alternately and continuously to the summit of the ambulacrum, Pl. III, fig. 11, 14. In Pourtalesia Jeffreysi, therefore, not only the first plates of the bivium are single, not double, but they are, moreover, widely separated from the next in order, and the two ambulacra begin, as it were, anew, at about the posterior half of the body, each with the regular double alternate series of plates. But there, as where they commenced witht he two first single plates I, 1 and V, 1, the two ambulacra are again contiguous in the mesial line, the 1 *a 2* and V *b 2* touching each other by their foreparts for more than the anterior half of their inner margins, thereby excluding the interradials 1 and 4 from the posterior interradium 5. After that their hind portions separate, bending right and left, to give place to the sternum, Pl. I, fig. 2; II. 9; III, 10. The 1 *b 2* and V *a 2* are shorter, less irregular, but sub-pentagonal, slightly curved, and somewhat broader in front. Of the third pair the 1 *a 3* and V *b 3* are elongated, irregularly hexagonal and contiguous to the sternum and to the forepart of the episternum, while the 1 *b 3* and V *a 3* are broader, but much shorter, thus allowing the ambulacrum to bend upward at a right angle, Pl. I, fig. 3. Hence the fourth pairs lie at the basis of the ascending portions of the bivium. The 1 *a 4* and V *b 4* are hexagonal, with their hind-portions widening and extending beyond the posterior limits of the ambulacrum, so as to border inwardly upon the episternum 5 *b 3* and 5 *a 3*, then to fill out on either side the episternal angle, and to join the whole length of the first pre-anals 5 *b 4*, 5 *a 4*, and the greater part of the second,

5 *b* 5, 5 *a* 5. Being thus disposed, the I *a* 4 and V *b* 4 are traversed by the subanal fasciola, and thereby brought alone to correspond to the group of from two to six or more ambulacral plates of I *a* and V *b*, from the sixth onwards, which, in the Prymnodesmic Spatangidæ, are prolonged and salient inwards, so as to fill, within the subanal fasciola, the reentering episternal angle, and to determine the upward flexure of these ambulacra, and which, by marking off, throughout, as ventral, the foregoing plates and limiting their number everywhere to five, constitute a prominent and most significant feature [1]).

The ambulacrals I *b* 4 and V *a* 4 of Pourtalesia Jeffreysi nearly equal in size these just described, and are more regularly hexagonal. In the two succeeding pairs, the fifth and sixth, the plates of I *a* and V *b* are shortened, to give place to the circum-anal region of the odd interradium, while the fifth plates of I *b* and V *a* are narrowed anteriorly in connexion with the curvature of the ambulacrum. From the seventh, and onward, the following pairs have their plates nearly equal, only those of the posterior rows slightly smaller, distinctly hexagonal, and slowly diminishing in size. In the specimen described the fourteenth pairs are terminal.

According to an almost universal rule, the ambulacra of the bivium ought to ascend so as dorsally to join the calycinal system. From this the Collyritidæ, of Oolitic existence, make the sole exception hitherto known, having their calycinal system dismembered by the interjacence on either side of the unreduced interradia 1 and 4, which sever from it the radial pieces I and V, and leave them in connexion with the respective ambulacra. And from their erect position and convergence it follows that their tops, with these radials, are brought in close contact, or so near each other, as to be separated only by a narrow plate, which is one of a row of slender, longitudinal, irregularly arranged plates stretching from the periproct to the calycinal system. At a first glance this structure seems to be revived in Pourtalesia Jeffreysi, but on closer inspection notable differences become apparent, Pl. *1*, *fig. 1, 3; III, fig. 11*. The bivium, far from having a vertical position, leaning backwards, so as to overhang the postern slope, as in Collyrites, stretches forward longitudinally, and converges but slightly, the two ambulacra being separated all along by the odd interradium 5, a pair of whose plates intervenes between their summits, while the lateral interradia 1 and 4, in joining from either side, combined with elements of the odd interradium, 5, keep them widely apart from the calycinal system. Their summits, a pair of moderately sized plates, not abruptly diminished as in the trivium, are situated at about the foremost third of the whole length of the test. Of radial (»ocular») pieces not a trace is seen.

From all this it follows that two of the fundamental and universal characteristics of the Echinoidean ambulacra, their joint participation in the formation of the peristome, and the uninterrupted sequence of their plates, are set aside in Pourtalesia.

---

[1]) Etudes, p. 15, pl. XXXII, fig. 200,—XLII, fig. 232.

The third, no less essential characteristic, the disposition of the ten ambulacral rows, not in conformity with the bilateral arrangement of the ambulacral system, but referable to an axis other than its actual antero-posterior one, is even as fully discarded in Pourtalesia. This disposition is most plainly seen in the Spatangidae. It is as follows[1]). If a Spatangean, of any genus or species is held in supination, that is with the ventral surface upwards, and with the odd interradium backwards, and if the ten ambulacral plates of the peristome are then counted from left to right, — that is, from the right side of the animal to its left, — beginning with the ambulacrum of the bivium marked I; if, at the same time, in each of the ambulacra: I, II, III, IV, V, thus gone over, the row of plates first touched is marked a, the second b, it will be found, that the peristomal plates I a, II a, III b, IV a, V b, are the larger ones, and provided with two pedicellar pores, $i. e.$ they are binary, bi-porous, while the peristomal plates I b, II b, III a, IV b, V a, are smaller, and each provided with only one pedicellar pore, $i. e.$ are simple, uniporous. The identical disposition of these same plates is found in the Echinoneidae, Cassidulidae, Holastridae, that is in all the Edentates. In the Dentiferous Echinoids the same law is maintained, though differently expressed. Among the Echinoconidae[2]) it is manifested by the peristomal plates I a, II a, III b, IV a, V b, binary in the genus Echinoconus, being always larger, and succeeded everywhere by a single plate, placed between each of them and the first triad, while the peristomals I b, II b, III a, IV b, V a, are smaller, and directly contiguous to the first triad. In the Echinidae[3]) its existence is obvious, and the same formula holds true, masked though it be by the seemingly radiate disposition of the parts. Out of the ten peristomal plates, all of them composite, the I a, II a, III b, IV a, V b, are larger than the I b, II b, III a, IV b, V a. All Echinidae possess, on their buccal membrane, five pairs of minute free plates, each plate bearing, in the adult, a pedicellar pore. In the very young Toxopneustes droebachensis, only two millimeters in diameter[4]), out of these ten plates, those five which correspond to the ambulacral rows I a, II a, III b, IV a, V b, are larger, but still for a time are without pores, while the five other plates, that answer to the ambulacral rows I b, II b, III a, IV b, V a, though smaller, already have received theirs. In the Cidaridae[5]), in other respects so widely different from the Echinidae, out of the ten ambulacral plates surrounding the oesophageal opening, those five that belong to the rows I a, II a, III b, IV a, V b, exceed in size the other five that appertain to the rows I b, II b, III a, IV b, V a, while the plates of these last-named rows are, all around, the first to detach themselves from the margin of the corona, which is thus continually broken up and renewed. Finally, in the Clypeastridae[6]), the last arrived, in which many a primeval feature is vanishing or even effaced, the peristomal plates of the rows I a, II a, III b, IV a, V b, are distinguished by their superior size from those of the rows I b, II b, III a, IV b, V a, the difference, however, in a few cases having become very slight.

Thus, it is seen, in whatever group of the Echinoidea the structure of the ambulacra is examined, out of the ten plates composing the peristome, the five: I a, II a,

[1]) Études, p. 13 - 39, pl. III—IX, XIV, XVII—XX, XXII—LII. [2]) Ib., p. 20, pl. XIV, [3]) Ib., p. 20, pl. XVII, XVIII. [4]) Ib., p. 27, pl. XVII, fig. 148. [5]) Ib., p. 28., pl. XX. [6]) Ib. p. 32., pl. XLIV—LII.

III b, IV a, V b, always differ in a marked manner from the other five: I b, II b, III a, IV b, V a, be it in size, in outline, or in the number of their pedicellar pores, and the two sets follow each other, all around the stoma, everywhere in the same order. And this invariably recurring biformity of the ambulacra in their peristomal beginnings, of a never failing validity through the whole of the Echinoidea, recent and extinct, that have been examined on this point, is also more or less distinctly recognisable all through the entire length of each ambulacrum, and more so in the older types, in which the seemingly radiate disposition of the parts is predominant, than in those of a later date. In Cidaris the plates of the rows I b, II b, III a, IV a, V a, in every ambulacrum are in advance of those of the rows I a, II a, III b, IV a, V b, by an entire plate or half a one[1]), and in the very young and minute Toxopneustes dræbachensis, the seventh plate is begun in each of the rows I b ... V a, while there are yet only six in each of the rows I a ... V b^2. But in the types of later appearance, the Neonomous, in which the radiate form largely makes way for a decidedly bilateral disposition, as in the Cassidulidæ, Collyritidæ, Holastridæ, Spatangidæ, the tendency towards a gradually more and more decided symmetry in external outline between the two lateral ambulacra of the trivium, II and IV, and between the two bivious, I and V, seems to invalidate the biformity of their composition, and leave it in full force solely in the peristome. There it, therefore, continues from the antique Cidaridæ till it all but vanishes in the Clypeastridæ, of Tertiary origin, always suggesting, in a manner not yet understood, the previous existence of a skeletal axis diverging from the actual antero-posterior one, being at an angle with it, and dividing lengthwise the ambulacrum IV and the opposite interradium. If five homologous points in I a, II a, III b, IV a, V b, are connected by straight lines, and also homologous points in I b, II b, III a, IV b, V a, two irregular pentagons are inscribed within the peristome, disposed in such a manner that each of them is divided by this axis, $\alpha\omega$, into two parts, one trapezoid and the other pentagonular, the areas of which are equal; and that, if one of them is made to revolve half a circle on the axis $\alpha\omega$, it covers the space left by the other[3]).

It results from the arrangement thus detailed, that the two bivious ambulacra are symmetrical towards one another with regard to the disposition of their constituent elements. Within the trivium the front ambulacrum, III, in so far has a medial character, as by its peristomals it is symmetrical on one side towards the ambulacrum II, on the other towards the ambulacrum IV. But these latter, the two lateral ambulacra of the trivium, are, with regard to the disposition of their elements, unsymmetrical towards each other, thus testifying to the inherent obliquity of the Echinoidean ambulacral system. In both the principal types of the Echinoidea, however, this obliquity is outwardly concealed: in the Archæonomous, the dentiferous forms, Cidaridæ and Echinidæ, by the apparently quite circular and radiate arrangement of the skeletal systems, the central position of the mouth, and the verticality of the stomato-proctic axis, all correlatively bound up with one another and rigidly maintained; in the later, the

---

[1]) Etudes, p. 30. [2]) Ib., p. 21, pl. XVII, fig. 140. [3]) Ib., p. 37, pl. XVII, fig. 140.

Edentate forms, — contrasting with the former in the pliancy they manifest during their successive appearances and vanishings, — by their progressively developed bilaterality, by the variously inclined, or even horizontal stomato-proctic axis, and by the symmetry, in general outline, between the two paired ambulacra of the trivium, as well as between the two of the bivium.

When Pourtalesia Jeffreysi is examined on this point, *Pl. II, fig. 9; IV, 15, 16*, it is found at once that the two paired ambulacra of the bivium are symmetrical towards each other in their general outlines. This is manifested, as regards the two single plates with which the ambulacra I and V begin, I 1 and V 1, no less by their outlines than by the condition of their pores. They are therefore in complete accordance with the general rule. But, contrary to that same rule, the two ambulacra of the trivium, II and IV, also present this same symmetry in the disposition of their component elements. The plates II a 1 and IV b 1 are evidently counterparts, and so are II b 1 and IV a 1, in size, form, number and character of their pedicellar pores. And yet, according to the law pervading the whole of the Echinoidea, those same plates ought to differ in these respects, belonging, as they do, to different series: II a 1 and IV a 1 to the series I a ... V b, and II b 1 and IV b 1 to the series I b ... V a. This is an essential and important anomaly. It is also very remarkable that, in presence of so profound a transformation, the front ambulacrum, III, alone remains intact, presenting the normal external form and internal composition, together with the legitimate condition of the pedicellar pores, bearing a single pore on its smaller peristomal plate, III a 1, and two on the larger plate, III b 1. While, in all the rest of the Echinoidea, the composition of the peristome is expressed by the common formula:

I a, II a, III b, IV a, V b: large, biporous;
I b, II b, III a, IV b, V a: small, uniporous.

in Pourtalesia Jeffreysi the peristomal series, if arranged according to the size of the plates, would be:

I, II b, III b, IV a, V: large;
I, II a, III a, IV b, V: small;

and the different size of the paired trivious ambulacrals has no relation to the number or character of the pores. The seven plates: I, II a, II b, III a, IV a, IV b, V, are all uniporous, III b alone is biporous. It is evident, therefore, that the obliquity hitherto found inherent, everywhere and without exception, to the constitution of the ambulacral system of the Echinoidea, is evanescent in that of Pourtalesia Jeffreysi, its paired radii II and IV, I and V having their elements disposed solely with relation to the antero-posterior axis of the body, and not to a subordinate deviating axis ao, as in all other Echinoidea. The elsewhere all-pervading obliquity is on the point of disappearing, but a trace of it is still left in the front radius, III. which has, as normal, its a plate uniporous, and its b plate biporous.

Now, bearing in mind the unvarying constancy of the ambulacral characteristics in all the numerous genera and species so highly diversified in other respects, with which we are familiar, it seems that we might be allowed to expect their contrasts, so strikingly set forth in Pourtalesia Jeffreysi, to possess an equally pervading validity as characteristic of the entire genus and its allies. But a careful examination of the specimens sent me by Sir WYVILLE THOMSON, fragmentary as they are, has taught me that, to a great extent at least, this is not the case. Already in Pourtalesia laguncula AL. AG., Pl. VI, fig. 37—41, some important differences present themselves. The front ambulacrum, III, retains its normal structure. The two paired ambulacra of the trivium, II and IV, are very like those in Pourtalesia Jeffreysi, the two first plates of the first pair being minute and wedge-shaped, and each provided with a single pore, the second pair II a 2, II b 2 and IV a 2, IV b 2, suddenly expanding, so as also to join the aboral margins of I b 1 and I a 1, and V a 1 and V b 1. Both ambulacra continue very broad, until, dorsally, they contract rather suddenly, ending at the calycinal system with a minute terminal plate. Pl. VII, fig 52. Thus in this species, as in Pourtalesia Jeffreysi, the trivious ambulacra present throughout their whole extension a continuous sequence of plates, and their summits attain the calycinal system. In the bivium all this is otherwise, yet nearly in the same manner as in Pourtalesia Jeffreysi. Whereas in that species the pairs of plates I a 1 and I b 1, as also V a 1 and V b 1, have respectively coalesced into a simple compound plate, I, V, on either side of the middle line, the same plates are separate in Pourtalesia laguncula, fig. 37—40, the joint outline, presented by each pair, corresponding with that of the single plate in Pourtalesia Jeffreysi. But while, in this latter species, the single compound plate is provided with one pore only, in the former the two: I a 1 and I b 1, as also V a 1 and V b 1, each of them retains its pore, that of I a as well as that of V b being single, not double, as they ought to be. While in Pourtalesia Jeffreysi the I 1 and V 1 are contiguous along the middle line, they are separated in Pourtalesia laguncula by the wedge-shaped interradial 5 1, permitting them to come near each other at the very bend only of the ventral margin of the niche, but driving them asunder by its triangular aboral expansion. In the same manner as in Pourtalesia Jeffreysi, these I a, b 1 and V b, a 1 are widely separated from I a, b 2 and V b, a 2, by the interposition of the interradia 1 and 4; and the I a 2 and V b 2, contiguous in their adoral half, so as to exclude these interradials from the interradial 5 2, the sternum, then bend right and left, to give room to that plate, and to the episternum, 5 a and b 3. The disposition of these plates thus very much resembles that seen in Pourtalesia Jeffreysi, the I a 4 and V b 4 being traversed by the fasciola. In like manner, on the dorsal surface, Pl. VII, fig. 52, the bivious ambulacra are separated from one another by the odd interradium 5, nor do they join the calycinal system, being kept widely apart from it by the interradia 1 and 4, meeting from either side. They terminate with small, and rather suddenly diminished plates.

In Pourtalesia ceratopyga AL. AG., Pl. VII, fig. 48—50, the disposition of the first plates of the ambulacra I and V appears to be identical with that in Pourtalesia laguncula, the labrum 5, 1 separating I a and V b. Each plate also has only a single pore, but the row of the eight pores is not visible from the ventral aspect, as they are placed on the flattened margin of the incurvation, fig. 49. The mode of connexion of the labrum with the rest of the interradial system could not be made out, the specimen unfortunately being broken at the critical point. But, as stated above, there exists a decided peculiarity in the condition of the interradials 1 and 4, of which, on either side, a narrow plate, 1 and 4, is seen keeping apart the IV from the V, and the II from the I, *fig. 48*, and this plate on the left side is pushed forward so as to approach the flexure and to compress and reduce the IV *b 1*; on the right side it keeps farther back, and the II *a 1* is fully developed.

Echinocrepis cuneata AL. AG., *Pl. VII, fig. 53*, repeats the mode of disposition of Pourtalesia ceratopyga, the interradial 5, *1* separating the two bivious ambulacra, the interradials 1 *1* and 4 *1* being placed between I and II and between V and IV, and all the four ambulacral plates on either side being uniporous.

Pourtalesia carinata AL. AG., *Pl. VI, fig. 42—46*; *VII, 47*, presents the same arrangement, a small and narrow interradial plate intervening on either side between the first pair of I and that of II, as also between the *a, b 1* of V and of IV. Here also, as in Pourtalesia laguncula and Pourtalesia ceratopyga, but unlike Pourtalesia Jeffreysi, the I and V each commence with two plates, and the I *a* and V *b* are biporous, as according to rule. But, what is more, it is plainly shown in the fragment examined, that the 2 of V is not separated from its plate *1* by the intervenience of the interradials 4, but really contiguous to it, *fig. 42, 46*, part of the interradial 4, 2 coming into view between V *a* and IV *b*. It cannot be doubted that the like might be seen on the right side, if the specimen were entire. This diversity is of great moment. The plates I *a*, II *a*, III *b*, IV *a*, V *b* are biporous, while the I *b*, II *b*, III *a*, IV *b*, V *a* are uniporous, which is in complete accordance with the general rule. If I have succeeded in following rightly the very indistinct continuation of the plates beyond the curvature, the labrum, 5 *1*, ought to be extended to the peristome, having all along on either side the I *a* and V *b*, while of I *b* and V *a* the pointed terminations alone are to be seen just inside the margin of the niche, and still less of II *a* and IV *b*, the II *b* and IV *a* ending in the very bend, so that no trace of them is visible inside.

From all this it appears that the old order, reigning among the ambulacral plates of the peristome and their pedicellar pores, is not all at once abandoned by the Pourtalesiadae. It is exchanged for a new order only reversibly and, so to speak, hesitatingly. Pourtalesia carinata retains unaltered the otherwise universal Echinoidean formula:

I *a*, II *a*, III *b*, IV *a*, V *b*: biporous;
I *b*, II *b*, III *a*, IV *b*, V *a*: uniporous,

while Pourtalesia Jeffreysi, Pourtalesia laguncula, Pourtalesia ceratopyga, and Echinocrepis cuneata, all present a single pore only in each of the peristomal plates I, II, IV, V, which thus, in that respect, become symmetrical on either side of the labrum, the III alone remaining as of old. In none of the five species examined are all the interradials admitted into the peristome. In four of them the labrum, of considerable size, intervenes between I and V, and in three of these the interradials 1 and 4 tend to separate the I from the II, and the V from the IV. In one species alone, Pourtalesia Jeffreysi, the labrum, 5 *1*, is greatly reduced, and the I and V close with one another behind it, so as to exclude it completely from the rest of the perisomal system. All this recalls in a certain degree what is seen among the Clypeastridae, another type of late appearance. In these[1], of the peristomal ambulacrals none are biporous, all

[1] Études p. 32, pl. XLIV, LII.

the ten being uniporous, and much alike in the disposition of their pores, and the peristomal formula is sustained, in the greater number of genera at least, solely by the superior size of the first plates of I *a*, II *a*, III *b*, IV *a*, V *b*, or, more distinctly, of the corresponding second plates, one genus, however, Arachnoides, being exceptional even on that point. The relations between ambulacrals and interradials are also various, the latter preserving their series uninterrupted in Echinocyamus and Laganum[1]), while in Encope and Clypeaster, Echinarachnius and Arachnoides Zelandiæ[2]), the first plate of all is alone admitted into the peristome, as is also in Mellita and Rotula[3]) the first plate of 1, 2, 3, 4, while the interradium 5 remains entire, whereas in the adult Arachnoides placenta[4]) all are excluded, the 5, I alone appearing in the vicinity of the peristome.

I have given the insignificant name of Sphæridia[5]), Spherids, to certain sense organs, of function as yet obscure, present in all forms of the Echinoidea, the Cidaridæ, and perhaps Echinothuriadæ, excepted. They are very minute, calcareous, generally globular or pyriform, pedunculated bodies, articulated to little knobs of the test, and composed, like the spines, of an axial reticular tissue, and external compact layers of transparent glossy substance, and covered with a thin connective tissue, an epithel and a ciliated cuticule. They belong exclusively to the ambulacra, and to the adoral portions of these. In the greater number of the Echinidæ they are uncovered and mostly numerous, being found single, one only in each ambulacrum, in the genus Echinocidaris[6]) alone, which, together with the allied form, Coelopleurus, deviates from the Echinidan type in other respects also, in the sub-petaloid ambulacra bearing branchial pedicels, in the quadri-partition of the central piece of the calycinal system, in the anomalous forms of the spines. The Clypeastridæ offer two types: one, represented by the plurality of genera[7]), in which there is only a single spherid for each ambulacrum, more or less concealed in a cavity; and another, to which belong Clypeaster and Arachnoides[8]), having in each ambulacrum two spherids contained in crypts hollowed out in the substance of the test. In a like manner the multiple spherids of Cassidulus[9]), at first free and uncovered, successively become overgrown by the superficial layer of the calcareous substance of the test, until the site of each is marked merely by a very minute opening.

In all these groups, in which the bilateral disposition of the skeletal systems is often but slightly, though unfailingly expressed, the spherids are distributed by equal numbers, or nearly so, between the five ambulacra, which are also nearly of the same structure. In the Spatangidæ[10]), on the contrary, where the bilateral differentiation of the ambulacra in a trivium and a bivium, apparent already in the Holastridæ of the Older Cretaceous period, is gradually carried out in a decided manner,

---

[1]) Etudes, p. 32, pl. XLIV, XLV. [2]) Ib. p. 32, pl. XLVI, XLVII, L, LII. [3]) Ib. pl. XLVIII, XLVI. [4]) Ib. pl. LI. [5]) Ib. p. 1—11, 36, pl. I—V, VII—X, XVII. [6]) Ib. p. 7, pl. X, fig. 91, 92. [7]) Ib. p. 6, pl. VIII, fig. 68—73. [8]) Ib. p. 6, pl. VIII, fig. 74—78. [9]) Ib. p. 6, 36, pl. VII, fig. 61—66. [10]) Ib. p. 6, 36, pl. III, fig. 32—40, IV, 42—45; V. 48.

the spherids, mostly uncovered. — Lovenia alone having them recondite, — are often more or less unequally disposed, generally with some relation to the distribution of the phyllodean pedicels. Thus they generally are fewer on the front ambulacrum, III, in a greater number, though arranged in the same manner, on the two paired ambulacra of the trivium, II and IV, and most numerous, and not seldom somewhat differently disposed, on the bivium, as may be seen more particularly in Moira, Schizaster, Brissus, Plagionotus. Appertaining, as they do, to the ambulacral system, they obey, in their mode of appearance during the development of the individual, the law governing the growth of that system. Accordingly, in the very young animal the first spherid appears on each of the plates I b, II b, III a, IV b, V a, the second on plates I a, II a, III b, IV a, V b, and so forth, and in the same order also they are shed in the Echinidae [1]), and grown over in the Cassidulidae [2]). Consequently, in the Spatangidae, the plates bearing the first spherids are those having a single pedicellar pore, while the second spherids appear on the biporous plates.

All this is very different in Pourtalesia Jeffreysi. There are only four spherids, Pl. IV, fig. 15. Of these the two are placed one on each of the two first single plates of the bivium, I 1 and V 1, not far behind the pedicellar pore, close to the external suture, in a depression partly extending to the adjoining plate of the trivium. In the same manner the two other are placed on the plates II a 1 and IV b 1 of the trivium. They are all sub-globular, those of the first pair somewhat larger than those of the second, and all are uncovered. With the spherids of the Spatangidae they agree also in their proximity to the suture, and in the leaning over it, a feature observable in the first spherids of the young of these, Pl. XV, fig. 172, 174, 175, but soon lost [3]). The plates II b 1, IV a 1, and the whole of III, are devoid of spherids. Of the plates I, 1 and V, 1, the former represents the two peristomals I a 1, I b 1, and the latter the two V a 1 and V b 1. in other Echinoids, and as these two pairs are always symmetrical towards one another on both sides of the middle line, in their joint outline as with regard to their component elements, the position of the two larger spherids in Pourtalesia Jeffreysi is fully in harmony with the general law. But, according to that law, the first spherids of the ambulacra II and IV ought to have appeared on II b and IV b, that is to say: unsymmetrically, whereas in this Pourtalesia they are placed symmetrically towards each other, as detailed above, fig. 15. These spherids, therefore, like the rest of the ambulacral elements, are disposed solely in relation to the actual antero-posterior axis of the skeleton. They are also developed exclusively on that reduced part of its ventral surface which is in close contact with the ground on which the animal lives. Their size is relatively considerable. In a specimen of 34 mm. one of the larger spherids measures 0,26 mm. in length, and 0,20 mm. in transverse diameter, and one of the smaller 0,23 mm. and 0,20 mm., in the same dimensions. Compared to a spherid, 0,26 mm. in length, taken from a specimen of Meoma ventri-

---

[1]) Études, p. 37, pl. XVII, fig. 141—147.   [2]) Ib. p. 36, pl. VII, fig. 61—66.   [3]) Ib. pl. III, fig. 32, 33, 34.

cosa LAMK. of 160 mm., and to another of 0,15 mm., from an Echinocardium flavescens O. F. M., measuring 28 mm., the relation between the length of the spherid and that of the whole skeleton is

             in Mcoma ventricosa   as 0,16 to 100,
             in Echinocardium flavescens as 0,53 to 100,
             in Pourtalesia Jeffreysi   as 0,76 to 100.

The increased volume of each single spherid appears in some degree to make up for their reduced number, and its efficiency to depend, in some measure, on the extent of its ciliated surface.

The fragments given me by Sir WYVILLE THOMSON enabled me to examine these curious organs in three more species of Pourtalesia: P. lagnncula, P. carinata and P. ceratopyga of AL. AGASSIZ, Pl. VI, fig. 37, 38, 40, 41, 44; VII, 47, 48, 49, 50. In these, as in P. Jeffreysi, the entire set is brought together on the sub-labial parts of the first plates of the four ambulacra I, V, II, IV, there being none on the frontal, III. P. laguncula has four spherids, one on each of the ambulacrals I a, I b, V a, V b, Pl. VI, fig. 37, 38, 40, 41. They are pear-shaped, more lengthened in proportion than those of P. Jeffreysi, and placed in slight depressions close behind the first pedicels. In P. carinata, Pl. VI, fig. 44; VII, 47, their form is the same. I counted nine in all, one on each of the five first plates of I b, V a, II a, IV b, IV a, and two on I a and V b, but it is probable that some more were lost. The pedicellar portion of each plate is raised, and produced aborally into a projecting point, to which the first spherid is attached. In P. ceratopyga, Pl. VII, fig. 48, 49, 50, they are likewise pear-shaped, and still more numerous. I counted twenty two of them, twelve on the right, ten on the left, but there had no doubt been twenty four. The plates I a 1, I b 1, V b 1, V a 1, had four spherids each, II a 1 and II b 1 had each two, and IV b 1 also two, but on IV a 1 none could be detected, probably from its two spherids having being lost.

Thus the spherids of the Pourtalesiadae from one species to another seem to differ more widely in number than those of the other Echinoids. But, whether few or many, they are always found stationed exclusively on a restricted part of the sub-labial region, formed by the ambulacra I, II, V and IV, and absent on the part of the peristome that is elevated above it, ambulacrum III, while in Echinoids generally, in which the whole of the peristomal region is ventral, they are distributed all around, on all the five ambulacra, and missing only higher up, on the sides and on the back. Of whatever nature, therefore, the special changes in the surrounding water may be, that their ciliated epithelium has to watch for, these changes seem to be of essential moment to the animal, solely when they take place in the vicinity of the mouth, or between the under surface and the ground, on which the animal has to find its food.

The pedicels of the Echinoidea, of paramount importance as organs of touch, of locomotion and prehension, and, in some forms, of respiration, are, however, easily overlooked, and have been much neglected, even in the latest works. Réaumur [1]) was the first who, early in the last century, observed them in a living Echinus and described some of their functions. But he was led to state that every single perforation, »trou», of the ambulacrum answered to a pedicel, and consequently that there were as many pedicels as perforations. He also seems to have supposed that they are extended from the interior and drawn in again through the pores. Sixty years afterwards these errors were corrected by J. A. Gyllenhahl, [2]) in the highly remarkable paper in which he demonstrated the animal nature of the fossils then named »crystal apples», »calcareous nodules», or »Aetites», and ranged by Linnæus among minerals, but which he proved to be »petrified animals of the genus Echinus or its nearest allies». He described two species, the Echinus pomum, now Sphæronis pomum, and Echinus aurantium, now Echinosphæra aurantium, both well-known forms of Cystoidea. Of the former he says:

»Tentaculis procul dubio numerosissimis instructum (iisdem licet ipsis, prout mollioris substantiæ, adeoque petrificationis incapacibus, non potuerint non omnino privata fuisse fossilia individua): Cutis enim undique pertusa est poris minutissimis, orbiculatis: Quorum gemini semper collocati sunt intra cancellum minutum; inæquilateri-angulatum; fundo convexum; plerumque oblongum et in singula extremitate pororum altero pertusum».

This he explains thus:

»As »the tentacles» are to be understood those soft and elastic filaments which in all other Echini are attached to the surface of the test, each over a pair of small perforations. All the species of Echinus hitherto known possess cancelli on the surface of the test, corresponding with those described above in outline, in the convexity of the bottom, and in the test being pierced, within every single cancellus, by two minute perforations, one at each of its ends, the cancellus commonly being of an oval form. These two pores afford the communication between the internal parts and the tentacle, the basis of which occupies the entire cancellus, and consequently covers both pores. In the new fossil species now described the cancelli are somewhat deeper than in most other Echini, but in some of the irregular Echini I find those around the mouth to agree with them in this respect also.»

And he adds, against Réaumur:

»I have examined Echini of different species, such as they had been taken out of the sea and afterwards dried, and these I have placed in warm water in order to make their substance swell and resume its natural shape, and thus I found that, instead of there being one tentacle to each pore, there is one tentacle corresponding to each pair of pores.» . . . »It follows that the pores are twice as numerous as the tentacles».

It will be noticed, that Gyllenhahl had an idea that in some of the Echini irregulares of Linnæus, the pedicellar pores near the œsophageal opening were somewhat different from the rest. To the eminent Dane Otto Frederic Müller belongs, however, the discovery, as early as in 1776, of the peculiar structure, in Spatangus purpureus, of its circum-oral pedicels, of which, in the following year, he published a magnified figure,

---

[1]) Histoire de l'Académie Royale des Sciences. Année MDCCXII. Avec les memoires de mathématique et de physique pour la même année. Paris 1714. 4:o, Mém. p. 136, pl. 8.

[2]) Johan Abraham Gyllenhahl, in his twenty second year, communicated to the R. Swedish Academy of Sciences the above quoted memoir: Beskrifning på de så kallade Crystall-äplen och kalkbollar, såsom petreficerade djur af Echini genus, eller dess närmaste slägtingar. Kongl. Vetenskaps-Akademiens Handlingar för år 1772, Vol. XXXIII, p. 239. Translated into german in: Der Königl. Schwedischen Akademie der Wissenschaften Abhandlungen aus der Naturlehre, Haushaltungskunst und Mechanik, auf das Jahr 1772. Aus dem Schwedischen übersetzt von Abraham Gotthelf Kästner. Bd. XXXIV, p. 231. Leipzig 1776. -- J. A. Gyllenhahl, elder brother of Leonard Gyllenhaal, the eminent author of »Insecta Suecica», was born in 1750 and died in 1788, as Director of the Copper-mines at Åtvidaberg in Ostrogothia.

as good as any given since.[1]) He was also acquainted with another sort of pedicels, namely those belonging to the frontal ambulacrum of Echinocardium flavescens, and possessed figures of these, made by his brother and draughtsman C. F. Müller. These figures, however, were not published till long afterwards, in 1789, by Abildgaard[2]) who was well aware of the distinctness of the frontal pedicels from those surrounding the mouth. It will seem that O. F. Müller had regarded both as being of one and the same sort, when he made use of their structure, very happily after all though, as an essential character distinguishing his genus Spatangus: »*tentaculis penicillatis*», from the genus Echinus: »*tentaculis simplicibus*». [3]) This is indeed the first important step towards a rational dismemberment of the great Linnæan genus Echinus, and O. F. Müller is to be considered as the real author of the natural genus Spatangus since adopted by Lamarck. The name, borrowed from Aristoteles, had been in use with the Museographers of the pre-Linnæan era for certain artificial divisions.

It is, however, mainly to the account given by Johannes Müller[4]) of the various kinds of pedicels occurring in the Echinoidea, that we have to turn for the principal source of information respecting these important organs. After having remarked that not all the regular Echinoidea are homoiopodous, that is, have the whole of their pedicels terminating in a sucking-disk, as Duvernoy had presumed, but that certain genera, as Echinocidaris, Astropyga, Diadema, and Colobocentrus, have the dorsal pedicels simply pointed and flattened, and, the last named genus excepted, plaited on the sides, thus suggesting a respiratory function, he proceeds to give the following general description of these organs, as they occur in the Spatangidæ. In this group four different kinds of pedicels may be distinguished: 1) simple locomotive pedicels with truncated or rounded tops, destitute of sucking-disks; 2) locomotive pedicels provided with a terminal circular sucking-disk, either crenulated at the margin and strengthened inwardly with radiating calcified laminæ, or divided into radiating processes containing calcareous rods or lamels; 3) tactual, penicillate pedicels, ending in expanded brushes of club-shaped filaments, inwardly sustained by calcareous rods; 4) branchial pedicels, ambulacral gills, having the shape of triangular leaflets with plaited sides. In one and the same ambulacrum there may be found two or even three of these kinds succeeding one another, between the peristome and the dorsal pole. Wherever a fasciole is present, one kind of pedicels is peculiar to the area it circumscribes. In the genus Spatangus Joh. Müller recognises three kinds: tactual, locomotive and branchial. The circum-oral pedicels of all the five ambulacra are tactual and penicillate, the rest of the ventral ones simple and locomotive. Within the sub-anal fasciole there stand on either side three

---

[1]) Zoologiæ Danicæ Prodromus, 1776, p. XXIX. — Zoologia Danica, I. t. VI, fig. 5, 1777; latin letter-press, in 8:o, 1779, 1, p. 11; in fol., 1788, p. 5; danish letterpress, in fol., 1781, p. 19. The erratum, Zool. Dan. Prodr. p. XXIX: »ano infero», is here corrected to »ano laterali».

[2]) Zool. Dan. III, p. 17, t. XCI, fig. 4. »Terminantur disco radiato, radiis clavatis, alternis longioribus. Tentacula vero, quæ poros ad circumferentiam oris transeunt fasciculo penicillato filamentis capitatis composito terminantur». Abildg.

[3]) Zool. Dan. Prodr., p. XXIX.

[4]) Ueber den Bau der Echinodermen. Abhandl. d. K. Akademie d. Wissensch. in Berlin, 1854, sep. p. 26, pl. III.

penicillate pedicels, belonging to the inner rows of the bivious ambulacra, the fasciola traversing their plates. The front ambulacrum, which is never seen to bear gills, has simple locomotive pedicels, continuing all up to the calyx. But then in this genus the peripetalous fasciola is absent. Brissopsis, Schizaster etc., on the other hand, are provided with a peripetalous fasciola, and Echinocardium with an internal fasciola, and, within the boundary of either, the frontal radius presents a set of peculiar pedicels with crenulated or stellated disks, but outside of it only simple locomotive pedicels. In Brissopsis and Schizaster the disks contain radiating laminae,[1] as likewise the fingerlike processes of Echinocardium.[2] The internal fasciola of this latter genus traverses not only the front ambulacrum, but also the tops of the four petals, and the apical parts of these that fall within the fasciola, bear no branchial leaflets, only very minute simple pedicels.

The penicillate circum-oral pedicels of the five ambulacra JOHANNES MÜLLER found similar in all the genera examined, and, in all of them, subanal penicillate pedicels, in Brissopsis, as stated above, three on either side within the sub-anal fasciola, in Schizaster canaliferus, which is pryamadete, seven on either side, at a distance from the periproct, not between it and the posterior fasciola, but in front of the latter.

To this account may be added the previous researches of ERDL and VALENTIN, and those of subsequent observers, as AL. AGASSIZ, HOFFMANN and PERRIER.[3]

In my former memoir on Echinoidea I abstained from entering upon any detailed description of these organs, and gave only a short notice of their structure and distribution in Brissopsis lyrifera[4], and of the primordial pedicels in Toxopneustes droebachensis[5]. I expected to have, sooner or later, richer materials to examine. Although this hope has but partially been realised, as it is of some importance to compare the pedicels of Pourtalesia to those of the Spatangidae, in particular, and as I shall have no more occasion to revert to the subject, I here give what has hitherto been attainable to me, from which it will appear that these organs, overlooked as they have been, are well worth a much closer investigation than what I have been able to bestow upon them.

To the whole region around the peristome DESOR gave the name of *gloscelle*[6], retaining that of *phyllodes* for the part of each ambulacrum contiguous to the stoma, often distinguished by a somewhat expanded surface, and always by the presence of

---

[1] l. c. pl. III. fig. 6, 7.
[2] l. c. p. 29, pl. III. fig. 4, 5.
[3] VALENTIN, in Agassiz, Monographies d'Échinodermes, IV, p. 37, pl. 4, Echinus; 1842. — ERDL, Wiegmanns Archiv, VIII, 45, Taf. II, »Echinus saxatilis«; 1842. — ALEXANDER AGASSIZ, Rev. of the Echinidæ, I, p. 693, with numerous figures. — HOFFMANN, Zur Anatomie der Echinen n. Spatangen, Niederländisches Archiv für Zoologie, I, 1871, p. 75, 80, pl. X, fig. 78, 88—90. — PERRIER, Recherches sur les Pedicellaires et les Ambulacres des astéries et des oursins; deuxième partie, Ann. d. Sc. nat., 5:me ser., XIII, 1870, p. 1, 64; Ech. irréguliers; pl. 6, fig. 2, 3, 5: Amphidetus; 4, c—e, 7, e: Spatangus; 6, 8, 9: Brissopsis; 10: Brissus; ib. XIV, n:o 8: Echinoneus.
[4] Études, p. 10, pl. I. fig. 1.
[5] Ib. p. 27, pl. XVII, fig. 149—152.
[6] Synopsis des Échinides fossiles, 1858, p. 247. In creating these appellations Desor had in view the Cassidulidae alone, but they are equally applicable to the corresponding parts of the Spatangidae.

conspicuously large pores. The pedicels belonging to this region may be called phyllodean pedicels. In all the species examined the tubular shaft of these pedicels terminally expands into a circular convex disk, which, in the great majority, bears numerous capitate filaments covering its whole surface, Pl. VIII, fig. 64. They are disposed in concentric circles, and longer and more closely set at the margin, slightly shorter towards the centre, thus forming, with their tumid tops, almost a section of a sphere. Each filament contains a prolongation of the clear and homogeneous layer of the tube, and, imbedded in it, a slightly arched calcareous rod, by which the filament is kept rigid and in supination, Pl. VIII, fig. 55, 56, 58, 60. This rod, in the great majority of species, rises more or less centrally from a circular basis of areolar texture, in its immature state not unlike the wheels so frequent in Holothuriae, Pl. XI, fig. 121. On its under side it presents a prominent nave, Pl. VIII, fig. 63, while on the upper side a number of its fibres unite in forming the rod, which in some species is linear, in others at first contracted, then in most cases slightly widening, again attenuated and obtuse at the top, sometimes faintly clavate: dense and smooth, as in Brissopsis, Schizaster, Echinocardium, or presenting internal traces of meshy texture Pl. VIII, fig. 59, 60, and a rough, even spiny surface, as in Meoma, Lovenia, Spatangus. In Urechinus Naresianus, fig. 56, the rods are rather strong, not solid, but areolate throughout. Generally the conformation of the rods resembles a simplified miniature of that of a spine or radiole.

On the structure of the tumid tops of the filaments in Brissopsis lyrifera, I formerly made some observations, Pl. IX, fig. 80, 81, 82. From a thin layer, a plexus surrounding the homogeneous central substance, numerous nervous fibres are seen to traverse the connective tissue towards the inside of the external tegument, and there to form nucleated multipolar cells in close proximity and connexion with the bases of very minute, scattered, rigid and motionless hair-like processes on the external surface, which is devoid of vibratile cilia. From this structure the tactual function of the phyllodean pedicels appears to be fully confirmed; I give it here with a view of inducing further research, and at the same time will draw attention to the peculiar form of the tops of the filaments in Metalia, Lovenia and others, observed in specimens too long preserved in spirits to bear with a closer examination, Pl. VIII, fig. 61, 62.

From this description of the phyllodean pedicels, as I have observed them in the greater number of known genera, only three of these have presented exceptions, possibly more apparent than real. In Aceste bellidifera Wyv. Thoms., Pl. VIII, fig. 67, 68, which in some of its characteristics shows a certain analogy to Schizaster and Moira, even in the strangely forward position of the œsophageal opening, — an exaggeration of a feature not altogether foreign to them, — I found the disks of the phyllodean pedicels crowned only with a double marginal circle of filaments, leaving the central part naked, and raised into a high, rounded protuberance, which, when seen from above, presents distinct traces of five converging plicatures. Palæostoma mirabile Gray presented forms very similar, Pl. XVI, fig. 192, 193. In Palæotropus Josephinæ n. were found, among the regular phyllodean pedicels, some, fig. 72, that presented the same aberrant structure. It will be seen further on, that this structure is peculiar to the subanal pedicels, and it may be that in the cases here mentioned it is assumed by the aborally most distant among the phyllodean pedicels.

The mode of development and the growth of the phyllodean pedicels may be seen, partially at least, in very young specimens. In the young Abatus cavernosus, still astomous and aproctic, Pl. XIV, fig. 163, there are five in the ambulacra I and V, two of which are in the I *a 1* and two in V *b 1*, one in each of I *b 1, 2, 3*, and of V, *a 1, 2, 3*; in II and IV: two in *a, 1*, one in *a 2*, and one in each of *b 1, 2, 3*; in III: two in *b 1*, one in *b 2*, and one in each of *a 1, 2, 3*. They are all simple, rounded, elevated knobs. The young of Echinocardium flavescens O. F. M., Pl. XV, fig. 172, measuring only 1,7 millimeter without the spines, having the pentagonal peristome placed only a little before the middle, with the newly-formed oesophageal opening in its very centre, and presenting the five first spherids, one in each of the uniporous plates *1*,[1]) has fifteen phyllodean pedicels: two in each of the bi-porous plates, one on each of the uni-porous. The following plates are also provided with pores, but the pedicels beginning to form over them could not be discerned, probably from their too great transparency. Each of the fifteen pedicels presents a short tubular shaft, and a simple, tumid, semi-globular head, in the centre of which is seen a roundish, convex lamina of calcified reticular tissue, fig. 176. In a specimen only a trifle larger, 1,9 mm., fig. 175, the head of the pedicel of one of the uniporous plates, V *a*, fig. 177, has become ovate, and two circular wheels have begun to form on its centre-piece, one of them directed against the small end of the head, the other, smaller, nearly opposite, and on their outer sides the calcified fibres are seen to interlace and protrude. In the pedicel of V, fig. 175, 178, two rounded lobes have grown out, and to each of them there is a corresponding wheel, on the point, as it appears, of coming off the central network, and out of its fibres the rod is seen to rise outwardly. Similar changes are seen in the young specimen of Abatus cavernosus, in which the oesophageal opening is just on the point of forming.[2]) In another specimen of Echinocardium flavescens, of 3 mm., fig. 174, which has the oesophageal opening moved a little behind the centre of the pentagon, the second pair of plates, in each of the paired ambulacra, presents their newly-formed pedicels. The disk of the older pedicels has now expanded into two or three lobes, fig. 179, 180, each containing a wheel, free from the central network, and with a lengthened rod. Underneath are seen the long, arcuated, spiny, transverse spicules of the ring. The central network seems not so large, relatively to the expansion of the disk, as it was at first; in adult specimens it is absent, as generally among the Spatangidæ, a store used up by the growing rods. A specimen of 5,3 millimeters has disks, fig. 181, with eight clavate filaments, forming a marginal circle, and one that seems to begin another, inner circle. Their number appears to increase rapidly; a Spatangus purpureus of 14 millimeters already presents the same number as one of 51 millimeters.

[1]) Études, p. 36, pl. III, fig. 33—35.
[2]) See woodcut p. 26.

It follows from what has been detailed here, that the phyllodean pedicels of the great majority of the Spatangidæ, when forming, begin with a circular top, strengthened by a central calcareous network, that is, by a contrivance like that which is permanent in the Archæonomous Echinoidea, and chiefly subserves locomotion, but that they soon pass through this stage, as transitory, and develop into organs of a higher function, that of touch.

The distribution of the phyllodean pedicels among the five ambulacra, and the form of the phyllodes, are different in the different genera. The two bivious ambulacra I and V always symmetrise with one another in this, as do also the two paired ones, II and IV, while the front ambulacrum III, the odd one, stands alone. Whenever the two series a and b differ in the number of their phyllodean pores, it is the uniporous series, I b, II b, III a, IV b, V a, that presents the additional pore, all in accordance with the universal rule. The two paired ambulacra of the trivium, II and IV, present the most highly developed phyllodes, and the greatest number of phyllodean pedicels. In Maretia planulata these are seen to number eleven in each series, in Meoma ventricosa ten, in Brissus Scillæ nine, in Desoria australis eight, in Agassizia scrobiculata seven, in Spatangus purpureus six, in Breynia australasiæ, Plagionotus pectoralis, Faorina chinensis and Schizaster fragilis, five. On the other hand there are only four in Brissopsis lyrifera, Moira atropos and Abatus Philippii, three in Micraster cor anguinum, Kleinia luzonica, Echinocardium cordatum and Lovenia elongata. But still the number always equals, often exceeds that of the corresponding pores in the bivium. In the frontal ambulacrum the number of phyllodean pores is often less than in the bivium, in a few cases it equals them, and in still fewer exceeds them slightly, as in Brissus Scillæ, Plagionotus, Brissopsis, Maretia planulata. It follows from this that the floscelle has its greatest extension in the transverse direction.

In each phyllode the pedicels are largest in the proximity of the peristome, the more remote gradually becoming smaller, and less rich in filaments. They are, however rather suddenly replaced by simple pedicels, small and slender, terminating in a conical or truncated top, which, in most cases, is surrounded by a waved margin, as in Brissopsis lyrifera, Pl. IX, fig. 83, 84, Moira atropos, Pl. X, fig. 110, Lovenia elongata GRAY, fig. 107, 108, Schizaster japonicus AL. AG., fig. 111, and thus somewhat like the pedicels in Rhynchopygus pacificus AL. AG., Pl. XI, fig. 118, 119. These simple ventral and lateral pedicels become very slender and minute, more particularly in the bivium and the paired trivious ambulacra, and their pores are very small, all up to the petal. In the bivium, however, this holds good only with regard to the exterior rows of plates, the I b and V a. The two interior rows, I a and V b, very generally have their series of simple pedicels interrupted by the sudden appearance of the stout, peculiar, subanal pedicels discovered by JOHANNES MÜLLER. Introduced in the earlier Spatangidæ, the Prymnadetes, in an uncertain and, as it were, a hesitating manner, these pedicels become in the Prymnodesmians a constant and striking feature. The subanal fasciola, in traversing the bivious ambulacra,[1]) marks off their five foremost plates, 1—5, and

---
[1]) Études, p. 15, 59; pl. XXXII, fig. 200, — XLIII, fig. 232.

never more nor fewer, as ventral, the sixth of the inner row being intermediate, half ventral, half lateral, resembling the preceding in the size and position of its pore and the form of its simple pedicel, but extending itself inwardly like the succeeding, while the seventh + *x* following, have their pores transferred towards their opposite, inner extremity, and their pedicels, specialised in a peculiar manner, thus brought within the fasciola. This is the momentous modification of the Spatangean skeleton, brought on for the first time in Micraster during the Middle Cretaceous era. Generally, if not throughout, the subanal pedicels are penicillate, as stated by JOHANNES MÜLLER, and, at the first glance, they appear to be like those of the phyllodes, only that the disks are somewhat smaller, the filaments more unequal, as if disposed in five groups, and their terminal heads more tumid. On a closer inspection, however, this similarity is found to exist in but very few genera, as far as is hitherto ascertained, only in Echinocardium, in Lovenia, and perhaps in Breynia. In these the filaments are seen to cover the whole surface of the disk, though not quite so densely as in the phyllodean pedicels. In Echinocardium also the rods are much stronger, more particularly in E. cordatum PENN., *Pl. VIII, fig. 57*, in which species they are rather thin near the base, and from thence increase in thickness, so as to become four times as strong as those of the phyllodes, spindle-shaped, and nearly solid. The heads of the filaments, among which the marginal ones are the longer, are very tumid. So they are in Lovenia also, the rods being likewise stronger than those of the phyllodean pedicels, *Pl. VIII, fig. 59, 60*. But, unlike these, the great majority of other genera present a different arrangement. In Spatangus, Maretia, Brissopsis, Kleinia, Brissus, Metalia, and, as it seems probable, in Eupatagus and Linopneustes, among the Prymnodesmians, in Agassizia, Schizaster, Abatus, Hemiaster among the Prymnadetes, the pencil is made up of a few circles only of filaments, placed round the margin of the disk, so as to leave bare its central part, and within this there rises a cupola-shaped or even subglobular protuberance, surrounded by an open circular space, and commonly presenting on its top a central depression, in which about five folds are seen, indicating about five convergent, more or less distinct lobes. In Brissopsis the central protuberance sometimes shows eight to ten such lobes, nearly closing over the middle, sometimes, when subjected to pressure, taking the shape of a waved brim all around a flattened cup supported by five calcified areolar lamels, *Pl. IX. fig. 85*. So it is also in Brissus. In the like manner, the large central protuberance in Kleinia luzonica presents four or five triangular converging lobes almost closing over the middle, while in Spatangus purpureus it is relatively small, but high, apparently without any distinct lobes, supported by a convex areolar lamina, and surrounded by a broad circular space, and a marginal crown of filaments with very strong rods and very tumid heads.

In Agassizia scrobiculata VAL., *Pl. VIII, fig. 65*, the inner filaments are short, and the central protuberance, rising vertically and convex above, presents five triangular, thin, converging lobes, supported beneath by five coarsely areolar, calcified laminae. In Schizaster japonicus AL. AG. the whole of the central surface is occupied by the convex protuberance, presenting three to eight subtriangular, convergent, apparently very thick lobes, separated by deep grooves, and in some cases forming in the middle a funnel-shaped depression.

The structure thus described, the central protuberance, provided with flexible lobes resembling lips, sometimes found closed, sometimes open and expanded, in a certain degree calls to mind the sucking mechanism seen in Starfishes and Archæonomous Echinoids, as also in many other Echinoderms. If an Asterias rubens is brought to fasten some of its pedicels on a covering-glass, and this is placed under the microscope after the pedicels have been cut off, their tapering tops, destitute of any calcareous support, are found to be flattened against the glass, thus forming temporary disks, and their central parts are seen to be drawn in conically into the tube, by the action of some of its longitudinal muscles. If covering-glasses are strewn about in a vessel where specimens of Toxopneustes drœbachensis are kept alive, these readily take to lifting some of them, and keeping them hanging on their backs, perhaps mistaking them for fragments of dead shells, like those they are said to make use of in disguising. Preparations for the microscope are thus obtained of the disk in adhesion, the pedicels of this species keeping their hold more persistently after amputation than do those of the Starfish. If the glass is detached by pulling, some disks will let go their hold, each leaving behind a circular mark, a thin film made up of fragments of its cuticula, spread all around a clear spot in the centre, where there had been no adhesion. But other pedicels will part, and their disks, left adhering to the glass, *Pl. XI, fig. 112—115*, present within the broad circular and regularly waved margin, a flat surface, *fig. 113*, in whose centre an angular depression is seen to give off radiating, gradually less defined plicatures. Beneath this depression bundles of delicate muscular fibres come in sight converging from below, *fig. 112, 114, 115*, by the action of which the central part is drawn in. It will appear that suction is brought about in consequence of the capacity of this depression being thus increased.

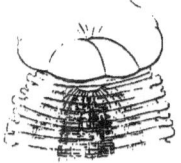

Sucking pedicel of Asterias rubens L.

Experiments on living Spatangi are necessary, before it may be safe to conclude from a certain resemblance in structure to a similarity of function, but meanwhile it seems at least allowable to look upon the subanal pedicels, in the genera enumerated above, as a combination of a marginal, tactual, with a central, sucking apparatus, and the whole as a union of a feeler and an instrument of prehension.

For locomotive purposes most of the Spatangidæ, being normally burrowers, chiefly use the strong oar-like spines of the sternum, and are never seen to climb the walls of glass-vessels, as do the true Echinids by means of their powerful pedicels. In close accordance with the amount of muscular exertion thus displayed by the last named, stands the superior solidity of the calcareous lamels and spicules that underlie the adhesive surface of their disk. These have been described by various authors. In Toxopneustes drœbachensis, *Pl. XI, fig. 112*, four reticular laminæ, concentric and adjacent to one another, and, if I am not mistaken, united by short muscles, inwardly inclose a circular open space, and outwardly send out strong points, at regular intervals, answering to the reentering angles between the marginal undulations. Their inner margins and their outer circumference are raised above the rest of the surface. Very similar lamels are seen in Echinoneus, Pl. XI, fig. 116, 117, which is homoiopodous. Close under this circlet of areolar lamels there lies, in the last named genus, fig. 117, as well as in Echinoids generally, fig. 114, 115, another set of calcareous ossicles, composing what may not improperly be named the foot-ring. This is for the most part composed of a single series of lengthy and arcuated spicules, outwardly smooth, inwardly areolar and frequently spinose, and placed transversely in such a manner as to overlap one another and to form together a quadrangle, or much more commonly a ring, encircling the tubular shaft. And, lastly, there follows, through the whole length of the shaft, the series of the well-known minute, numerous, arcuated and fusiform spicules.

The pedicels of the Spatangidæ possess calcified tissues answering to those in the Echinidæ just described. Their phyllodean pedicels, however, seem to be devoid, in the adult, of anything comparable to the strengthening lamellæ universally present in the suctorial disks of the Echinidæ. It has been shown above that in the phyllodean disk of a very young Echinocardium flavescens, a calcified network is primarily deposited, evidently corresponding to that seen in the sucking-disk of the young Echinus[1]), but also that it gradually diminishes, being, as it seems, dissolved and converted into the permanent form of the filamental rods, while the tactual function of the disk is preparing by means of the successive development of additional filaments. And long before these have reached their due number, the primary net-work has disappeared, at least I have searched for it in vain in the adult. It seems to be replaced, very generally, if not universally, by radiating vertical septa, Pl. VIII, fig. 64, composed of areolar lamels of irregular form, fig. 78, in some way connected with the annular spicules to be described hereafter. And likewise, when the subanal pedicels are constructed upon the model of the phyllodean, as in Echinocardium and Lovenia, there is no trace of strengthening horizontal laminæ.

On the other hand, when the disk of the subanal pedicels is provided with a central protuberance, apparently adapted for sucking, as in the genera enumerated above, this protuberance is often, though, as it seems, not always, underlaid with calcified laminæ, which, however, nowhere possess the solidity or the regular form observable in Echinids. Thus in Brissopsis lyrifera, Pl. IX, fig. 85, there are five such separate, but contiguous laminæ, in Agassizia scrobiculata, Pl. VIII. fig. 65, likewise five, of a somewhat triangular shape, in Brissus compressus LAMK., fig. 74, five, minutely areolar, contiguous, outwardly bi- or tri-lobate, while in Brissus mediator n., fig. 75, and Maretia planulata LAMK., they seem to form a convex, continuous expansion, outwardly of a more open texture, inwardly closer, supported on the underside by slender radiating ribs. — In the simple slender pedicels, ventral as well as lateral and frontal, the like structure obtains, a terminal combination of about five areolar lamellæ forming a somewhat convex layer, beneath the surface of the top.

[1]) Études, p. 28, pl. XVII, fig. 149, 150.

It follows from the general description here given, that the subanal pedicels, even in the antique form of Hemiaster, are penicillate, either totally, or, in most cases, partially, semi-penicillate, that is: partly suctorial, partly sensitory, the central space being occupied by a labiate elevation, and the periphery bearing clavate filaments. It is therefore rather surprising to find two genera distinctly different from the rest in this regard.

Palæotropus Josephinæ n.[1]), which deviates so widely from the Spatangean type, by its simple ambulacra, dorsally apetalous, and by the absence of branchial pedicels, — of the usual form at least, — but which is still provided with at least semi-penicillate phyllodean pedicels, presents, within the subanal fasciole, on either side, two plates, 7 and 8, bearing pedicels, *Pl. VIII, fig. 73*, larger than the rest, but devoid of the usual marginal crown of filaments, and presenting only a circular disk with a waved margin, strengthened by about eight areolar, subtriangular, converging lamels. In Meoma grandis and M. ventricosa a similarly exceptional structure occurs. The phyllodean pedicels are normal, very strong, and rich in filaments. Within the bivium they are such in I *a*, plates *1* and *2*, in I *b*, plates *1, 2, 3*; in V *a*, plates *1, 2, 3*, in V *b*, plates *1* and *2*. Then come, abruptly, very minute, simple pedicels, each terminating in a small disk, the diameter of which is less than that of the tube. It has a distinct, but thin and rather narrow margin, and within that a convex area, in which are seen four or five converging lobes, leaving a small bare space in the centre, and underlaid with an equal number of lamels of rather coarse and open network. The pedicels continue such in V *b*, as also in I *a*, by the plates *3, 4, 5, 6*. With their respective plates 7 they come behind the incomplete subanal fasciola, but remain unaltered, only very sligtly larger in plates 7, 8 of V *b*, and 7, 8, 9 of I *a*. These are the only two exceptions known to me, from what appears to be the general rule.

The number of typical or modified subanal pedicels differs in the different genera, and among the species of one and the same genus. If the figures given in my former work, of the skeletal structure of the Spatangidæ are consulted, it will be found that in all the Prymnodesmians figured,[2]) Palæotropus, Micraster, Brissus, Meoma, Spatangus, Brissopsis, Kleinia, Echinocardium, Plagionotus, Breynia, Maretia, Lovenia, the sixth plate of I *a* and V *b*, though extended mesially so as to reach within the fasciola, retains the minute pore of the simple pedicel in its place, near the outer margin and outside the fasciola, while the true subanal pedicels begin in the seventh plate, their large pores being transferred towards the inner end of the plate, and within the fasciola. The same holds good in Metalia and Eupatagus, not figured there, and, in fact, in every species of the Prymnodesmians hitherto examined, from which it may be allowable to conclude that the same conformation is maintained in the genera Cionobrissus, Homolampas, Linopneustes, Argopatagus, of AL. AGASSIZ. Among the Prymnadetes it is otherwise.[3]) The order is even different in different species of the same genus. Thus, in Schizaster fragilis and Sch. Moseleyi, the subanals begin with the se-

---
[1]) Études, p. 17, pl. XII, fig. 105; XIII, fig. 108—113; XXXII, fig. 200.
[2]) Ib., pl. XXXII, fig. 200, — XLIII, fig. 232.
[3]) Ib., p. 16, pl. XXVI, fig. 185, — XXXII, fig. 197.

venth, in Sch. japonicus and Sch. gibberulus with the fifth, in Abatus cavernosus with the eighth, in A. Philippii with the seventh. In Agassizia scrobiculata and Faorina chinensis they commence with the sixth, in Hemiaster Fourneli with the seventh, in Desoria australis with the tenth.

Among the Prymnodesmians perhaps the greatest number of subanal intra-fasciolar pedicels occurs in the genus Brissus, they being as many as nine on either side in Brissus carinatus Al. Ag.[1]), and at least five or four in Brissus Scillæ and Brissus Garretti Al. Ag. Breynia australasiæ has six in I a, seven in V b, the old Micraster cor anguinum five on either side, Plagionotus pectoralis and Kleinia luzonica four. In Meoma ventricosa, Brissopsis lyrifera, Echinocardium cordatum, Lovenia subcarinata, Maretia planulata, there are three, in Spatangus purpureus and Palæotropus Josephinæ only two. Among the Prymnadetes the diversity is greater, Agassizia scrobiculata possessing five or six, Abatus Philippii, Desoria australis, Faorina chinensis three, Hemiaster Fourneli Des. as many as eight.

A very young specimen of Brissopsis lyrifera, measuring only 4,6 mm. in length,[2]) has the plates 6, 7, 8, 9 of I a and V b extended within the fasciola, and the three: 7, 8, 9, bearing semi-penicillate pedicels, all which is as in the adult. The number of intra-fasciolar pedicels, normal to each species, therefore, seems to be obtained at a very early age, so that specimens, inferior in size and presenting fewer subanal intra-fasciolar pores ought not, on that account, to be taken for juvenile stages of species possessing a greater number of such pores, and to which they in other respects may have some resemblance. At the same time, however, it is not to be overlooked that the number of these pores is sometimes, but rarely, seen to vary slightly in one and the same species, and that even in the same specimen there may be one more in I a than in V b, or *vice versa*. But these are accidental variations, and, with proper care, the number of subanal intra-fasciolar pedicels may be used, with perfect confidence, as a specific character.

Various, with regard to size and form, as are the pedicels of the bivium, the frontal pedicels, those of the ambulacrum III, are still more so. In this the phyllodean pedicels are soon succeeded by simple pedicels. Wherever their succession is not interrupted by a dorsal fasciola, they continue unaltered and of minute dimensions all up to the calycinal system. Thus it is in Spatangus purpureus O. F. M., Maretia planulata Lamk. and Maretia alta Lütken. In Maretia planulata, *Pl. X, fig. 104*, they taper into a rounded tip, within which are seen reticular lamels. In Spatangus purpureus those next to the phyllodean pedicels rise abruptly from a large and tumid base, while the following, up to the calyx, are slender and very small, and similar to the simple lateral pedicels of Brissopsis, *Pl. IX, fig. 83, 84*, or those of Meoma, *Pl. VIII, fig. 70, 71*, described above, terminating in a small disk, with highly flexible margin. In most cases the dense pigment of the top prevents observing its internal structure, but, when long macerated in weak spirits, it sometimes happens to retain the calcareous skeleton still coherent, *Pl. X, fig. 105*. Then it is seen, that at the base of the flexible margin

---

[1]) Revision, pl. XXXI, a, fig. 3, 4.   [2]) Etudes p. 16, pl. XXXVII, fig. 218.

there lies a ring of strong, transversal, arcuated and branched spicules, and that the central part is sustained by about five, finely areolar, converging, and convex laminae.

Among the genera provided with a peripetalous or an internal fasciola, such continuance of simple pedicels all through the length of the frontal ambulacrum has been observed only in Meoma and Lovenia. In Meoma ventricosa and M. grandis, both of which huge species have a well-marked, though narrow peripetalous fasciola, the frontal pedicels, Pl. VIII, fig. 70, surprisingly minute, present the same uniform simple structure all along, from the phyllode to the calyx, just as those of I a and V b do within the subanal fasciola. The central convexity is lobate, much as in the subanals of Schizaster, and the spicular structure is that just described in Spatangus. Very minute are also the simple frontal pedicels within the internal dorsal fasciola of Lovenia, Pl. X, fig. 107, 108, and similar in structure to those of Spatangus.

Among the Prymnadetes, Hemiaster expergitus n., Pl. X, fig. 92,[1]) the most ancient generic type among recent Spatangidae, presents, within the peripetalous fasciola, middle-sized pedicels, terminating in a flat disk, slightly waved at the margin, strengthened by ten or eleven elongated, reticular, calcareous lamels, which in their outer, larger and horizontal portion are of a more open texture and lacerated at the margins, in the inner, tapering and feebly rising portion, more compact, smooth-margined and contiguous, leaving a clear space in the centre. Slightly different from this is the terminal disk in Abatus Philippii, fig. 91, not much exceeding the tubular shaft, circular and sustained by areolar lamels up to twelve in number, sub-triangular, rather flat throughout, more dense and less rough-margined in their inner tapering portion. But it is in the singular Palæostoma mirabile and in the group formed by Schizaster, Moira and Aceste, that this structure of the terminal disk is more highly developed, the pedicels at the same time attaining unusual dimensions, so as to make their rows form a very striking feature of the frontal ambulacrum. In all of them the disk is wide, and strengthened by numerous radiating laminae. In Palæostoma, Pl. XVI, fig. 194, it is octo-stellate, and the laminae, outwardly lanceolate, have their inner portions broad and spade-like. In Schizaster fragilis, D. & K., Pl. X, fig. 100, its margin is digitate, deeply divided into from fifteen to twenty three rays, expanded at the top, each of them for about half or two thirds of its length supported inwardly by a long, nearly linear lamel, lacerated at its growing end, otherwise nearly smooth-margined, with its inner portion slightly rising, and tapering to an obtuse point. The same reappears in Schizaster japonicus AL. AG., fig. 101, 102, 103, in which the margin is less deeply digitate, and the lamellae, even exceeding thirty in number, are very long and narrow, and have their inner ends slightly dilatated. In Moira atropos, fig. 94, 95, on the other hand, the inner contiguous portions of the lamellae are broad, spade-like and smooth-margined, thus contrasting with the outer portion which is narrow, linear and jagged. In Aceste bellidifera WYV. THOMS., fig. 96, 97, 98, which has received its name from the size and singular appearance of these pedicels, the broad expanse of the disk is only slightly waved in front of each of the twenty to twenty seven rod-

---
[1]) Études. p. 13, pl. XII, fig. 114—120; XI, fig. 93, 94; V, fig. 46, 47

like, narrow laminae, with shortened, acutely triangular inner portions, and lengthened, slightly widened, and spinous outer portions. In Aceste, Moira and Schizaster japonicus another peculiarity is met with. The inner portion of each lamella has its margins thickened and compact on the under surface, and produced on either side into a tooth, which in the Schizaster, *fig. 102, 103*, is strong and directed inward, in Moira, *fig. 95*, hardly perceptible. Between the thickened margins the under surface is concave, and the upper, in Aceste, raised into a projecting keel. *fig. 97, 98*. It is worthy of remark that in Schizaster fragilis scarcely a rudiment is to be seen of the whole of this conformation, which no doubt serves to extend the attachment of motor muscles.

Among the Prymnodesmians, Metalia, *fig. 106*, has frontal pedicels nearly like those of Abatus. A conformation, similar to that just described in Schizaster, reappears in Kleinia luzonica GRAY, whose long and well-developed frontal pedicels end in a large disk, deeply divided into thirteen to fifteen rays, corresponding to a like number of laminae, *fig. 99*, resembling those in Moira, only a little broader, of a more open texture, and more spiny at the margins. Their inner extremities are also spade-like, with two distinct marginal teeth. In Brissopsis lyrifera the strong frontal intrafasciolar pedicels likewise terminate in a large and flat circular disk, *Pl. IX, fig. 86—89*, with a waved margin, the regular undulations of which answer to an equal number of fifteen to eighteen radiating laminae, resembling those of Schizaster fragilis, subrectangular in their longer, external portions, compact, smooth-margined and tapering to an obtuse point in their internal contiguous portions, and devoid of the marginal teeth seen in Kleinia. The circular space in the centre generally is perfectly clear, — numerous observations had indeed made me assured that it were so invariably, till one specimen turned up, presenting the calcified lamina delineated in *fig. 86*. According to notes taken long ago, accompanying the figures here given of the disk, as it appeared in the living animal, these lamels are inclosed in the homogeneous substance, outside which is seen a complexity of connective tissue and nervous elements, together with interspersed pigmentary nucleated cells, *fig. 88*, some deep red, others yellow. This texture extends to the inside of the epithel. In the interstices between every two laminae there is seen an oblong granular body, opaque by transmitted light, white by reflected light, having all the appearance of a glandular mass, although, at the time, I could not find an excretory opening. In specimens preserved in spirits it has disappeared almost completely. It may perhaps secrete some viscous substance, by which minute animals are captured that live above the surface of the clay in which the Spatangus is deeply burrowing, while the tops of these highly extensible, prehensile organs are playing freely in the water high above. Alone among the species hitherto examined, Agassizia scrobiculata, *Pl. X, fig. 93*, has frontal intra-fasciolar pedicels similar to the subanal. Almost of the same size with these, they likewise end in a circle of filaments of unequal length, with rods as slender, and tops as tumid, surrounding a cup-like protuberance with five triangular lobes converging into a central depression, and overlying a rosette of radiating laminae.

Echinocardium presents a rather peculiar form of frontal pedicels. In Echinocardium flavescens O. F. M., *Pl. XI, fig. 127—130*, their structure was observed already by OTTO FREDERIC MÜLLER, and described by his editor ABILDGAARD [1]), as terminating in a stellate disk, the rays, fifteen in number, being clavate and alternately longer. They are robust, straight, obtuse at the top, slightly contracted at the base, and strengthened by an inner calcareous rod of peculiar conformation, conical, not rising from the centre of its basal circlet, but almost directly from its very margin, and made up of numerous longitudinal, linear and straight fibres, with short transverse connecting processes, but becoming compact near the point, *fig. 129*. The central part of the disk is a cup, *fig. 127*, the margin of which sometimes is waved irregularly, sometimes formed into lobes closing over it. In Echinocardium cordatum, Pl. *XI, fig. 120* —*126*, it likewise bears a cuplike projection, the lips of which present various forms, depending on their different degree of contraction, but it is surrounded by a marginal, single row of numerous, even up to forty, unequal, slender and clavate filaments, each containing a straight or very slightly arcuated, needle-shaped rod, *fig. 121*, composed of a small number of calcareous fibres rising from the margin of the basal circlet of network, but soon contracting, becoming nodular, swelling again, and spiny near the top. Neither of these two species of Echinocardium presents any trace of a central network at the bottom of the cuplike projection. In Breynia Australasiæ LEACH, Pl. *XI, fig. 131*, the long and slender frontal pedicels, within the peripetalous and internal fasciola, are provided at their truncated, not disciferous ends, with a few marginal, very short, conical processes, evidently answering to the filaments of others, each supported by a strong and solid calcareous rod, with traces of reticular texture only at its base, and somewhat resembling the rods in Echinocardium flavescens.

The shafts of the pedicels are prolongations of the external tegument, each rising over a geminous pore. With the exception of the branchial pedicels, they are cylindrical tubes, flexible and extensible in an eminent degree. In Brissopsis lyrifera, Pl. *IX, fig. 90*, I found the wall to be made up of: an external layer, *a*; a thick layer, *b*, consisting of connective tissue and nervous elements, with imbedded pigment cells, red and yellow; a thin, homogeneous, transparent layer, *c*, in which the calcareous spicules are deposited; another, *d*, of delicate, transverse, muscular fibres, and, within that, a much stronger one, *e*, of longitudinal muscles; and, innermost, *f*, a rich plexus of multipolar nucleated cells, the true extension of which I could not make out at the time, and which seemed to occupy, to a great extent, the lumen of the tube. This structure was observed in the tubular shafts of the pedicels of the front ambulacrum, and it appeared to hold good in the others also.

The transverse spicules of the homogeneous layer *c* are disposed into longitudinal rows. Generally they are the most minute of all the various calcified deposits, sometimes numerous, and then densely packed in the contracted state of the pedicel, in other instances rather scarce, even apparently wanting in the phyllodean pedicels, rarely so in the subanal, frontal or ventral. They are more or less arched, sometimes bent, as in Echinocardium cordatum, III, Pl. *XI, fig. 120*; slender, slightly fusiform, nearly smooth, as in Metalia, III, Pl. *X, 105*; Maretia, III, *104*; Palæotropus, subanal,

[1]) See above p. 43.

Pl. VIII, 73; very minute in Moira, ventral, Pl. X, 110; muricate, but rarely areolar, in Spatangus purpureus, III, 109; Meoma, III, Pl. VIII, 70; Breynia, III, Pl. XI, 131; Brissopsis, ventral, Pl. IX, 83; Abatus, III, Pl. X, 91; Echinocardium, III, Pl. XI, 123, 128. All through the length of the tube they are generally of the same shape, but near the top they regularly all at once assume peculiar shapes, and combine in forming the foot-ring, annulus, psellion, under the terminal part. In some the elements of this ring are simply enlarged modifications of those of the shaft, presenting an annular complication of lengthened, arched, overlapping spicules, sometimes prickly, Brissus, Pl. VIII, fig. 74, sometimes outwardly almost smooth, inwardly spinous and emitting, at regular distances, strong spikes, Brissopsis Pl. IX, 85, or connected with centripetal spokes, as in Brissus, Pl. VIII, 75, or in the phyllodean pedicels of Maretia, 64, 78, which are composed of series of irregular flakes. In others the ring consists of areolar prickly lamels, small in Spatangus, III, Pl. X, 109, in Lovenia, III, 107, 108, larger, subtriangular, as in Echinocardium flavescens, III, Pl. XI, 128, phyllode, 130. In others again, as in the subanals of Lovenia, Pl. VIII, 76, Abatus, 77, in the frontals of Breynia, XI, 131, and in Rhynchopygus, XI, 119, the ring is formed by a single series of detached, irregularly rounded, areolar scales. Echinocardium cordatum in this regard deviates in a most extraordinary manner, not only from its congener E. flavescens, but from all the rest of Spatangidae. The tubes of the phyllodean pedicels are devoid of spicules, and the ring is represented by a few small sigmoidal ones only; in the shafts of the subanals there is a single row of similar spicules, most of them rather broad in the middle and areolar, and the tubes of the pedicels of the III, within the fasciola, present two rows of similar small and slender, slightly muricate spicules. In the subanals, as well as in the frontals, there is no trace of a true ring, but close under the top one single spicule, or in some cases two spicules, suddenly become of an enormous size, Pl. XI, fig. 120, 123, lying across the tube, and even exceeding with their pointed ends the diameter of the crown of filaments, and sometimes simple, sometimes expanded in the middle, areolar and spinous, fig. 122, 124, 125. These gigantic spicules, larger generally in the frontal pedicels than in the subanal, are seen as well in the common European Echinocardium cordatum PENN. as in that called E. australe GRAY. It is difficult to conceive their probable use, unless they may be some sort of stinging apparatus, a weapon added to the tactual and prehensile parts of the pedicel.

The diversities in form and in function exhibited by the pedicels are represented more or less distinctly by corresponding modifications of those special parts of the skeletal framework which surround the canals, by which they communicate with the ambulacral system in the interior. These parts were called cancelli by older authors: I shall venture to propose for them the appellation of peripodia.

It was, no doubt, a bright thought of J. A. GYLLENHAHL, in those days, now more than a hundred years ago, to assimilate the »cancelli» of the »crystal apples» to those of recent Echini, and on that account to transfer their bearers to the animal kingdom, ranging them under the great natural genus Echinus, then recently instituted by LINNÆUS. And so close is in reality, on either side, the general conformity in structure of the geminous pores, as to cause the lineage of the Archæonomous Echinoidea to gravitate forcibly towards that group of antique Cystoidea of the Silurian era, different as these no doubt were in other respects, in the total absence, — at least in the adult, — of a calyx, and in the distribution of the pores all over the perisome. There seems also to be little reason for doubting the pedicellar character of the geminous pores in Sphæronis, Eucystis, Glyptosphæra, Protocrinus, Mesites, the less so since the want of a decisive proof in this regard is supplied, in some degree at least, by the occasional preservation of the actual pedicels in a contemporary form of Echinoids, Botryocidaris Pahleni FRED. SCHMIDT, of the older Silurian era. A specimen of this most remarkable type, for the inspection of which I have to thank the liberality of its learned author, distinctly shows, in several places, long cylindroid bodies, having one of their ends in close connection with an ambulacral, geminous pore, even so as to cover it, and for the rest of their length

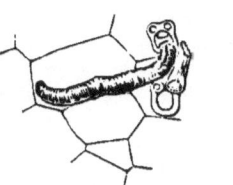

Pedicels of Botryocidaris Pahleni FR. SCHMIDT.

lying variously bent across the plates, with their free ends gradually tapering into rounded tips, and thus like the simple pedicels of one of our Echinoids. They even exhibit traces of having had their tubes strengthened by series of arcuated spicules.

The peripodia, so I venture to call them from analogy, of those archaic Cystoidea and of Botryocidaris, and, generally, of the Archæonomous Echinoidea, are built mainly upon the same model: a wall, more or less raised, incloses an elliptical or lengthened depression in which, in the great majority of forms, two nearly equal perforations open, placed on the longitudinal diameter and separated by a septum, or bridge, of varying breadth and form. In the genera of Cystoidea named above, their distribution is somewhat various. In Sphæronis and Eucystis the whole perisome is densely crowded with them, all or nearly all pointing adorally with their longer axis; in Protocrinus they are strewn less dense-

Sphæronis pomum GYLL.   Glyptosphæra Leuchtenbergi VOLB.   Protocrinus fragum EICHW.   Mesites Pusirefskii NIK.

Peripodia.

ly over the whole exterior, the grooves excepted, and point mainly in the direction of the mouth, still with a tendency to deviate; in Mesites they are confined to the perisome and variously divergent. In Botryocidaris they are confined to the ambulacra, and point all one way. This is also the case with the ambulacral peripodia in all the rest of the Echinoidea, the direction of their longer axis being towards the mouth, those of the branchial peripodia of the petala excepted, which normally are transverse.

In *Pl. XII, fig. 132—149*, an attempt is made to give a general idea of some important modifications of the peripodia among the Neonomous Echinoidea. The series begins with the homoiopodous Echinoneus [1]), *fig. 132*, which, as in other parts besides, retains an Archæonomous character in the structure of its disciferous pedicels and their peripodia, very like those of an Echinus, geminous, with the pores nearly equal. In the Cassidulidæ, *fig. 133*, the new order has set in, the peripodia of the five petala being branchial, and very different from those of the phyllodes. In Cassidulus these last are deep, oval depressions, with the bottom sloping towards the adoral end, near which is the single perforation. In the Spatangidæ, including the Collyrites and Anancites, the phyllodean peripodia, by their superior size, gradually become more and more prominent, at the same time assuming a character of their own that corresponds to that of their pedicels specialised into organs of sense. They are shown in *fig. 134 — 148*, all IV *a 1*, ear-shaped expansions, contrasting with the rest of the surface by a compact and glossy texture, generally of an obovate outline, the longitudinal axis pointing adorally, and mostly towards the mesial suture of the ambulacrum. Within this expansion, the boundary line of which is slightly impressed, while its surface is in some forms convex, in others flat or even depressed, the perforations, as long as geminous, are placed on the longitudinal diameter, the adoral perforation, which is always present, mostly being the larger of the two, while the aboral has a tendency to abort. Thus it seems to be the rule, that in the early types, the Adete, Meridosternal [2]) forms, both perforations are maintained. In Holaster seaniensis COTTEAU, *fig. 134*, they are separated by the highest part of the convex surface, and in Anancites ovata, *fig. 135*, minute, and kept apart by an ovoid protuberance, — and so it is in both the two peripodia of IV *a 1*. The distal peripodium of Hemipneustes, *fig. 136*, shows only a trace of the aboral perforation, while in the proximal it has disappeared. In Echinopatagus, *fig. 137*, one of the earliest of Amphisternal [3]) forms, the perforations of IV *a 1*, reduced in size, are geminous, the bridge being almost as in the Echini. Among the Prymnadetes the two perforations are maintained in Hemiaster, *fig. 138*, and in Faorina, *fig. 142*, in others the aboral perforation aborts. How this is done may be observed in Schizaster japonicus, *fig. 140*, or in Sch. Moseleyi. The aboral perforation contracts, and is moved towards the adoral, while the bridge gradually narrows, till at last it opens, and the two make one, the trace of the passage being overgrown with calcareous tissue. In fullgrown specimens of Schizaster fragilis there are still some geminous perforations left, in Sch. gibberulus and in Moira atropos they are all simple. So they are also in adult specimens of Agassizia and Desoria, while in Abatus Philippii a process obtains similar to that in Schizaster japonicus. Lastly, among the Prymnodesmians, the latest and the most advanced of Neonomous Echinoids, the geminous pore, strictly kept up even as far as from Melonites, and discarded in a few only of the Prymnadetes, their elders, is replaced, as it seems universally and normally, by a single perforation. So it is in Micraster, Brissopsis, *fig. 143*, Brissus *fig. 144*, Spatangus *fig. 145*, Lovenia *fig. 146*, Maretia *fig. 147*, Echinocardium, *fig. 148*, and in Meoma, Plagionotus, Breynia, Eupatagus. It is a change that implies a certain amount of modification in the vascular apparatus. —

---

[1]) Études, pl. IX. [2]) Μερίς, piece. [3]) Ἀμφίστερνος, with two breast plates.

Palaeostoma mirabile, *fig. 139*, presents deeply sunk phyllodean peripodia, with the two perforations not separated, but united by an open slit. The specimen examined is, however, young and still retains this juvenile character, the pore being at first simple, not geminous.[1]

When the entire series of Adete, Prymnadete and Prymnodesmian Spatangidæ is viewed as a whole, the common characters of their phyllodean peripodia is apparent: their general form, their great size relatively to that of the other peripodia bearing tubular pedicels, the parallel direction of the two peripodia of the biporous plates, the gradually prevailing abortion of their aboral perforation. The similarity is in fact such as to justify the conclusion that the principal characteristic of the modern Spatangidæ, the penicillate phyllodean pedicels, was present already in the earliest Adete forms, in Collyrites, Holaster, Anancites, Hemipneustes, Cardiaster.

Where the penicillate pedicels are succeeded by the much smaller simple pedicels, the peripodia, again with geminous perforations, at once become very minute. In the Meridosternal Adetes, as in Collyrites, Anancites, Hemipneustes, they continue so in the five ambulacra all up to the petala, in Holaster and Cardiaster through the middle part of the front ambulacrum, and in the four paired ambulacra, I and V, II and IV, up to their petala, thus suggesting the probable absence, in these old types, of peculiar subanal pedicels. These appear in the Amphisternal Spatangidæ in I *a* and V *b*, supported by peripodia always larger than the corresponding in I *b* and V *a*, though in a various degree. Already in Echinopatagus, Hemiaster, and in Palaeostoma, that of V *b* surpasses that of V *a*, and in the great majority of recent forms, Prymnadete as Prymnodesmian, the difference is more or less marked, *fig. 140 — 148*. But, as far as my present knowledge extends, the structural differences of the subanal pedicel, penicillate, semi-penicillate, or simple and devoid of filaments, are not distinctly associated with corresponding diversities in the peripodium. The penicillate subanal of Echinocardium is supported by a peripodium not very unlike that of the simple pedicel of Meoma, and the similarities or dissimilarities between the subanal peripodia of different genera appear to bear no very close relations to the resemblances or diversities between their pedicels. The like seems not far from being the case with those of the front ambulacrum. There is some resemblance between those of Hemiaster, *fig. 138*, and of Schizaster, *fig. 140*, — they are lengthened, narrow, and bridged over by a convex protuberance, — and that of Palaeostoma, *fig. 139*, is not very different —, and these three genera have frontal pedicels with large radiating lamels in the disk; but the nearly similar frontal pedicels of Brissopsis, *fig. 143*, have very different peripodia. Those of the simple frontals in Spatangus, Maretia, Lovenia and Meoma are minute, those of the more complicated, as in Agassizia and others, are much larger.

In the greater number of Neonomous forms, Cassiduline and Spatangean, the pedicels of the dorsal portions of the ambulacra are transformed into but slightly extensible, generally triangular branchial leaflets. These portions of the ambulacra,

[1] Études. pl. XVII, fig. 151.

the petala, are in themselves uninterrupted, »open« continuations of the ambulacral series of plates, thus in Cassidulus, in the Adetes, in Spatangus, Micraster, Maretia, Echinocardium, Lovenia. When, in others, as in Agassizia, Meoma, Brissopsis, Kleinia, Brissus, Eupatagus, Plagionotus, Breynia, they are »closed« inferiorly, this is an accidental feature, the constriction being caused solely by the pressure exerted by the peripetalous fasciola.[1]) The petaline plates are longitudinally narrow, extended transversely, and the peripodium, generally placed towards the external margin, incloses with a narrow rim the always geminous, widely separated, transversely placed perforations, and unites them with a slender compressed ridge or with a furrow, a more or less distinct suture marking the junction of the margins from either side. Upon the whole a structure like this is found prevalent in the great majority of forms coming into view from the first appearance of the Cassidulidæ. But among the Spatangidæ their exists a group, of a few genera, differing widely enough in other respects, but held together by a common character, the absence of petala. They are Apetalous; whether Abranchian further researches will decide. Their ambulacra, instead of being, in their dorsal portions, deepened and crowded with compressed plates, in order to give room to numerous gill-leaflets, are all along even with the general surface, and only gradually contracting up to the top, and their plates, as high as they are broad, or nearly so, are regularly hexagonal, the pores being very minute, placed centrally or subcentrally, and the pedicels small and simple. These genera are Palæotropus, Argopatagus; Urechinus; Cystechinus; Genicopatagus; Aceste, Calymne, Aerope. They are all abyssal.

In the vast majority of Echinoidean forms, Archæonomous and Neonomous, — and presumably in the whole of them, — it is seen that the adoral and inner perforation of the peripodium is prolonged into a short and narrow slit, cut through the wall, and that this slit widens below into a separate but smaller perforation. This is very distinctly seen in the Cidaridæ, Echinidæ, Echinoconidæ, Echinoneidæ, and, above all, in the phyllodean peripodia of the Spatangidæ. In those of the Cassidulidæ, as generally in the subanal and frontal, as well as petaline peripodia, it is less distinct, but mostly to be recognised as a minute notch in the wall. This is the particular little foramen that gives passage to the branch of the ambulacral nerve which is seen, on the inside of the plate, to enter the pore along with the vessel, and, as easily, on the outside, to emerge from it and distribute its branchlets, all through the connective tissue, to the external organs.[2])

Such is a sketch of the pedicels in the most prominent of Neonomous Echinoidea, as they are variously specialised in order to meet requirements more varied than those essential to the earlier types: developed into delicate organs of touch, or combining with tactual function that of prehension, modified for purposes still obscure, or evidently subservient to respiration. I have dwelt at some length on these diversities, with a view not only to add a few facts more to those known already, but mainly to

---

[1]) Études p. 62 [2]) Ib., p. 8, pl. II, fig. 29, 30, 31.

bring out strongly the great contrast exhibited in this point by the Pourtalesiadæ. For while these, in other regards, have not a little in common with the Spatangidæ, and share a few features with the Cassidulidæ, they differ widely from either in being homoiopodous. Their pedicels are all simple, and differ in size only, the phyllodean and the upper frontal pedicels being larger than the rest, which are very minute, *Pl. IV, fig. 16, 21, 22; VI, 40, 41; VII, 50*. They all terminate in a rounded or slightly tumid top, which, in some states, is surrounded by a narrow circular brim, not unlike that of Rhynchopygus, *Pl. XI, fig. 118, 119*. The very dense pigment of their tissues so obscures its structure that I could not even make sure of the existence of calcareous spicules. The peripodia, *Pl. I, fig. 5, 6, 7; IV, 15, 24; V, 27, 29; VI, 44; VII, 47; XII, 149*, not unlike those of the Cassidulidæ, are sunk, and the two perforations confluent in the phyllodean and frontal ones, separated in the minute subanals of V b. In the ventral, subventral and lateral plates of the ambulacra the diminution of the peripodium relatively to the entire surface of the plate is carried to the extreme, it being hardly discernible over the greater part of the ambulacrum, and far inferior in size to the smallest of tubercles. The ambulacra are also all apetalous and perfectly even with the perisome, and all this, combining with peculiarities of the interradial areas described above, tends to soften down the elsewhere salient diversities of the two predominant systems, and to give to the whole surface of the skeleton the character of smoothness, which the Pourtalesiadæ have in common with their fellow-habitants of the great depths, the Apetalous Spatangidæ.

IV. THE CALYCINAL SYSTEM.

The homologies of the calycinal system in Crinoidea and Echinoidea. Tiarechinus. Salenia. Its modifications during geological development. Echinoconidæ. Spatangidæ. Its decay in the Pourtalesiadæ.

Years ago it occurred to me, as it had to others, that the general resemblance of the »apical» system in the Cidaridæ, Saleniadæ and Echinidæ, to the calyx of certain Crinoidea, might be a morphological fact of importance with regard to a true perception of the homologies of the skeletal constituents in the Echinoderms generally. For such is in reality the conformity between the respective parts of both structures, that, when once perceived, it must leave a strong impression of some hidden meaning well worth understanding, and often enough it may have called forth reflexions that far less often were recorded. LOUIS AGASSIZ [1] once remarked, as of peculiar interest, »the correspondence between the development of the calcareous central network» of the disk in the young »Startfish and the stem of Pentacrinus»; the arrangement of the five plates »surrounding it and those alternating with them that will form the five

---

[1] Twelve Lectures on comparative Embryology delivered before the Lowell Institute, in Boston, December and January 1848—49. Boston, Flanders & Co. 1849; p. 17, 22, 24, 25.

rays, and so on, with successive little plates in all the genera»; »the correspondence between the plates that protect the eyes in the Starfish and the smaller perforated plates of the upper disk of the Echini», as well as that between the »ovarial» plates of these and »the angles between the rays in the Starfish.» AUSTIN [1]) was of opinion that, in Cidaris, the ambulacra — in which he seems to have included the »ocellar» pieces — »terminate near the apex, which is composed of five plates, each of which has a central opening or ovarial aperture. These pieces united may be considered as the dorso-central plate, in the centre of which the vent is situated». He nowhere mentions the five genital plates of the Echinoids as collectively representing the dorso-central plate of Marsupites. ALEXANDER AGASSIZ, [2]) from his study of the »abactinal» system in the young Starfish, arrived at the conclusion that its central plate is a solidified homologue of the basal plates, and that the set of five plates in the angles corresponds to the interradial plates, and the arm-plates themselves to the radial plates of the Crinoid. BEYRICH [3]) considered the apical system, with regard merely to its position, as the analogon of the Crinoidean calyx. But in no instance the comparison was more than mentioned incidentally, well worthy as it seems to be of an examination in detail.

It was at a very remote geological period that the classes of the Echinoderms branched off from their ancestral trunk, at the same time inheriting in common certain important characteristics, the actual presence of which still holds together their diversified forms. Whenever, therefore, we are called upon to compare the leading features of one class to those of another, we do well to trace them back, as near as we can, to that common source, for, close as presumably were, at that starting point of diverging existence, their mutual resemblances, most of their members have ever since been going on modifying themselves, each in its own way, some by slow degrees, others rapidly, every time that a new branchlet of the group has been developed, and it has become a delicate task to parallel features that perhaps have been only slightly altered in some type of long-continued existence, with those deeply changed in another, and that, may be, within the course of a much shorter time.

Typically the »apical» system of the Echinoidea is a radiate structure composed of: a central pentagonal ossicle; contiguous to each of its five sides one of five other, hexagonal ossicles, forming a closed ring; and, in the outer angle between every two of these, one of a second, external, set of five pentagonal ossicles. This is the general formula, which in the Echinoidea has remained, more or less altered, but always recognisable, from Palæozoic to recent time. If we look for it in the Crinoidean calyx, we find it profoundly obscured in the Cenozoic forms, and discernible enough in the Mesozoic, but it is only when we approach the older Palæozoic time that forms come in sight by which we are led to expect to see it clearly expressed in some early genus, coeval in a certain degree with the oldest of the Echinoidea. It seemed to me that

---

[1]) Ann. Nat. Hist., 2:d Ser., VIII, 285, 288; 1855.
[2]) Proc. Am. Ac. Arts and Sc., 1863, Apr. 14. Embryology of Starfish. Contributions to the Nat. Hist. United States, V. 1864. 50; Reprint 1877. 62.
[3]) Ueber die Basis der Crinoidea Brachiata, Monatsberichte Akad. Wiss. Berlin, Febr. 1871.

a near approach to a calyx of that simple description was to be seen in Cyathocrinus, and one of its species, Cyathocrinus (Poteriocrinus) geometricus GOLDF. was therefore selected to open a series of figures [1]) by which, — while leaving to others the more difficult task of unravelling the perplexedly diversified composition of the Crinoidean calyx, — I endeavoured to exhibit the homologies between the constituents of the calyx in that Palæocrinoid and those of the apical system in typical forms of Echinoidea. It then appeared that this system is not an assemblage of parts, each contrived for the special purpose of subserving the function of an internal organ, one as a temporary appendage of the excretory opening, another as an accessory of the system of aqueous circulation, others as bearers of the organs of vision, and others again as mere holders of the outlets of the sexual organs, but that, in reality, the apical system is by itself an independent whole, morphologically equivalent to each of the two other systems, the perisomatic and the ambulacral, constituted of three elements, intimately combined and normally disposed radiately in regard to its centre. And these elements, which are rarely seen simultaneously present in the adult, I ventured to point out as homologous: the central one to the whole of the pentagonal Basis (JOH. MÜLLER) of the Crinoidean calyx; the five ossicles of the proximal set called »genital» in the former, to the Parabasalia (JOH. MÜLLER) in the latter; and the five outermost ossicles in the Echinoid, usually termed »ocellar», to the Radialia (JOH. MÜLLER) of Cyathocrinus. [2]) And it was shown that the same homologies hold good in the Asteriadea.

If this view is well based, as I believe it is, it follows that a terminology has to be found, which may be applied equally in the different classes, and which designates homologous parts by identical appellations. Now, among the numerous denominations proposed by authors, three have been more widely used. The constituents of the calyx are termed

in Cyathocrinus: by

MILLER:	Pelvis.	Costalia.	Scapulæ.
JOH. MÜLLER:	Basis.	Parabasalia.	Radialia.
HERB. CARPENTER:	Infrabasalia.	Basalia.	Radialia;

in Echinoidea: by

AUTHORS:	Central plate.	Genital plates.	Ocellar plates.

The position of the calycinal system, while basal in the Crinoidea, is culminating in the Echinoidea and the Asteriadea, and consequently any appellation involving the notion of a basal position must be avoided. On the other hand, the terms: genital and ocellar, besides being expressive of incidental relations peculiar to the Echinoidea and partly to the Asteriadea, cannot by any means be applied to the homologous parts in the Crinoid. For these reasons, and to avoid multiplying terms already too numerous, I proposed to retain the old name of costals MILLER — the quaint allusion it implies being long forgotten — for that of parabasals JOH. MÜLLER, and thus to define the calycinal system, or the calyx, in the Cyathocrinidæ, the Echinoidea and Asteriadea,

---
[1]) Études, p. 80. — [2]) Ueber den Bau des Pentacrinus, p. 31.

as typically composed of a *central* ossicle, five *costals*, and five *radials*.[1]) I shall make use of the same terms here, without fear of being misunderstood. When future science shall have lying before her, for comparison, numerous forms now undiscovered, and the perplexities of the present shall have cleared up, the final terminology will come of itself.[2])

What the calyx is to the antique Crinoid, its homologon is not to the Echinoid, — its constituents were inherited morphologically, not their modes of subserviency to the physiological activities of the animal —; along with the enormous change in conditions of existence there have arisen essential alterations of the entire structure. In the Crinoid, as in the Echinoid, the calyx is normally opposite to the mouth. In the stalked Crinoid, which feeds by means of ciliary agency, the mouth is directed upwards, and the calyx, on the darkened side, is the fundamental support on which the body rests, permanently or temporarily, enclosed on all sides by its perisome, with its radiating grooves. In the Echinoid, when first seen by us already long since adapted to a free and ground-feeding life, with the mouth directed downwards, the calycinal system, permanently adnate, is carried uppermost, towards the light, on the top of the back, and there, covering probably the dorsal part of the perisome, nor-

Cyathocrinus alutaceus
ANG.

Tiarechinus princeps
LAUBE.

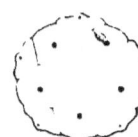
Salenia sp.

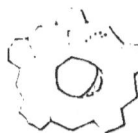
Echinus sp. young.

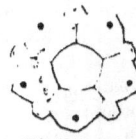
Cidaris Merceyi
COTTEAU.

mally meets the ambulacra radiating from the mouth, at their growing extremities, but never lifts or supports them.[3]) In consequence of the thus inverted posture, the inner organs of the Echinoid are to a great extent transposed and brought into relations to the calycinal system widely contrasting with those existing in the Crinoid. Relatively to the other skeletal constituents the calyx holds its legitimate position, but under it, owing to altered conditions, an assemblage is brought together of organs of primary importance: those of vision, — apparently foreign to the Crinoidean type, at least not to be looked for in a homologous place —, those of generation, of aqueous circulation, and of excretion. And thus, in the Echinoid, the calycinal system is rendered, to no small extent, a disputed ground, each of these organs tending to penetrate its substance, and to gain access to the surrounding water.

Of all the Echinoidea at present known Tiarechinus has the most antique looking calycinal system, *Pl. XIII*. It is large enough to cover the greater part of the dorsal

---

[1]) Études p. 73.
[2]) It is well known that MILLER was inconsistent in the use of the term *crostals*, but it has always been considered allowable to suggest the use in a strict sense of a term elsewhere vaguely applied.
[3]) Études, l. c.

aspect, and distinct from the interradia by a faint linear impression, discernible in the largest of the specimens examined only; above it the calyx is slightly raised. The central ossicle, or what may have filled its place, is lost, and a nearly pentagonal open space is left in the centre, or rather anteriorly. The five costals are very large, the posterior one, 5, somewhat smaller than the others; they are all hexagonal, with the outward side slightly truncated for the reception of the narrow middle plate of the corresponding interradium. The costals 1 and 3 each bear a slightly tubular pore, apparently sexual, placed towards the inner margin. Water-pores were not to be found. The radials are pentagonal, each contiguous to the top of an ambulacrum; there is no trace of an ocular pore, if this be not marked by a slightly larger granule observable in two or three of them. The whole calyx is covered with a dense granulation similar to that of the interradia, but without any indication of linear arrangement. The whole, costals and radials, appears as if of one piece, the sutures being excessively fine, and to be elicited only by the treatment mentioned above. The relative magnitude of the entire system, the prominent share it takes among the constituents of the skeleton, the forms and proportions of its parts, are such as forcibly to recall the calyx of some Palæocrinoid, and to justify a desire to turn the Echinoid upside down and to see the calycinal system in its imaginary original position, when it formed a part of some remote ancestral type. In this aspect the resemblance becomes still more striking.

Tiarechinus princeps Laube, with the mouth upwards.

In the remarkable group of the Saleniadæ[1]) the three constituents of the calycinal system, the central pentagon, the costals, and the radials, are all simultaneously persistent in the adult. The madreporite, the sexual openings, and the organs of vision, are in possession of their respective ossicles. The system is generally seen to expand largely, covering a great extent of the dorsal surface, and to exhibit, in forms of Mesozoic existence, a highly elaborate sculpture, repeating almost every characteristic observed in the calyx of Crinoids of preceding, Palæozoic, ages, but apparently of none from later times, as though in token of a common descent, and a yet not very remote epoch of separation. The granulation seen in Acrosalenia, the deep impressions crossing the sutures in Peltastes, the strong straight ridges connecting the centres of the ossicles in Goniophorus, the impressed points at their sutures and angles in Salenia, often continued on either side into parallel lines, are features well known in the Palæocrinoidea and present also in the Cystoidea, but evanescent in the Crinoidea of Secondary and later ages.

In the oldest of the known genera, Acrosalenia[2]), the periproct at first but slightly touches the central disk or even fails to attain it. Placed closely within the posterior margin of the costal 5, its large aperture is widened lengthwise, sometimes leav-

---

[1]) Etudes, p. 27, 70, 78, pl. XIX. fig. 177; XXI.
[2]) It is hardly necessary to mention that the figures here given are taken from the works of M. Cotteau in the »Paleontologie Française« and elsewhere, all unsurpassed models of research and elucidation.

ing anteriorly a part of the costal irregularly fractured, while expanding it posteriorly beyond the other costals[1]). During the next periods the periproct, always placed on the antero-posterior axis and regularly transverse, in Peltastes, which appears in the

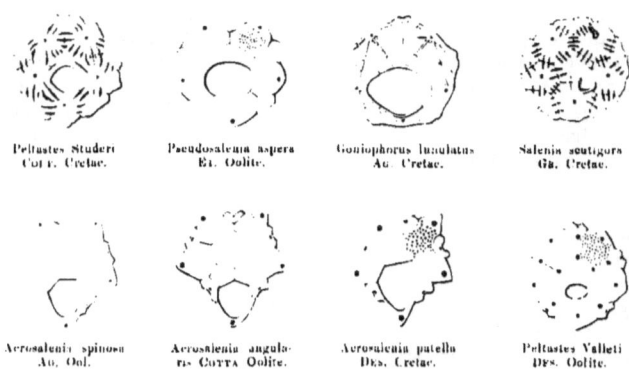

Peltastes Studeri Pseudosalenia aspera Goniophorus lunulatus Salenia scutigera
Corr. Cretac.   Et. Oolite.   Au. Cretac.   Gh. Cretac.

Acrosalenia spinosa Acrosalenia angularis Acrosalenia patella Peltastes Valleti
Au. Ool.   Cotta Oolite.   Des. Cretac.   Des. Oolite.

Middle Oolite, affects slightly and equally the costals 1, 4, 5, and the central disk, while in Pseudosalenia, of the same time, it erodes it deeply, permitting the costal 5 to resume nearly its normal shape. In Goniophorus, of the Middle Cretaceous time, it expands so as to take in great parts of the surroundings. In Salenia proper, which may be followed from early Cretaceous time up to the present period, and in Heterosalenia of the later Cretaceous, the periproct is for the greater part cut out from the costals 1 and 5, and thus, while slightly entering upon the central disk, is drawn over to the right, on the axis 1—3, thus conforming to the rule now prevalent in the majority of the Echinidæ and, partly at least, among the Asteriadea, of having the excretory opening placed excentrically, to the right of the antero-posterior axis. In view of these marks of a gradual advance, in the Saleniadæ, during their geological development, of the periproct, from the hindmost limits of the calycinal system to near its centre, there is some reason for inferring the probable existence, at a remote period, of Exocyclic Salenian forms combining a calycinal system of a nearly intact Crinoidean character with a periproct placed in the interradium of the bivium, perhaps even towards its ventral surface[2])

Be this as it may, in all the known Echinidæ, the Saleniadæ not excepted, in the earliest forms as in those of the present era, the periproct is endocyclic. In one of the oldest groups, the Cidaridæ, the Crinoidean character of the calyx is still strongly

---

[1]) Compare Acrosalenia miranda GAUTHIER, Echin. foss. de l'Algerie. II, p. 86, pl. XX, fig. 109, 110.
[2]) The little known Upper Silurian Cystocidaris ZITT. (Echinocystites Wyv. Th.) is described as having the periproct interradial.

marked. One, however, of its three constituent elements is no longer persistent in the adult; the central disk is substituted by a pliant membrane paved with numerous minute ossicles, in the centre of which is the excretory opening. In this strictly orthoproctic group the outline of this membrane still remains pentagonal, as determined by the rectilinear margins of the costals, while in most of the Echinidæ the partial resorption of these margins, combined with the excentric position of the excretory opening, tends to conceal, in no small degree, the original existence of a central disk. Now we know, however, that in the calyx of the Echinidæ, and most probably also in that of the Cidaridæ, during the transitory astomous and aproctic stage of the very young animal, the central disk exists in its legitimate position relatively to the other constituents of the system, but only for a short time, and soon to be resorbed, in part at least, upon which its place is filled by the anal membrane. Its structural and morphological identity with the central disk of the Saleniadæ cannot be doubted, and, like that, it is not in the remotest manner referable, morphologically or physiologically, under the appellation of an anal or subanal supplementary plate, to the digestive apparatus, indeed no more so than, in the Saleniadæ, the portion of the respective costals, which necessarily has been removed in behalf of the formation of the periproct, and in like manner replaced by an anal membrane, which thus coexists with the nearly intact central disk. The difference is, that, in the Cidaridæ

Salenia hastigera Ag. Ag. Calycinal system.

and the Echinidæ, unlike what takes place in all the Saleniadæ, the excretory opening breaks out, not wholly or partially outside the central disk, but from under it, and thus induces its destruction as such. The anal membrane supplying its place may possibly be a dependency of the perisome.

As long as the excretory opening continues endocyclic, a certain degree of stability maintains in the disposition of the calycinal system. Costals and radials are constantly present in the normal number of five, and distinct sutures mark their mutual limits. The water-pores penetrate the costal 2 alone and very rarely exceed it, the sexual organs open regularly by a pore in each costal, and there is an orbit, simple or double, in every radial. It is evident that the internal organs, in sharing among themselves the constituents of the calycinal system, balance each other in an equal manner. In the Cidaridæ and the whole numerous group of Echinidæ it has continued so to the present day.

But this state of stability in the calycinal system is broken, as soon as one or the other of the organs it covers begins to move[1]. The excretory opening is the first to alter its position, it is followed by the madreporite and the sexual pores, but the eyes remain stationary. Already in the time of the Lias there existed, at the side of Cidaridæ, Echinidæ and Saleniadæ, the group of the Echinoconidæ[2], true Gnatho-

[1] Études, p. 76.
[2] Ib., p. 79.

stomous Echinids, — with the ambulacra all alike, and the peristome, central and circular, presenting five pairs of branchial indentations, — but exocyclic, the periproct having passed from its old site at the centre of the system, into the odd interradium. In consequence of this movement the costal 5 had been destroyed, but in the course of time is regenerated, and even its sexual pore returns, all nearly according as the periproct becomes more distant, and has been so for any length of time. Thus in the oldest, Pygaster, with the periproct sub-calycinal, the 5 is completely wanting; in Pileus, of the Middle Oolite, the periproct is dorsal, submarginal, and the costal 5 is restored, but destitute of sexual pore; in the Oolitic species of Holectypus, with the periproct marginal or ventral, it is present, but imperforate, whereas in the Cretaceous, in which the excretory opening is ventral and farther distant from the calyx, the sexual pore exists, and thus the system has once more become normal. In Discoidea, of Cretaceous origin, the periproct is ventral and the costal 5 present, imperforate in the lower beds, perforate in the Turonian; in Echinoconus and Anorthopygus the vent is posterior, subventral, and the costal 5 present, but without a pore.

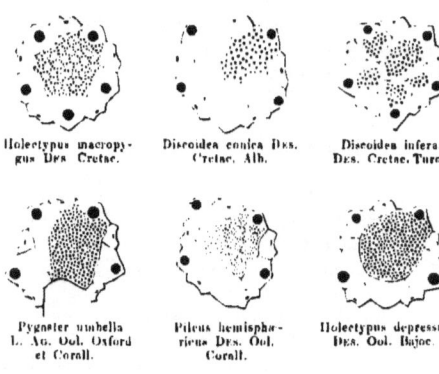

Holectypus macropygus Des Cretae.
Discoidea conica Des. Cretae, Alb.
Discoidea infera. Des. Cretae, Turon
Pygaster umbella L. Ag. Ool. Oxford et Corall.
Pileus hemisphæricus Des. Ool. Corall.
Holectypus depressus Des. Ool. Bajoc.

In like manner, among the Atelostomes, where the excretory opening can be said to have just left the calyx, as in the old Echinoneid genera Galeropygus and Hyboclypus, in the Oolitic Pyrina, the central part is irregularly broken up, or compressed; in forms of later appearance it aborts, and the four paired costals and the radials I and V close from either side. In Clypeus, the oldest of Cassidulidæ, the gap left by the retreating periproct is filled by an extraordinary prolongation of the almost always contiguous radials I and V, and there is hardly a trace of the costal 5; when the vent is removed farther back, these radials are again normal. Thus these three groups on their first appearance present distinct marks of the passage of the vent out of the limits of the calyx, and, while in their further development it continues its receding movement, the damage it has caused is at least partly repaired.

Future research will perhaps afford evidence that the filtering apparatus of the aqueous system primordially had its legitimate site in the central disk, and that it was displaced forward through the pressure exerted by the periproct advancing from the posterior interradium. Be this as it may, certain it is that, in the Mesozoic period, the movement, in the opposite direction, of the excretory opening was followed by the beginning of a retrograde movement of the madreporic filter. As early as in Pygaster, the oldest of Exocyclic Gnathostomes, it is seen to have entered the central part of the calycinal system, effacing the suture which limits the costal 2, and such is its condition in all known Echinoconidæ[1]), except that in Discoidea it is seen to spread to all the five costals[2]). When the Atelostomata make their first appearance, as Echinoneids, the madreporite is restricted to the costal 2; it is more expanded centrally in the Cretaceous Pyrinæ than in the Oolitic; in the recent Echinoneus[3]) it is central, and the sutures effaced. In some few of the oldest of Cassidulidæ, in which the centre is fractured into irregular detached pieces, it is limited to the costal 2; in the great majority of species it occupies the centre, expanding it largely. In the recent Cassidulus all the sutures are obliterated.

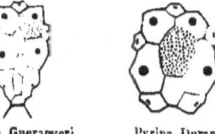

Pyrina Guerangeri Corr. Oolite. Bajoc.

Pyrina Durandi P. & G. Cretac. Turon.

The growing deviation from the original Gnathostomous type reaches its highest point in the Spatangidæ. Introduced by the Collyrites, of Oolitic existence, they make their appearance early in Cretaceous time as Holastridæ. Deeply contrasting with the Orthoproctic plan of construction: the circular ambitus; the central and circular peristome not modified during growth, and formed out of ambulacral and interradial plates of both series, at equal parts in either; the seemingly radiate disposition of the areas, ambulacral and interradial; the specious homocentricity of the spines; the general uniformity of the pedicels, only exceptionally or in part branchial; — all features present already in the ancient Cidaridæ, consistently maintained up to the present era by them and by numerous Echinidæ, and but slightly, if at all, modified in a few forms[4])—, the evolution of the Spatangidæ is pervaded by an increased and largely diversified tendency towards the differentiation of the skeletal elements into modifications unseen before, only in part begun by the Echinoneidæ and the Cassidulidæ. The gradual lengthening of the whole framework, the forward movement of the trivium, the increasing growth and differentiation of the abdomen and of the bivium, more and more overcome the inherited globosity; the alimentary canal extends horizontally, its œsophageal opening advancing, while the excretory aperture retrogrades; the bilateral symmetry becomes apparent, betraying a dawning approximation towards a vermiform disposition; the trivium and the bivium are more distinctly constituted: in the former the ambulacrum III is specialised as the front ambulacrum, and provided with pedicels of a peculiar structure, in the later genera at least not subservient to respiration, while the II and IV are paired and made counterparts in outline, though still unsymmetrical with regard to their constituent plates, and the I and V are made symmetrical inwardly as well as in their outlines; the peristome, consisting of biseriate ambulacrals and single interradials, is originally pentagonal, but nearly always becomes modified during growth; of the perisome, the four lateral interradial areas are distinctly disposed into two pairs, the symmetry of the anterior pair, 2 and 3, being perfect, while that of the posterior, 1 and 4, is qualified, in 1 a, or in 1 a and 1 b, by an heteronomous disposition un-

---

[1]) See woodcut on the preceding page. [2]) Études, p. 81, pl. XV, fig. 133. [3]) Ib. pl. XV, fig. 131.
[4]) Ib. p. 26, pl. XVIII, fig. 153—158.

known in the whole of the Gnathostomata as well as in the older Atelostomata, obscurely marked in the Holastridæ, manifest in the true Spatangi; the odd interradium, 5, at first, in the Holastridæ, nearly similar to the other four, has its ventral plates separate, transversely triangular: Meridosterni, but later, in the higher genera, formed into two large collateral sternal plates: Amphisterni: the fasciolæ, a feature unseen before: Adeti, at first are vaguely extant: Prymnadeti, or marginal alone, then the peripetalous fasciola is added, till, towards the end of the Cretaceous period, the subanal appears: Prymnodesmii, in the higher Spatangidæ always traversing adorally the sixth plate of I a and V b, and marking off the first five plates as ventral, the following as abdominal and dorsal; the spines are bristle-like, generally curved, tending backward, where not otherwise directed by the fascioles; the pedicels, which in Echinoneus are disciferous and similar to those of the Endocyclic Gnathostomes, and homotypic all over, in Cassidulus simple, in the petals only modified into branchials, attain in the Spatangidæ their highest development as diversely adapted organs, those of the phyllodes penicillate, the subanal mostly sub-penicillate, the lateral simple, the frontal variously constructed, and those of the petals, where these exist, branchial.

While these and other changes are successively introduced in the structure of the Spatangidæ, the two main constituents of their skeleton, the interradial system and the ambulacral, hold their own, and keep up their relative parts in the evolutional labour, their elements gradually assuming novel and almost refined forms[1]). It is not so with the third constituent, the calycinal system.

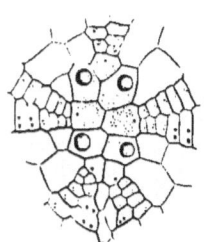

Hemipneustes radiatus GM. Calycinal system.

When the Collyrites appear, the first of the Spatangidæ, and after them the Holastridæ, the excretory opening is posterior and distant, and the calycinal system in the condition presented by some Echinoneidæ of the Oolitic period, as *e. g.* by Hyboclypus. It is generally more or less lengthened, and the only trace of the passage of the periproct is the total suppression of the central disk and the costal 5. In this state it remains in the Adete, Meridosternate forms: Amancites[2]) Offaster, Holaster, Cardiaster, Hemipneustes, introduced at the beginning of the Cretaceous period and continued into the Eocene; it is still seen, in the seas of the present time, at great depths, in the Adete Cystechinus AL. AG., and in Urechinus AL. AG., Pl. XXI, *fig.* 239—242, which is said to be provided with a subanal fasciola. It is shortened, but tightly closed by the contiguity of the costals 1 and 4, in the forms with a true, but yet imperfectly developed sternum: Toxaster, Heteraster and Enallaster; it is short and subcircular, closed behind by the costals 1 and 4

---

[1]) Observe the contrast between the plain and rigid angularity of the plates in Micraster, Études, pl. XXXIII, of Cretaceous existence, and the freedom of outline, even elegance, observable in corresponding parts in later Prymnodesmian types, Tertiary and recent, such as Echinocardium, pl. XXXIX; Plagionotus, pl. XL, Breynia, pl. XLI, Maretia, pl. XLII, Lovenia, pl. XLIII. The contrast is less striking between Hemiaster and the later Prymnadetes, ib. pl. XXVI—XXXII, fig. 197.
[2]) Études, pl. XI, fig. 96, 97, 98.

and the radials 1 and V, in the old subglobose forms with a normally constructed sternum: Epiaster, Isaster, and the typical species of the abundantly developed Hemiaster, Pl. *XVIII*, *fig.* *221*, *222*, while in other species[1]), from the middle Cretaceous era, it is closed also, but solely by the radials 1 and V, the costals 1 and 4 having separated, in this respect like the calyx of Micraster[2]), the first of Prymnodesmians, continuing from the middle Cretaceous into the Tertiary period. In all these forms the madreporite is strictly confined to the right anterior costal, 2. They may be conveniently comprised under the common name of Ethmophracti[3]). But, of them all, as far as our knowledge extends, no generic type has survived up to the present time save Hemiaster, while the abyssal depths contain some genera of Ethmophracts, as Calymne, Urechinus and Cystechinus, that more or less recall those ancient forms.

For in the latter half of the Cretaceous era an important change took place in the structure of the calycinal system of the Spatangidæ. It has been seen that, when, in the Echinoconidæ, the periproct had retreated far back from the calyx, the costal 5, which had been suppressed, was reinstated again, and that the normal condition returned even so far as to allow the efferent duct of the corresponding sexual gland to perforate it. In a similar manner also among the Spatangidæ, the central disk and the costal 5 make their reappearance, the former separating the costals 1 and 4, the latter disjoining the radials 1 and V, but never receiving a sexual pore. At the same time the madreporic filter, no more held back by the excretory apparatus, but free to move and expand, spreads its pores, as formerly in the Cassidulidæ, into the now extended space of the central disk, and from thence into the costal 5. The Spatangidæ provided with a calyx of this description may be distinguished as Ethmolysii[4]). The madreporite, while it penetrates the substance of the costal 2, the central ossicle and the costal 5, obliterates the sutures which separated them, as it did the suture between the 2 and the central in the Echinoconidæ, Echinoneidæ and Cassidulidæ, and those three ossicles, so strictly kept apart in the Endocyclic forms, are here united into one unbroken area, contiguous anteriorly to the interradium 2, and posteriorly to the interradium 5. It will appear that Linthia and Schizaster[5]) from the middle Cretaceous time to our time, Prenaster from the end of the Cretaceous period and far into the Eocene, Macropneustes in the Eocene, were the first in which this change took place, and associated with them may perhaps be found some species rightly belonging to Abatus[6]), Pl. *XVIII*, *fig.* *220*. In three of these oldest genera of the Spatangidæ Ethmolysii: Schizaster[7]), Prenaster, Macropneustes, the costal 5 is not extended far beyond the posterior limits of the system, and in Schizaster the madreporite takes its due by more or less crowding with its pores the costal 2, so as to cause the abortion of the efferent

---

[1]) Mainly, or wholly, algerian See COTTEAU, PÉRON et GAUTHIER, Echinides fossiles de l'Algerie, IV, Cenomanien, VI: Turonien.
[2]) Etudes, Pl. XI, fig. 95.
[3]) Ἠθμός, filter; φρακτός, fenced.
[4]) Λύσιος, deliverer.
[5]) Schizaster antiquus COTTEAU, Bull. Soc. Géol. VI, 567.
[6]) Compare Abatus Philippii, Etudes, pl. XI, fig. 99
[7]) Schizaster fragilis, Ib., pl. XII, fig. 102.

duct of the corresponding sexual gland. In Prenaster and Macropneustes, the next, it will appear, to assume the modified structure of the calycinal system, the costal 5 also keeps within its precincts, while the reduced press of the filter on the costal 2 admits of the normal presence of its sexual pore. But in the great number of genera of later appearance, while this pore is constantly maintained, the cluster of water-pores is seen to have withdrawn from this costal and to have retreated backward, expanding the combined area of the central ossicle and the costal 5, which thus are made to form a prolongation reaching beyond the posterior limits of the calycinal system and far into the interradium 5[1]). This is the case in the great majority of recent Spatangidae: Faorina, Agassizia among the Pymnadetes, Brissus, Metalia, Rhinobrissus, Cionobrissus, Meoma, Spatangus, Homolampas, Palaeopneustes, Brissopsis, Kleinia, Echinocardium, Plagionotus, Breynia, Maretia, Lovenia, Eupatagus, among the Prymnodesmians.

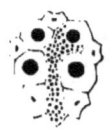
Macropneustes Pellati
Cotteau.

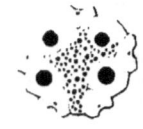
Prenaster Julieri
Desor.

The diversity between the calycinal system of the Ethmophracti and that of the Ethmolysii, striking as it is, has nevertheless been overlooked. As long ago as in 1845 Philippi described and figured three species of Spatangus from the antarctic sea of South America, and proposed for their reception a new subgenus: Tripylus, principally characterised by possessing only three sexual openings. He named them Tripylus excavatus, Tr. cavernosus, and Tr. australis. The first was referred by L. Agassiz to Agassizia Val., while Troschel, who examined the original specimens of all three, made it the type of a new genus: Hamaxitus, and Gray and Al. Agassiz retained for it the primitive appellation: Tripylus. For the two other, Tr. cavernosus Phil. and Tr. australis Phil., placed by L. Agassiz in Brissopsis, by Gray in Faorina, Troschel created a new genus: Abatus[2]), remarking at the same time, that if only one species had come under

[1]) Études p. 12, Pl. XII, fig. 100, 101, Brissopsis: 106, Meoma; 107, Echinocardium.
[2]) The following is the nomenclatural history of the species of

Abatus Troschel.
Wiegmanns Archiv. XVII, (1851), 72.
1. Abatus cavernosus Philippi.

1845.	Tripylus cavernosus Phil.	Wgm.	Arch. XI, 345, t. XI, f. 2.
	Brissopsis	" "	1847.	Agass. & Des. Cat. R., Ann. Sc. Nat., 3e Sér., VIII, 15, sep., 121.
	Faorina	" "	1851.	Gray, An. Nat. Hist., 2d ser., VII, 132.
			1855.	Gray, Cat. rec. Ech. Br. Mus., 57.
	Hemiaster	" "	1872.	Al. Agassiz, Rev. Echin., 132, 587. t. XXI c, f. 1, 2.
			1876.	Al. Agassiz, Proc. Am. Ac. Arts a. Sc. Boston, XI, 231.
			1879.	Edg. A. Smith, Phil. Trans., Vol. 168, 271.
			1880.	Studer, Zoolog. Anzeiger, 544.
			1880.	Studer, Mon. Ber. Berl. Akad. 861.
			1881.	Al. Agassiz, Rep. Chall. Echinoidea, 179, pl. 20, a.
1845.	Tripylus australis Phil.	l. c.	347, T. XI, f. 3.
	Brissopsis	" "	1847.	Agass. et Des., Cat. R. l. c.
	Faorina	" "	1855.	Gray, Cat. Br. Mus., 57.
	Hemiaster	" "	1872.	Al. Agassiz, Rev. 132, 586, pl. XXI c, f. 3.

his notice, he doubtless would have referred it to Hemiaster DES. This became also the view taken by AL. AGASSIZ, and since 1872 every author who mentioned these two species, treated them as living representatives of that genus, thus associating them with a host of long known fossil forms that once peopled the seas of the Cretaceous and Tertiary periods, and with their more lately added recent congeners, Hemiaster expergitus LOV.[1]), discovered by SMITT and LJUNGMAN during the cruize of the Josephine in 1869, H. gibbosus AL. AG. and H. zonatus AL. AG., both dredged by the Challenger Expedition[2]). Now these three species of the existing seas are true Hemiasters fully sharing the well-known characteristics of that highly natural genus, the subglobose form, elevated in its posterior region, a calyx of four costals, the madreporite confined to the costal 2, the 4 and 1 and the radials I and V closing from either side, in strict accordance with the mode of conformation universally prevalent within the calycinal system during the older Mesozoic period. These species are, as it were, apparitions from a former world, relics surviving from an evolutional stage long passed through, and very different from the altogether modern Abatus, with its moderately convex test, its calyx with five costals, the 5 being reproduced between the radials I and V and bearing the madreporic filter, thus set free, on its unimpeded retrograde movement. An extraneous form like this[3]), if suffered to remain in the otherwise homogeneous group of true Hemiasters, is sure to vitiate its integrity, and the mixed assemblage thus set up for a natural genus, if taken on trust, cannot fail to mislead when the question is to trace out comparatively its former geological and actual geographical distribution. The few survivors hitherto found of the once numerous genus Hemiaster inhabit temperate and tropical parts of the Atlantic and Pacific oceans, the Caribbean and Brazilian Seas, through that of the Azores towards Madeira and the Iberian peninsula, the Sea of Japan and that between New-Guinea and Australia. Abatus, on the other hand, is an antarctic form.

1851. Faorina antarctica GRAY, Ann. Nat. Hist. I. c. 132.
          1855. GRAY, Cat. Br. Mus., 57.
1876. Hemiaster cordatus VERRILL Bull. Un. St. Nat. Mus. Washington, N:r 3, 6*.
   Hemiaster sp.   1876. WYV. THOMSON, Journ. Linn. Soc. XIII 67.
1877. Hemiaster Philippii »GRAYa, WYV. THOMSON, Voy. Challenger, II, 227.
  Obs. Abatus cavernosus PHIL. appears to be the female, Ab. australis the male. GRAY remarks, Cat. Br. Mus. 57, that the three, Faorina antarctica, cavernosa and australis, perhaps are only one species. Tripylus Philippii GRAY is generically different, probably an Agassizia, as also Tr. excavatus PHIL.

2. Abatus Philippii LOVÉN.

1871. Abatus Philippii LOVÉN, Öfversigt af K. Vet.-Akad. Förhandl. N:r 8, 1065, 1070.
          1874. LOVÉN. Études s. les Échinoïdées, pl. XI, fig. 99; pl. XXIX, f. 188—190.
   Hemiaster » » 1873. AL. AGASSIZ, Bull. Mus. Comp. Zool. III, r:o 8, 189.
          1874. AL. AGASSIZ, Zool. Results Hasler Exp. I, 20.
  Obs. The synonymy is doubtful, because the sexual pores are said to be »two or three«, and »if a third exists it is the right anterior one, usually, but sometimes the left«.

[1]) Études, p. 13, pl. XIII, fig. 114—120.
[2]) Rep. Chall. Ech., p. 184, pl. XX, fig. 1—16.
[3]) Another stranger is Hemiaster elongatus of Indian Tertiaries. It is a Palæostoma.

A due attention paid to the development of parts during the growth of the individual animal has more than once reconciled discrepancies as great as that of the calycinal system in the Ethmophracti and the Ethmolysii, the Mesozoic type and the Cenozoic.

In the young of Abatus cavernosus, *Pl. XIV*, *fig. 164*, *164 A*, the calycinal system, relatively large, presents five radials I, II, III, IV, V, each bearing a tentacle, and four costals, 1, 2, 3, 4, among which the 2 has become already the site of the madreporite. The central and open part is overlaid, within the general envelope, by a membrane in which are seen detached minute calcified laminæ, presumably rudiments of the central ossicle and the costal 5, nowhere extant among the Ethmophracti, but here to be developed. *Pl. XVIII*, *fig. 220*, after the backward passage of the excretory end of the alimentary tube.

Young Spatangi, with the mouth and the vent opened, and living free on the bottom of the sea, very early present a calycinal system completed by the presence of the central disk and the costal 5. Different stages of Echinocardium flavescens O. F. MÜLLER, Spatangus purpureus O. F. M., and Brissopsis lyrifera FORBES, *Pl. XVII, XVIII, XIX*, may serve as examples showing the development of the calycinal system and the movement of the madreporic apparatus in the Spatangidæ Ethmolysii. Of the first-named the calycinal system is represented *Pl. XVII*, *fig. 197—207*, as it appears in specimens of different dimensions, from mm. 3,5 : 3 to mm. 36 : 32. In the youngest the five radials are present with their ocular pores. The whole system, up to the individual size of mm. 30 : 26, is more or less distinctly pentagonal. The central ossicle together with costals 2, 3, 5 are united into one continuous middle area, extending through the whole length of the system, with the radial III in front, the radials IV and V and costal 4 on the left, and radials I and II together with costal 1 on the right. At first, *fig. 197, 198*, the madreporite is a single pore placed nearly in front, then there are two or three pores, *fig. 199—205*, of which the last added is more towards the middle; in a specimen of mm. 14,5 : 12, *fig. 205*, out of five pores two are posterior. Meanwhile the costals, at the total size of mm. 10,5 : 9 and mm. 12 : 10, *fig. 203, 204*, have been provided with sexual pores, at first so minute as easily to be taken for madreporic pores, but becoming larger according as the reproductive organs are developed. At mm. 30 : 26, *fig. 206*, the swarm of madreporic pores lies more than half behind the middle, and at mm. 36 : 32, *fig. 207*, nearly the whole of it behind the costals 1 and 4, and the costal 5 has been driven backward into the interradium 5; but still its intact margin is seen to limit the pressure of the pores. And during this transference, in this species as in those next to be described, the middle part, expanded as long as occupied by the growing madreporite, contracts again when it has passed, yielding to the pressure exerted by the interradia.

A series of young stages of Spatangus purpureus O. F. M., from mm. 5 : 4 to mm. 24 : 21, presents similar modifications, *Pl. XVIII*, *fig. 209—219*. There is the same drawing together of the sexual openings and narrowing of the middle area, after the recession of the madreporic filter, which is richer in pores than that of Echinocardium, and much more expansive, so much so as largely to invade, at mm. 53 : 50, the costals 1 and 4, to fill to the very brim the costal 5, stretching it to the utmost and leaving no trace of an intact margin, and even to detach one or other of its pores to the further side, into the interradial area 5, *fig. 219*.

The presence, outside the costal 5 and within the corresponding interradium, of a single pore of the madreporic filter, at first seems nothing more than an accidental anomaly. On a closer inspection, however, it looks otherwise. In a specimen of Brissus canariensis HAECKEL *ms.* I observe a dense group of six pores within the interradium 5, on the left from the costal, and a set of specimens just at hand of Brissopsis lyrifera presents not a few cases of the same disposition, *Pl. XIX, fig. 223—231*. In the adults of this well-known species the sexual apertures are normally four, and one of them is in the costal 2. In a specimen of mm. 9 : 7, *fig. 223*, the system is made up of the five radials, the costals 1, 3, 4 distinguished by definite sutures, and the costals 2 and 5 together with the central ossicle united into one piece, the madreporic filter here as elsewhere effacing the sutures. Only one minute pore is to be seen, in the direction of costal 2. Next, in a specimen of mm. 11 : 9, *fig. 224*, one more has been added, in the central part; in specimens of mm. 15 : 12, 15 : 13, 16 : 13, *fig. 225—227*, their number increases, occupying the centre and the costal 5. Then, while the central part contracts, the filter, always increasing the number of its pores, expands, and forces the costal 5 backward, beyond the limits of the system [1]). And while it thus takes more room, as the animal grows, it is sometimes seen to prevent the sexual organs from opening in the costal 2, *fig. 229*, sometimes to expand in 1 outside its sexual pore, *fig. 230*, or sometimes to migrate, in no small number, across the limits of the system and into the interradium 5, *fig. 228*, partly even into the ambulacrum 1 *fig. 231*. In a hundred specimens of Brissopsis lyrifera taken at random, all from one locality, I find ten presenting this anomalous disposition, the expelled pores being in most cases on the right side, in the *b* series of the interradium.

Thus the movement of the madreporic filter, the starting point and the terminus of which have marked different geological epochs, is seen to take place in the living animal within the brief space of a transitory stage of its development. In the adult of Hemiaster and of all the other Spatangidæ of early Mesozoic origin, the calyx presents a structure essentially different from that of the calyx in the adult of a Spatangus, or of any other form, of later or recent appearance, and very rarely a link of connection is found between the two. But in the last-named of these groups an evolutional process actually takes place, showing us how, in the individual, the calyx passes from the one state into the other, and permitting us, however vaguely, to surmise the nature of the modifications by means of which the same change may have been brought about in the species, and the Ethmolysii made to take the place of the Ethmophracti. The contending activities of the internal organs, of sensation, generation and circulation, which, after the removal of the excretory opening, in the earliest Spatangidæ still for a time combined to render permanent the site of the madreporite in the costal 2, and to hold back the restoration of the central disk and the costal 5, entered into a period of alterations that by degrees induced the setting free

---
[1]. *Études*, p. 12, pl. XII, fig. 100, 101.

of the regenerative energy of these long suppressed parts, and, in obedience to the predominant tendency of abdominal growth, prepared the recession, by the way thus laid open, of the perforating agency of the madreporitic tubuli. Accompanied by correlative changes in other parts; transmitted, with tendencies enforced, from generation to generation, from embryo to embryo, and resuming innumerable times its plastic work, this evolutional process, simultaneously operating in a number of individuals, always at an early stage never found fossil, resulted in the location of the madreporite in the restored costal 5 of the adult. Then a period of rest followed in the calycinal system, during which innumerable specimens were preserved recording the transformation, which thus may seem to have been accomplished in a relatively short space of geological time, and, as it now appears to us, suddenly. The seas of the present era harbour at least one transitional form, the antique looking Genicopatagus affinis AL. AG., in which the central disk and the costal 5 are reinstated, separating the I and V, and preparing the way for the madreporite, which still however remains in the aporous costal 2. It is an abyssal form, and such are probably all the recent Ethmophracti, while the Ethmolysii, which have but few representatives in the great depths, are littoral animals κατ' ἐξοχήν. It is among these that the madreporite, after a period of rest, in our days seems to show signs of once more moving, and of transgressing its latest line of demarcation.

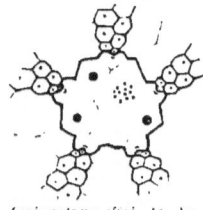
Genicopatagus affinis AL. AG.,
Calycinal System.

Further research, extending over a large number of specimens of these and other species, from different localities, will decide whether there be valid reasons for regarding this regression of the filtering apparatus beyond its old boundary as an evolutional stage and not as something accidental, as an instance of monstrosity. It is fully in accordance with what has been going on for ages within the calycinal system, through long series of succeeding species, only it is here carried a step farther, as though leading into a new phase of the morphological labour. In Mesozoic time the excretory opening moved out of the system into the odd interradium, and was seen to increase more and more the interjacent distance. After a while the madreporic filter followed its track, attaining, near the close of Cretaceous time, the costal 5. With the aid of a little imagination we might surmise that we actually witness how it exceeds the old terminus and begins its exodus, and indulge in the idea that, in a future geologically not very distant, the whole of the madreporite, in some species or other, will have settled within the odd interradium, while the central disk, together with the costal 5, cleared of the invading porosity, will have resumed their normal condition. Then this gradual displacement of the madreporic filter, combined with other correlative modifications of the external parts, accessory to internal changes of more directly vital importance, will have originated a new type of Spatangidæ. But this by the way, as mere speculation. One point alone is established beyond any doubt by what has been detailed here, namely that in reality the madreporite is not an integral element of the calycinal system, but an extraneous accessory, and that there exists no such thing as a »madreporic plate».

In like manner the conception of the costals as »genital plates» on a closer inspection ceases to be tenable. Subsequently to the appearance externally, in the young Echinid, of the madreporic filter, when the reproductive glands approach maturity, their efferent ducts penetrate from within the costals, and, in the adult state of the great majority of species, a sexual pore is found in each of these. To this there are but rare exceptions, such as Goniopygus, but in the Clypeastridæ not a few forms have their sexual apertures outside the costals, in the respective interradia [1]. In the Endocyclic Gnathostomes all the five costals are perforated, but four only in the earliest among the Exocyclic, in Pygaster, the fifth having disappeared along with the costal 5, at the outbreak of the periproct. And, though in Oolitic species of Holectypus the costal is restored, it is not until in the Cretaceous era that its pore reappears [2]), just as in Discoidea, of early Cretaceous origin, it reverts only in the Turonian time, — and this is the last instance known of its reinstatement, for among the Echinoneidæ and Cassidulidæ it never reappears. In these last-named the four sexual pores are far asunder, owing to the central expansion of the madreporite, they are drawn near together laterally in the narrowed and lengthened calycinal system of the Collyrites and in the Meridosternous Spatangi, such as Anancites, Hemipneustes and others, and they are squared again in the shortened system af the Amphisternous Ethmophracti. In the Spatangidæ Ethmolysii, also, four is their normal number. In some cases, for instance in Spatangus purpureus, they seem to make their appearance very irregularly, all four being present in a specimen of the stage mm. 15 : 14. Pl. XVIII, fig. 213, but wanting in another of mm. 16 : 15, fig. 214, almost so even at mm. 19 : 18, fig. 216, highly developed at mm. 23 : 22, fig. 215, while the two anterior are only indicated in a specimen of mm. 24 : 21, fig. 217,- anomalies that possibly are apparent only, and may depend upon difference of sex. During the growth, also, one or even two of the pores are liable to give way in the struggle against the madreporite. In the costal 2, the old site of the filter, this not seldom prevails and causes the sexual pore to abort, sometimes accidentally, as in Brissopsis lyrifera, Pl. XIX, fig. 229, but regularly in certain species of Schizaster, as Sch. fragilis D. & K. [3]), Sch. Moseleyi AL. AG., in Tripylus, and in Abatus cavernosus PHIL., Pl. XVIII, fig. 220. In Abatus Philippii n. [4]), in Moira atropos LAMK., and in some other species of Schizaster, as Sch. canaliferus LAMK., Sch. japonicus AL. AG., it has disappeared in the costal 3 also. But among the Spatangidæ the sexual organs are never deprived of their outlets in the costals 1 or 4.

Thus the madreporite, with its internal apparatus of cavities, passages and canals combined into a solid calcified structure, by its expansion and regressive movement determines, in the Spatangidæ, the closing up of one or more of the sexual openings, and constantly that of the costal 5. In earlier types, when this same costal, oppressed for a time in consequence of the retrograde passage of the excretory ori-

---

[1]) Études, p. 80, Pl. XVI, fig. 136. Ib. p. 69. COTTEAU PERON ET GAUTHIER, Echinides de l'Algerie, V, p. 223, Pl. XVI, fig. 1—12.
[2]) See above, woodcut p. 68.
[3]) Études, pl. XII, fig. 102. In Sch. gibberulus AG. all four sexual pores are present.
[4]) Ib. pl. XI, fig. 99.

fice, had reappeared again, the corresponding sexual gland also, in the course of subsequent ages, was seen, in some forms, to recover its outlet. This could not have taken place, had not the sexual gland, though checked in its development, and kept back in a rudimentary state, continued, during a genetic succession of forms, its dormant life, ready to begin its work whenever the repressing influence should have passed. In the Ethmolysic Spatangidae, as long as the madreporite is crowding its pores in the restored costal 5, there is no chance for a sexual outlet; but,—assumed that its movement across the old boundary is in earnest the beginning of a migration,—if a form should be discovered anywhere, in which this migration were accomplished, and the madreporite settled, as a whole, in the interradium 5, it will be a great point to look for the return of the sexual outlet. Meanwhile the problem is near at hand of demonstrating the hidden existence of the fifth sexual gland, in a still embryonic condition abiding its time.

Organs of vision, -in the whole animal kingdom seen to come forward at places of commanding situation, irrespectively of morphological relations- , appear to be foreign to Crinoidean organisation. In the Asteridea, on the other hand, their existence has been proved beyond any doubt by Ehrenberg, their discoverer, by Haeckel, Greeff and others. A group of crystalline cones surrounded by pigment is seen at the extremity of each ambulacrum, and, connected with it aborally, a finger-shaped tentacle, both sheltered under the radial, which has been removed from its original site in the axillary angle between two costals, by the interposition of the largely developed perisome [1]). In the Echinoidea organs apparently identical, but not yet properly studied, are seen in corresponding places, each of the five radials presenting a pore serving as an orbit to the eye [2]), and close over it a simple tentacle. There both these organs appear very early, even before the madreporic filter, and the tentacle perhaps before the eye, Pl. XIV, fig. 164, 164 A, and there they are found, out of the field of contest.

For the madreporic filter scarcely ever attains the radials—, in forms geologically old and new, with a tenacity recalling that of the eyes of the Podophthalmous Crustacea, which maintain so invariably their station at the top of the appendages of the first somite, arrested in their development. When in the Collyrites [3]) the bivium is severed from the calycinal system through the interposition of the enlarged interradia 1 and 4, the radials I and V adhere to the respective ambulacra, on the insides of which the nerves descend from the central collar to the eyes.

These are the two principal forms of the calycinal system prevalent in the great majority of the Spatangidae: the Ethmophracti and the Ethmolysii. A third modification is of much less frequent occurrence. Palaeotropus [4]), which by its general outline, its ambulacra all apetalous, similar and level with the perisome, in some degree re-

[1]) Etudes p. 86, pl. LIII, fig. 256—260.
[2]) Ib. p. 66, pl. XI, XII, XV, XVI, XVII, XIX, XXI.
[3]) Ib. pl. XI, fig. 98.
[4]) Ib. p. 17, pl. XIII, fig. 108—113; XII. 105; XXXII. 200.

calls certain ancient types, and at the same time is so like its contemporaries in the structure of the peristome, the sternum, and the episternum traversed by the subanal fasciola, as also in the regular heteronomy of 1, *a*, presents a calycinal system, Pl. XVII, *fig. 208*, of a nearly pentagonal outline, in which the radials are distinct, the I and V being widely separated, while the costals are all coalesced into one piece devoid of sutures, and in which the madreporite opens anteriorly in the middle by a small fissure and some pores, while the genital ducts are only two, having their outlets at the tops of two large tubular eminences placed transversely against the interradia 1 and 4.

Palæostoma mirabile GRAY, Pl. XVI, deviates in a strange manner from nearly all the rest of the Spatangidæ [1]), by the fusion into one single plate of the second plates of the interradia 2, 3, 4, the heteronomy of 1 being effected through the union of the plates *a 2, b 2* and *b 3*; by the very irregular interradium 5, and by the pentagonal peristome with its five valves, and from Palæotropus in particular, by its distinct petals and by the absence of a subanal, the presence of a peripetalous fasciola. But with all this, Palæostoma offers a calycinal system evidently constructed upon the same model as in that genus, *fig. 184, 190*, with the five radials distinct, the I and V widely separated, and out of the costals the 3 alone defined by a suture, all the rest being coalesced into one piece; with the madreporic filter represented, in the young specimens examined, by a few punctures placed before the middle, and with the two huge sexual outlets, mammiform and prominent, occupying a considerable portion of the system, and placed transversely against the interradials 1 and 4, so as to prevent the retrograde passage of the madreporite. These two genera, Palæotropus and Palæostoma, are, therefore, in a general sense Ethmophracti, but after a peculiar manner, entirely different from that which characterises the older Spatangidæ comprised under this appellation. They may be called Perissogonea [2]). There is not in any other genus of the Echinoidea, recent and fossil, anything strictly comparable to this structure. In some points it recalls what is seen among the Exocyclic Gnathostomes and the earlier Ateleostomes. The radials I and V are kept asunder by the interposition of the costal 5, and the madreporite spreads its pores over the entire central area, without any tendency to move backwards or out of the calycinal system. Thus it is in Holectypus and Discoidea [3]), of Oolitic origin, in most of the Cretaceous Echinoconi, in the recent Cassidulidæ [4]), in the Clypeastridæ [5]), of Tertiary origin. In these two last the sutures have a tendency to be obliterated. But in all of them the sexual pores are five or four in number, and placed against their respective interradia, into which they not seldom are transferred.

---

[1]) Études, p. 12, 50, Pl. XII, fig. 103, 104; XXXII, fig. 197—199. — A fossil species of this genus, from the Nummulitic strata of Western Sind, has been described as Hemiaster elongatus DUNCAN and SLADEN, Mem. Geol. Surv. India, Tert. etc. Ser. XIV, Vol. I, 3, p. 78, pl. XIX, fig. 7—15. Calcutta 1882.
[2]) Περισσός, excessive, *l'ovή*, generative organ.
[3]) Études, p. 81, pl. XV, fig. 133, 132.
[4]) Ib., fig. 130.
[5]) Ib., pl. XVI, fig. 135—139.

The calycinal system of the Pourtalesiadæ is much more anomalous, and at the same time not a little unsettled. In the specimen of Pourtalesia Jeffreysi, Pl. I, fig. 1, the calycinal system is brought out of contact with the interradia 1 and 4 through the interjacence of the detached plates of 5. Its general form is that of an irregular pentagon. Its constituents are all coalesced into one piece, the madreporal filter spreading its pores over its central forepart. The radials are not to be distinguished. The four sexual apertures are displaced, not answering to their respective interradia, moved forward, those of 2 and 3 being near the ambulacrum III, and those of 1 and 4 almost opposite the II and IV. Another specimen, Pl. V, fig. 27, 28, 29, not very different from the first, has the madreporic filter occupying the hinder part of the central space, the anterior pair of sexual pores nearly answering to the interradials 2 and 3, the posterior being pressed forward so as to front the ambulacra II and IV. An impression, not unlike an orbit, near the end of ambulacrum III, fig. 29, possibly indicates the existence of a radial. In a third specimen, Pl. V, fig. 25, 26, the disordered condition of the system is still more obvious. The costals 1 and 4, separated from the rest by distinct sutures, adjoin the ambulacra II and IV, and are driven widely apart by an advanced plate of 5.

In Pourtalesia lagunculu, Pl. VII, fig. 52, much the same holds good. There are no traces of radials. The costals 1 and 4, bounded by distinct sutures, adjoin the ambulacra II and IV, the costal 1 being partly in contact with the interradial 1 b, there being only one advanced plate of 5, and that intervening between the costal 4 and the interradial 4 a. The sexual pores of the costals 2 and 3 nearly answer to their respective interradia. The madreporic filter occupies the central space.

In Pourtalesia ceratopyga, Pl. VII, fig. 51, the water-filter spreads over the greater portion of the system, partly to its outermost margins. The costal 1 is completely united to the rest, but on the left side the costal 4 is wholly separated, by the interposition of three plates detached from the interradium 5, and both costals adjoin the ambulacra II and IV, while the hind margin of the system is contiguous to the interradials 1 b and 4 a. The biviary ambulacra I and V, as in the foregoing species, terminate dorsally far apart from the calyx, and without any trace of radials.

The calycinal system of Echinocrepis cuneata, Pl. VII, fig. 54, is an irregular pentagon. The madreporite spreads nearly over the whole, excepting the costals 1, 3 and 4, which are however completely united to the rest, provided with sexual pores and not much displaced. The costal 2 is completely invaded by the filter, some of whose pores are seen on its very edge, even in the suture. The radials II, III, IV are absent, but the I and V very distinct, of a fair size, pentagonally lengthened, contiguous to each other as in the Ethmophract Spatangi, and to the terminations of the ambulacra I and V. They seem to bear eye-spots.

Thus in Echinocrepis the calycinal system still presents somewhat of a Spatangoid character, such as this is exhibited by Palæotropus and Palæostoma, in the disposition of the water-pores and the obliteration of the sutures, while, at the same time, another feature peculiar to the older members of the group [1], the contiguity of the

---

[1] Comp. Echinoconus conicus, Études, Pl. XV, fig. 134.

radials I and V, again presents itself. It is in Pourtalesia Jeffreysi, P. laguncula, P. ceratopyga that the disordered and unsettled condition of the system is brought to a degree not reached in any other Echinoid, recent or fossil. The smallness and irregular outline of the whole, the frequently total obliteration of the sutures, the abortion of the radials, the displacement of the costals 1 and 4, consequent upon the general forward movement of the parts, and accompanied, no doubt, internally by a displacement of the sexual organs, the severance of one of the costals, and the abnormal contiguity of 1 and 4 to the terminations of the paired trivious ambulacra, otherwise the legitimate site of the radials, all these more or less abnormal features are as many signs of approaching ruin. During the long range of geological time that lies between the Triassic Tiarechinus with its ancestral, large, and regularly radiated calycinal system, and Pourtalesia with that same system degraded, shrunk, and dismembered, the evolutional process is marked by the successive appearance of forms unseen before, each bearing in the condition of the calyx the criterion of its geological age. The large, regular and intact calyx of the Endocyclic forms, with five costals and five radials equally balanced, points back to the earliest aspect of Mesozoic, and even Palaeozoic life, when their joint-heirs, the Palaeo-Crinoidea, were in existence; the Exocyclic system, broken up posteriorly by the egress of the excretory opening, to Oolitic time; and, among the Spatangida, the Ethmophract system, of four costals, with the 1 and 4, and the radials I and V, or these last alone, closing from either side, is a badge of seniority, as the other one, the Ethmolysic, with the restored costal 5 separating the I and V, and the madreporite retrograding, is a sign of juniority. Future researches will decide whether we should be right in seeing in the dissolving calyx of the Pourtalesiæ an indication of a still later origin.

These, I believe, are some of the leading features in the history of the calycinal system, as one of the constituents of the Echinoidean skeleton. A large and powerful structure, closely specialised for a function of fundamental importance in the economy of some remote ancestral type, is inherited, in an early state, by a descendant in which, from a total change in the mode of life, the very purpose no longer exists for which it was originally contrived, and to which its parts were adapted. It long retains certain marked features which even to this day reveal its origin, but—unlike its Crinoidean sister-structure which, with functions unaltered, multiplies its components—it remains simple as from the beginning, and, superfluous as it has become, gradually declines in intrinsic vigour, and is given up to subserving activities that had no share in its previous existence. Invaded by contending organs and yielding to their various tendencies, it has its parts deeply modified and even to some degree suppressed, and, although still true to its type, and asserting, so to say, its unimpaired independence by redintegrating its injured frame, it dwindles nevertheless from age to age in every succeeding form, and is seen to fall into decay and dismemberment, and to lose one by one its characteristics, till at last little remains of its original constitution.

V. THE POURTALESIADÆ.

The characteristics of their skeleton. They constitute a distinct family equivalent to that of the Spatangidæ and the Cassidulidæ. Their geographical and bathymetrical distribution.

Eight species comprised in the genus Pourtalesia, one Echinocrepis and one Spatagocystis, make the whole of what is known at present of the little group discussed in the foregoing pages with regard to its skeletal morphology. It remains to expose its characteristics in a comprehensive form, and to determine its systematic position. In this attempt I feel all the inconvenience of being able to speak, from immediate observation, of but a single species in an entire condition, of three others in a fragmentary state only, and of having had before me no specimen at all of Spatagocystis. It so happens, moreover, that Pourtalesia Jeffreysi, the only species examined with some degree of completeness, appears to be, in certain respects, of a more advanced character than the rest, and therefore, as being less in harmony with their mode of conformation, perhaps not rightly to be regarded as embodying the typical features of the group. However, notwithstanding these shortcomings, and with the reservation therein implied, and calling to mind that this is not the first occasion, nor will be the last, when a species that chances to be the most familiar to us, is put forward as the type of its kind, I venture on the following description, with Pourtalesia Jeffreysi in the foreground.

The general form of the skeleton of the Pourtalesiadæ is more lengthened than that of most other Neonomous Echinoids, sub-cylindroid or ob-conical; anteriorly more or less truncate, sometimes broad; in the middle slightly tumid; posteriorly tapering; dorsally convex, sometimes even raised into a hump; ventrally rather flat. Below the slightly overhanging front the forepart is invaginated into the peritoneal cavity, so as to form a deep infra-frontal recess, a rudimentary mouth and buccal cavity, opening anteriorly and ventrally, having at its bottom the peristome, — a disposition unexampled anywhere else in the whole class, an incipient feature approximating to what obtains in worms. Posteriorly the body, in most of the species, terminates in a caudal prolongation, and then the periproct is subdorsal, as among the Cassidulidæ, or at least posterior; in one species, Echinocrepis cuneata, the body is simply pointed behind and the periproct subventral. The stomatoproctic axis is nearly parallel to the ventral plane.

The bilateral symmetry of the constituent elements is highly developed, while, at the same time, the dorsal side contrasts with the ventral in a strongly marked manner. In these points the Pourtalesiadæ depart from the Archæonomous type more widely than any other group.

The three skeletal systems, forming together an unbroken surface, are all present, in different states of development: the perisomatic system predominates; the ambulacral presents its five rays, while the calycinal system is seen to lose its character, and to verge upon decay.

The ambulacrum III with the interradia 2 and 3 constitute the shortened and blunted front part. They are of a relatively small size, normal in outline, adorally involuted and elevated above the ventral level, and thus, contrary to what obtains even in the majority of the Spatangidæ, excluded from touching the ground. The paired ambulacra II and IV, with the interradia 1 and 4, combine to form the lengthened middle part, the ventral surface, wholly post-oral and making nearly the half part of the total length. They are expanded and more or less anomalous in outline, and so is the bivium, which, along with the odd interradium 5, makes up the abdominal portion of the body. Thus far the Pourtalesiadæ upon the whole resemble the Spatangidæ, but, at the same time, present an amount of peculiar modification unparalleled among even the most advanced of these.

The peristome is built up solely of the first plates of III $a\ b$, $2\ b$, $3\ a$ and 5, involuted and raised above the ventral plane. It is upright, nearly vertical to the ventral surface, and the oesophageal opening a longitudinal slit in the buccal membrane. The II and IV, having their first plates excluded from the peristome, attain the calycinal system with the terminal plates of their continuously double series. The bivious ambulacra, I and V, are dismembered; in each of them the first plates, not received into the peristome, are united into one single plate, and the two compound plates thus formed, by being contiguous to each other and to the plates II $a\ 1, 2$ and IV $b\ 1, 2$, intervene between the labrum and the interradia 1 and 4, while they themselves are aborally widely separated from I, 2 and V 2, which, like the following, are double, their continuous series embracing the sternum and episternum, $5, 2, 3$, filling with their plates I $a\ 4$ and V $b\ 4$ the episternal angle, surrounding with I $5, 6, 7$ and V $5, 6, 7$ the periproctal region, and forming the flanks of the abdomen, but dorsally not reaching the calycinal system.

This breach of continuity in the ambulacra I and V, without parallel in the whole class, is seen only in Pourtalesia Jeffreysi, P. lagunculа, and Spatagocystis Challengeri. It is brought about by the interradia 1 and 4, which close together ventrally from either side and meet again dorsally, forming, between I, 1 and V, 1 and II and IV, anteriorly, and I and V posteriorly, a broad, unbroken, vertical ring all around the middle of the body, a structure unexampled among Echinoidea, and, combined with the rudimental buccal cavity, expressive of a tendency towards an annulose differentiation, latent, or but faintly developed elsewhere among Neonomous forms. But, as said above, a few only of the species present this striking peculiarity. In Pourtalesia carinata, P. ceratopyga, Echinocrepis cuneata, the interradia 1 and 4 do not join ventrally in the middle, and consequently do not form a continuous ring. Dorsally they meet together from either side in P. carinata and P. ceratopyga, but in Echinocrepis they are separated by the ambulacra I and V, almost as in the Spatangidæ.

The heteronomy of the interradium 1, so eminently characteristic of the Spatangidæ, and particularly of their later forms, is distinctly maintained, at least in Pourtalesia Jeffreysi and P. lagunculа, but wholly transferred to 1 5, its formula having become 1 b 2 + 3 4 a 2:4 a 3.

The obliquity indicating an imaginary discordant axis am, IV—1, and manifested, throughout the whole class, in the disposition of the ambulacral plates of the peristome, is fully maintained in one species only, Pourtalesia carinata, but discarded in P. Jeffreysi, P. laguncula, P. ceratopyga and Echinocrepis cuneata, in which the first plate of the III, uni-porous in a, bi-porous in b, alone presents a remnant of the otherwise universal formula, while the first plates of the paired ambulacra II and IV, I and V, are all symmetrical on either side of the mesial line, thus conforming to the growing tendency towards a strict bilaterality, and a gradually more decided contrast between the ventral side and the dorsal.

The posterior interradium, 5, is dismembered in Pourtalesia Jeffreysi, P. laguncula and Spatagocystis. Ventrally the 1 of I and V, the 1 of I and I, and the 2 of I and V, are interposed between 5, 1, the labrum, and 5, 2, the sternum. In P. carinata, perhaps also in P. ceratopyga and in Echinocrepis cuneata, the labrum is contiguous to the sternum. In P. Jeffreysi the labrum is very minute, in the rest of species observed large and expanding aborally. The sternum is all of one piece in P. Jeffreysi, the plates $a\ 2$ and $b\ 2$ having coalesced, while in P. carinata they appear to be separate. It is followed in P. Jeffreysi by the regular double Spatangean episternum, $5\ a\ 3$, $5\ b\ 3$, the pre-anals $5\ a\ 4—6$, $5\ b\ 4—6$, the expanded periproctal series, $5\ a\ 7—9$, $5\ b\ 7—9$, and by the dorsal sequence of plates gradually narrowing, and in P. Jeffreysi, P. laguncula, P. carinata, P. ceratopyga, and Spatagocystis, reaching the calycinal system, but by means of detached pairs of plates only, *enclaves* between the 1 and 4, where these close mesially, thus distantly recalling Collyrites.

The calycinal system, somewhat Spatangean in Echinocrepis by the radials I and V being distinct, contiguous and closing, and the sexual pore of the costal 2 abortive, in the other species, at least in Pourtalesia Jeffreysi, P. laguncula, P. ceratopyga, is subject to a degree of degeneration seen nowhere else. Its outline is irregular, the sutures obliterated to an extent unknown elsewhere, the radials have disappeared, and while there is no trace of a restored costal 5, the 1 and 4 are displaced forward nearly beyond the ambulacra II and IV, and the costal 4 even occasionally severed from the system by detached plates of the fifth interradium; and while thus the structural consistency of the system is giving way, its relative size is reduced, and it is drawn forward and widely removed from the bivious ambulacra.

Alone — with the Echinoneidae — among the whole of the Neonomous Echinoids, the Pourtalesiadae are homoiopodous. The pedicels, all ambulacral, are uniform, simple, not disciferous, none of them formed into branchial leaflets, the sub-oral and upper frontal pedicels larger than the rest, which are very minute.

The spherids are uncovered, more various in number than usual, but always stationed exclusively on a restricted part of the sub-labial region, on the first plates of the ambulacra I, II, IV, V, and absent on the frontal, III, — a characteristic without parallel.

The single fasciola present is sub-anal, but holds not the same relation to the plates of the bivium, as in the Prymnodesmic Spatangidae. In one species it aborts.

The spines are Spatangean, partly curved and oar-like, partly almost straight, all rather slender, not crowded, except on the sternum and on the palate of the buccal cavity.

These are the leading features that characterise the skeleton of the Pourtalesiadæ. They combine to make them eminently Neonomous, and different from the oldest of these, the Echinoneidæ. With the Cassidulidæ, of Oolitic origin, they have in common the caudal prolongation, the structure of the proctal part, and, in some degree, the simple form of the pedicels. With the higher Spatangidæ, the Prymnodesmians, they share in the abdominal lengthening of the body, the forward position of the oesophageal opening, the heteronomy of the interradium 1, the sternum and episternum, the fasciola, the form of the spines. They fail to attain the high standard of the Spatangidæ by the frequent abortion of the organs of vision, by the pedicels uniformly simple, not specialised into tactual, prehensile, branchial organs distributed on differently modified parts of the ambulacra. The line of modification followed by their special development goes in another direction, indicated by the cylindroid form of the body, the forward position and the degradation of the calycinal system, the incipient feature of a rudimentary mouth and buccal cavity, with the oesophageal opening and the peristome vertical, by the peristomal part of the frontal ambulacrum and the interradials 2 b 1 and 3 a 1 being raised above the ventral plane and out of contact with the ground; by the contrast between the dorsal and ventral segment heightened by this disposition as, also, by the entire set of sphærids and the larger pedicels being stationed on the sub-labial area; by the symmetrical disposition of the parts on either side thus being to a certain degree realised, almost to the disappearance of an otherwise universal obliquity indicating the existence of an axis am, IV—1; by the annular disposition of the interradia 1 and 4, forming a closed ring all around the middle of the body, and, as a consequence, the dismemberment and backward transposition of the fettered hind-limbs, the ambulacra I and V. These are characters in the Pourtalesiadæ, pointing, though remotely, towards animal forms of another and higher type, animals of annulose differentiation. The sum of these features, those shared with other groups as well as those in which they stand alone, demand the creation for them of a distinct family, systematically equivalent to that of the Cassidulidæ and the Spatangidæ: THE POURTALESIADÆ.

Geographically the Pourtalesiadæ are distributed over the whole of the oceans. P. Jeffreysi seems to belong to the Norwegian Sea, having been found by the Porcupine halfway between Færöe and Shetland, and by the naturalists of the Vöringen at Lat. 63° 6' N., long. 1° 20' W.; Lat. 63° 10' N., long. 5° E.; Lat. 67° 20' N., long. 9° E. P. miranda was dredged by DE POURTALÈS and by the Blake in the Straits of Florida. P. phiale was first found by the Porcupine in the Rockall Channel, then again in the Antarctic Sea, by the Challenger. P. lagunculaand P. rosea are from the Pacific; P. hispida, P. ceratopyga and P. carinata Antarctic, the two last reaching the coast of Chile. Echinocrepis cuneata and Spatagocystis Challengeri are Antarctic.

Bathymetrically the Pourtalesiadæ have been found at depths from 442 to 5300 metres, the average depth being 2900 m. Seven species were met with from this point and downwards, in Globigerina ooze, grey ooze, and red clay: Pourtalesia phiale, two habitats, mean depth 2900 metres; P. hispida, two habitats m. d. 3300 m.; P. carinata three habitats, m. d. 3500 m.; P. ceratopyga, three habitats, m. d. 3800 m.; P. rosea at 1750 m.; Echinocrepis cuneata at 2900 m.; Spatagocystis Challengeri, two habitats, m. d. 3250 m., the medium of their average depths being 3800 metres. Above the general medium depth of 2900 metres and up to 442 m., from the Globigerina ooze to the sandy mud mixed with pebbles, were found two species: Pourtalesia Jeffreysi, in four habitats, at a mean depth of 1300 metres; P. miranda, two habitats, m. d. 1200 m.; and one species alone, Pourtalesia laguncula, from 630 m., sandy mud, 5° C., down to 5303 m., red clay, 1° C., in five habitats, mean depth 3000 metres. At one locality, in the Antarctic ocean, half-way between the Cape and Kerguelen Island, at a depth 2926 m., four species were found living together at one locality, Pourtalesia hispida, P. carinata, Echinocrepis cuneata. Spatagocystis Challengeri; half-way between Kerguelen Island and South Australia, in one locality, depth 3570 m., three species, P. ceratopyga, P. carinata, Sp. Challengeri were found with one another; two species, P. phiale and P. hispida not far from there, at more than 62° S., depth 3611 m.; and two others, P. ceratopyga and P. carinata near the coast of Chile, at 4069 m. The rest were found single.

Thus, as far as our present knowledge goes, three species are Atlantic, and one of these also Antarctic; two were found in the Pacific and five in the Antarctic Sea; and of the ten species hitherto known none comes nearer to the surface than by 442 metres, while two descend to 1000 and to 2000 m., one to near 3000 m., three to between 3000 and 4000 m., three to between 4000 and 5000 m., and one to beyond 5000 metres.

The littoral region comprises the favoured zones of the sea, where light and shade, a genial temperature, currents changeable in power and direction, a rich vegetation spread over extensive areas, abundance of food, of prey to allure, of enemies to withstand or to evade, represent an infinitude of agents competent to call into play the tendencies to vary, definite in kind and limited in number, which are embodied in each species, and always ready by modifying its parts to respond to the influences of external conditions. In this region the great majority of marine forms are at home, of the Echinoidea all the highest types, the Cidaridae, Echinidae, Clypeastridae, Echinoneidae, Cassidulidae and the Spatangidae, Prymnadete and Prymnodesmian, and there live, with rare exceptions, the recent representatives of the fossil types of preceding geological periods. But not one among the known living species, not a single fossil [1]) among the multitudes imbedded in the sediments of former seas, had suggested the possibility of a combination of characters like that realised in the Pourtalesiadae, and science was not aware of its existence, until, a few years ago, dredge and trawl descended into the vast regions of the great depths, where life endures on hard terms, far beyond the

[1]) AL. AGASSIZ, in the list of known recent species, Rep. Chall. Echinoidea, p. 208, doubtingly adduces as possibly a Tertiary representative of the Pourtalesiadae, the fragment described by EDW. FORBES as Echinarachnius Woodii, Echinodermata of the British Tertiaries, Palaeontographical Society, 1852, p. 12, pl. II, fig. 6 a, 6 b. Professor F. JEFFREY BELL has had the kindness to examine for me the original specimen of FORBES, now in the British Museum. There seems to be no reason whatever for regarding it as having being part of something like a Pourtalesia. I arrived at the same conclusion from the inspection of another fragment, also from Crag, lent me by Mr ROBERT BELL, Chiswick.

furthermost limits of solar light and of vegetation, in stillness and cold all but unvaried, and where much of the available nutriment is contained in the sediment that sparingly and slowly sinks down from the richer zones. Such are the abysses where the Pourtalesiadæ have to lead their simple life, unapproached by many of the powerful agents at work above, and well may it be allowable to surmise that the very poorness of the conditions surrounding them, while leaving unawakened, and thus eliminating a variety of tendencies forcibly active in the inhabitants of more favoured regions, has set free one deep-seated tendency, all but dormant in them, the one towards a structural differentiation typical of a higher and different order of the Annulate Animals.

The Pourtalesiadæ are not alone among Echinoids to impart a peculiar aspect to the abyssal fauna. Like them the Phormosomas are eminently deep-sea forms, the ten species found by the Porcupine, the Challenger, the Blake and the Knight Errant ranging from 219 metres to 5030 m., the average depth of the genus being 2625 metres. In five out of the eleven Challenger stations where Pourtalesiadæ were dredged, they were found associated with Phormosomas. Higher up these are represented by species of Asthenosoma.

As, among land animals and those of the sea that live near the shore, certain types, properly belonging to and richly varied within the tropics, are found represented in our temperate and even cold regions by one or the other of their forms, perhaps somewhat modified, but still recognisable, thus also in the oceans, in a bathymetrical sense, certain types, properly littoral and highly developed in the favoured zones of light, have outposts in the dark depths, sharing with true abyssal forms their reduced conditions of existence.

In the adult state most of marine Evertebrates remain at their native station, wandering within its precincts. Their embryonic and larval age is their period of dispersal. Of numerous littoral forms, of different classes, tribes and orders, currents must occasionally carry away the free swimming larvæ from the vicinity of land far into the sea, and during the course of succeeding generations early stages of many a species will in this way have reached the wide ocean. There they will have sunk, their development accomplished, all through depths full of dangers and more and more ungenial, and a few of them will have settled on the bottom of the abyss, and fewer still will have come to thrive there. Among these some will have long retained their original character, and but slowly been modified, while others will have exhibited a latitude of variation unknown or rarely seen where they came from, but upon the whole there will be reasons for assuming the less altered forms to be newcomers, the more deviating to be old inhabitants of the deep. At present it is too early to enter into these questions, — when the whole of the materials now on competent hands shall have been worked out, and a general view of the facts obtained, the time will have arrived for knowing, whether the abyssal fauna may be derivable, in the way mentioned, as a whole, from the fauna of the littoral region, as from its original stock, both being recent and coeval, though widely separated, or, in part, from littoral forms no more existing, but fossil not far off. The results then arrived at will perhaps come to throw some light upon the relations of certain fossil forms now regarded as characteristic of separate geological periods.

Among Archaeonomous genera, Goniocidaris, Aspidodiadema, Echinus are represented within the deep-sea habitats of the Pourtalesiadæ, and along with them a few littoral Spatangidæ. Among the Prymnodesmians Kleinia, Maretia, Cionobrissus descend to associate with Pourtalesia lagunenla at depths of 630 and 1460 metres, and well-known species of Brissopsis, Echinocardium, Spatangus, and a species of Macropneustes, were brought up from considerable depths by the Challenger and the Blake, as also some genera and species unknown before. Linopneustes Murrayi AL. AG.[1]), found to live at 630 m. with Pourtalesia lagunenla, has the elongated labrum and short, angulate sternum of Maretia planulata, its episternum, its broad and naked ventral bivium with the three extended subanal plates, the same form of the plate *1* and *2 + 3* of the interradium 1, but its whole body is more convex, not so much tapering posteriorly, the petals, level with the perisome, are more open and gradually narrowing upward, and there is a narrow, peripetalous, peripheral fasciola of only three or four minute tubercles in the transverse row. The two species of Homolampas[2]), from 60 to 4500 metres, according to the figures and descriptions given by AL. AGASSIZ, also come near to Maretia, but the gradually narrowing petals are still more open, their plates are much longer in relation to the breadth, and their pores are minute and placed diagonally. Argopatagus AL. AG.[3]), an associate of Pourtalesia lagunenla at 1460 metres, to all appearance is not remotely akin to the foregoing, but apetalous, the dorsal ambulacral plates being nearly equilateral hexagons with the pores almost central. Palaeotropus[4]), which lives in depths from 150 to 686 metres, is eminently apetalous.

Among the Prymnadetes the ancient Ethmophract genus Hemiaster descends from 300 to 1463 metres, and there joins Pourtalesia lagunenla. The Ethmolysians are represented by two very remarkable forms of the group of Schizaster.

Aceste bellidifera WYV. THOMS.[5]) appears to be a true deep-sea form, its habitats being at 3500 and 5000 metres, the last shared with Pourtalesia rosea. Thanks to Mr JOHN MURRAY I can give, from actual observation, a description of its skeleton, *Pl. XX*. The pedicels have been described above, *p. 53, Pl. X, fig. 96—98*. In the dorsal aspect the outline of the body is ob-cordate, frontally drawn in so as to form a deep sinus, continuous with the large, broadly lanceolate depression that occupies the middle part of the anterior slope. The dorsal surface gradually rises backward to far beyond the middle; then the calycinal system, for a small apical space, is horizontal, the part behind it declining into the almost abruptly vertical, high, nearly flat, elliptical anal surface. The ventral side, level along the middle line, posteriorly suddenly bends upward at the suture between the sternum and the episternum; laterally it

---

[1]) Rep. Chall. Echin., p. 167, pl. XXV, XXV b.
[2]) Ib., p. 164, pl. XXIV.
[3]) Ib. p. 160, pl. XXII, fig. 1—6.
[4]) Études, pl. XXXII, fig. 200.
[5]) Voy. Challenger, I. p. 376. AL. AG. Rep. Chall. Echin., p. 195, pl. XXXII. fig. 7—14, XXXIII. a, fig. 1—7.

gradually passes into the rounded flanks. These general features are those of Schizaster canaliferus, the frontal sinus that of Sch. fragilis. — The perisome, upon the whole disposed like that of Schizaster[1]), is in some points considerably modified. The interradials 2 and 3, which, as in that genus, form the ridge bounding on either side the great dorso-frontal depression, enter the peristome, as normal, each with a single small plate, followed by a pair of larger ones, of which the outer one is broad, the inner narrow. Then come, in 2 *a* and 3 *b*, two fair-sized plates, and a terminal row of eleven or twelve very minute plates, that look as if coalescent into three or four slender and compressed, articulated plates, making the very top of the ridge. The 2 *b* and 3 *a*, of nearly equal breadth throughout, with the last four or five plates lengthened, form the inner slope of the ridge, adjoining the frontal ambulacrum. The interradia 1 and 4 are very much as in Schizaster canaliferus, Sch. japonicus and Sch. fragilis, the plate *1* being subtriangular and internally extended so as to reach the 2, while in 1 *a* the heteronomy is effected by the union of *2* and *3* into a single plate. In the interradium 5 the labrum is somewhat longer than in Schizaster or Moira. The sternum is less broad, the episternal angle distinct, the abdominal *a* plates a little behind the *b* plates, the periproct being formed by *b 5, 6, 7, a 4, 5, 6*; the anal membrane, *fig. 236*, covered with rounded scales, has the excretory opening somewhat above the centre. — In the ambulacral system the III, sunk in the large and open depression of the forepart, is lanceolate, very broad, even more so than in young Schizasters, and expanding aborally. The II and IV are narrow, their first seven pairs of plates of a fair size; they terminate, not with a petaloid, sunken expansion of transverse plates, but with a strongly compressed double series of minute plates, longer than they are broad, level with the adjoining interradia, and bearing pores placed adorally and diagonally throughout, indistinct or perhaps partly wanting in the intra-fasciolar portion of the inner row. The bivious ambulacra I and V are rather broad in the ventral part, I *a 2, b 3* and V *b 2, a 3* being larger than the rest, I *a 5* and V *b 5* entering the episternal angle, the terminal part gradually tapering, apetalous, the plates about as broad as they are long, sub-hexagonal, the minute pores placed near the adoral margin. — The peristome is normal, *fig. 235*, transversely oval, altogether anterior, upright, vertical, not ventral. The scales covering the buccal membrane are larger frontally, the oesophageal opening transversely oval, somewhat below its centre. The calycinal system, *fig. 237*, placed on the apex of the body, a little behind the three fourths of the total length from the front margin, comes more near to that of Schizaster canaliferus, *fig. 238*, than to that of Moira, in which the distortion of the system is carried very far. It is a little broader than it is long, the 1 and 4 being prominent. In the specimen described the 1 and 2, and the 3, 4, 5 are united severally, only one suture being visible, connecting the radials I and III. The 1 and 4 each have a large sexual pore. The madreporite is central. — The single fasciola, simple and undivided all around, answers to the peripetalous fasciola of Schizaster. Very nearly as in that genus it traverses III, *3, 4, 2 b 4, 2 a 4, 5, 3 a 4, 3 b 4*. II 7 and IV 7, 8.

[1]) Études, pl. XXXI fig. 194.

ascends lengthwise 1 *b* 4, 5, 6, 4 *a* 4, 5, 6, thus attaining 1 *a* 6, 4 *b* 6, and crosses I and V at *11* or *12*, and the odd interradium on its eighth pair of plates.

With the evidently Schizasterian Aceste bellidifera for a guide it is not difficult to see the affinity, though distant, of the very extraordinary Aerope rostrata Wyv. Th.[1]), another inhabitant of the great depths, from 1460 to 3200 metres. According to the figures and descriptions given, its body is much more elongate, the frontal ambulacrum much less sunk, the peristome clabiate and subcircular, not anterior, but ventral, at the third of the entire length; the labrum is very long, the sternum occupies the posterior third, the periproct is dorsal; the calycinal system has four sexual pores; the madreporite is central. The pedicels of III are those of Aceste and Schizaster, the fasciola has the same course, and the heteronomy of I appears to be the same. It is likewise apetalous.

Recent Echinoids coming near to the earliest Spatangidæ, Adete, Ethmophract, Meridosternous, were unknown to science, and indeed do not seem to exist in the littoral belt. It was the good fortune of the late Sir Wyville Thomson to bring to light, near Fayal, from a depth of 1850 metres the very singular Calymne relicta[2]), and to have to indicate, by a *nomen triviale*, the significance of the discovery. It looks indeed like a relic from the Older Cretaceous or even the Oolitic period, combining with a perfectly ethmophract calyx a general form like that of Collyrites elliptica or ovalis, a bivium widely separated from the calyx, a sternum composed of several plates. But it is provided with a peripheral fasciola, a feature not foreign, it seems, to Cardiaster. It is apetalous. Its near ally, Cystechinus Al. Ag., a deep-sea form from 1900 to 4070 metres, at 2900 m. an associate of Pourtalesia hispida, Echinocrepis and Spatagocystis, at 3950 m. of P. ceratopyga, at 4070 m. of that species and P. carinata, Adete, Ethmophract, Meridosternous and Apetalous, has its bivium dorsally joining the calyx.

Of the no less characteristic Urechinus Naresianus Al. Ag.[3]), *Pl. XXI, fig. 239—242*, I can speak from direct observation, thanks to the liberality of my English friends to whom I am obliged for the inspection of duplicate specimens from the Challenger Expedition. This species was brought up in the Southern Pacific and the Antarctic from depths of 2500, 2600, and 3300 metres, from 2926 m. in company with Pourtalesia hispida, P. carinata, Echinocrepis cuneata and Spatagocystis Challengeri, and by the Blake among the Lesser Antilles, from 772 and 2200 metres. In the dorsal aspect its outline is oviform, tapering behind, the surface entirely smooth, the calycinal system nearly central; the ventral surface almost flat, the interradium 5 slightly rising and convex, the subanal part somewhat prominent; the peristome, *fig. 240*, is slightly sunk, sub-pentangular, with the small oesophageal opening in the centre of the buccal membrane, which is covered with three circles of triangular scales, the outermost of which are by far the largest. The periproct, *fig. 241*, rather wide, sub-orbicu-

---

[1]) Voy. Challenger I, 380. Al. Agass. Rep. Chall. Echin. p. 192, pl. XXXIII, XXXIII *a*, fig. 8—12.
[2]) Voy. Chall. I, p. 396. Al. Agass. Rep. Chall. Echin. p. 155, pl. XXXIV.
[3]) Report Chall. Echinoidea p. 146, pl. XXIX, fig. 1—4, XXX, XXX *a*, fig. 1—14. Report Blake Echinoidea, p. 52, pl. XXVI, fig. 1—3.

lar, is posterior, somewhat sub-ventral; the excretory opening occupies the centre of the anal membrane which is covered with about five concentric rows of scales.

The ambulacral system is normal and closely resembling that of Anancites by its lanceolate, nearly uniform radii, all level with the perisome. The peristomal formula is normal. In the bivium the plates I a 2, 3, 4, I b 3, 4, 5, and V b 2, 3, 4, V a 3, 4, 5, are lengthened, and the I a 4 and V b 4 slightly expanded interiorly, so as to fill up the feeble re-entering angle offered by the corresponding plates of the posterior interradium, a structure commonly met with also in Holaster and other Meridosterni, and in the Prymnadetes, that is, in forms devoid of a subanal fasciola, and in no wise to be compared with the well-known wedge-shaped, extended plates $6 + x$, present in all Prymnodesmic Spatangidæ. Its deficiency in Urechinus is a sure sign of the absence of a subanal fasciola, of which not one of the several specimens carefully examined showed the least trace. There is, close under the periproct, a dense accumulation of ordinary miliary tubercles, not unlike that seen in the same position in some Brissi; it has no relation to the fasciola. In all the five ambulacra, the plates, from 4 or 5, are very much alike, up to 9 at least twice as broad as they are long, then longer in proportion to the breadth, and finally, from 12 or 13, approaching to a somewhat equilateral hexagonal form. The minute pore, from 9 or 10, becomes more distant from the adoral margin, gradually nearing the centre. Thus all the ambulacra are apetalous.

The perisome presents the almost exceptional peculiarity of having the paired interradia perfectly symmetrical, the two plates a 2 and b 2 of 2 and 3 being, as observed hitherto in Palaeostoma mirabile alone, united into single plates, and likewise the plates a 2 and b 2 of 1 and 4. By this last unique mode of coalescence these interradia have become symmetrical towards one another, and the heteronomy of 1 is discarded. Hitherto Collyrites apparently was alone in presenting this regularity, a feature that seemed to approximate it to the Cassidulidæ. In the Holastridæ, on the other hand, in Holaster, Anancites, Offaster[1]), Cardiaster, the heteronomy, rendered by the formula I a 2 $+ b$ 2 = 4 a 2 : 4 b 2[2]), is distinctly seen in well preserved specimens, though in others it may be difficult to make out. Of Hemipneustes striatus (GM.[3]) several specimens were subjected to repeated and careful scrutiny without yielding decisive evidence of the presumable heteronomy, and now, being convinced of the perfect regularity of the corresponding parts in Urechinus, I venture, though always with some doubt, to give the figure, on the next page, of that species, as another example of perisomal symmetry in that early group of the Spatangidæ, the Meridosterni, among which the asymmetry is still unsettled and, as it were, in its beginning, and far from presenting the definite and constant character it gradually assumes in the Prymnadetes and the more recent Prymnodesmians.

The odd interradium, 5, is rather narrow; the labrum, expanded aborally, is contiguous to I a 1, 2 and V b 1, 2. The plate 5 b 2 simulates, as it were, by itself

---

[1]) See the woodcut on the next page.
[2]) See above p. 15.
[3]) See the wood-cut.

a small sub-pentangular sternum, contiguous to I *a 3* and V *b 3*, followed by 5 *a 2*, which is entirely separated from *1*, while *a 2, 3, 4* and *b 3, 4, 5* form together a slight re-entering angle, and *a 6—9, b 5—8* are periproctal, *10—16* dorsal, lengthened, sub-hexagonal.

Hemipneustes radiatus Gm.

When the successive modifications of the interradium 5 of the Spatangidæ are followed from the first appearance of the group to our days, it is seen that in the earliest, Collyrites [1]), after the labrum there begins a double row of alternating plates, in which the plates of the *a* series are posterior to those of the *b* series, the same order of sequence that holds good throughout the whole of the Spatangidæ. There is no appearance of a true sternum. In Hemipneustes the ventral plates of either row, from the *b 2* inclusively, extend triangularly across the interradium, so as to bring their points within a short distance from the opposite ambulacrum, and

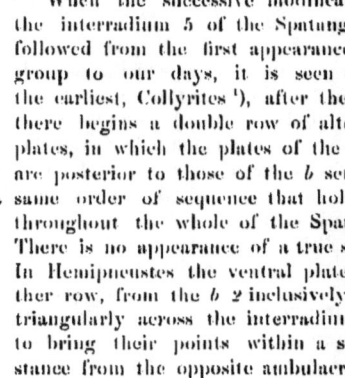

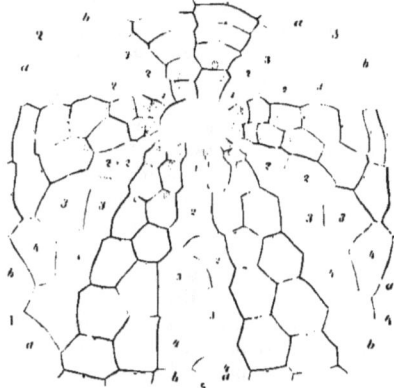

Offaster corculum Goldf.

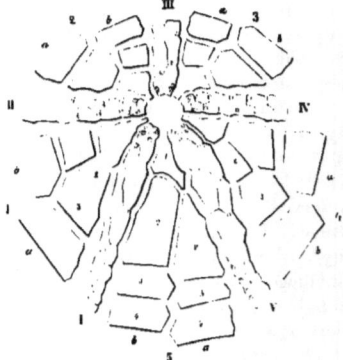

Echinospatagus Ricordeanus Cotteau.

to leave only a minute part of *a 2* in contact with the labrum, the middle suture thus becoming a zig-zag line of very wide turns. In Holaster [2]), Cardiaster, Anancites [3]), Offaster, this structure is so far modified that the *b 2*, still more expanded trans-

[1]) Etudes pl. XXIII.
[2]) Ib. pl. XXV.
[3]) Ib. pl. XXIV.

versely, occupies the whole breadth of the interradium, assuming a trapezoidal form, and fully attains the ambulacrum V, to which it becomes largely contiguous. By this means the $a\ 2$ is pushed back, widely out of contact with the labrum, but retains, like the two or three pairs of ventral plates, the triangular, pointed shape and the very oblique alternation, while the pre-anal, abdominal and dorsal plates, in proportion as they are distant aborally, and become shorter and broader, hold a less oblique position.

The large sternum of the higher Amphisternous Spatangidæ so universally consists of two equal symmetrical halves in regular juxtaposition, as to seem hardly to give room for a query whether it may not, after all, owe its form to a direct modification of that of the Meridosterni. However, it will seem to me, — notwithstanding the incompleteness of my materials, — that there really are indications of such a possibility, of its having originated through a gradual transposition of the obliquely placed $a\ 2$ and $b\ 2$ of the Meridosterni. The Adete Echinospatagus no doubt is rightly numbered among the Amphisternous Spatangidæ, but the plate $a\ 2$ of its sternum, inferior in size, triangular and asymmetrical, hangs behind the b plate, as if retarded in its growth, and anteriorly would not attain the labrum, did not this come to meet it with a lateral prolongation of its aboral margin. It may be allowable, from the whole of this singular feature to look back for the existence of earlier forms, perhaps undiscovered yet, still more evidently transitional, showing how the $a\ 2$, moving forward, first began to interpose itself between the $b\ 2$ and the ambulacrum V, at the same time exchanging its transversely cuneate shape for one more fitting its work and the place it was striving to occupy. If so, the two halves of the sternum of the higher Spatangidæ ought not to have been formed simultaneously, but in such a way that the $b\ 2$ alone had first been transformed into the future right plate, and, after that, the $a\ 2$ into the left one. And this supposition appears to acquire some degree of probability, when, leaving Echinospatagus behind, we look forward at the modifications displayed by the Spatangidæ of later appearance and higher order, modifications all of which are continuations of what has been observed in those of a lower. Thus among the Prymnadetes, some genera, as Palæostoma [1]), Hemiaster [2]), Agassizia, Schizaster, are seen to exhibit what may be regarded as marks of this movement, in the $a\ 2$ being behind and attaining aborally with a narrow point only the meeting labrum. Among the Prymnodesmian forms the earliest, Micraster [3]), still shows these traces of the asymmetry, but through the whole series of the higher, Tertiary and recent genera [4]), the symmetry and the exact juxtaposition of $a\ 2$ and $b\ 2$, of the episternals $a\ 3$ and $b\ 3$ the pre-anals $a\ 4$, $b\ 4$, and even of one or other of the anal pairs of plates, as $a\ 5$, $b\ 5$, is thoroughly established: their sutures have become rectilinear by the disappearance of the posterior inner truncation, and the angular middle suture is confined solely to the still alternating rows of abdominal and dorsal plates.

---

[1]) Études pl. XXXII.
[2]) Ib. pl. XXVI, XXX, XXXI.
[3]) Ib. pl. XXXIII.
[4]) Ib. pl. XXXIV—XLI.

I have hazarded here this attempt to explain the origin of the Spatangean double sternum in the hope that other observers, more fortunate in possessing richer materials, will deem it worth a strict examination. At present, this theory may eventually be found to stand the test or not, the plate marked 5 *b* 2 in the skeleton of Urechinus Naresianus AL. AG. is to be set down as homologous to the 5 *b* 2 in that of Offaster, Anancites, Holaster, Hemipneustes, and its 5 *a* 2 homologous to their 5 *a* 2. This striking character of the interradium 5 in the earliest among the Spatangidæ, thus met with again in Urechinus; its calycinal system, ethmophract and lengthened as in Collyrites and the Holastridæ; the absence of any heteronomy in 1, and the complete symmetry of the interradia 1 and 4, recalling Collyrites and apparently Hemipneustes; the coalescence of *a* 2 and *b* 2 known hitherto in the certainly very old-fashioned Prymnadete, Palæostoma, alone; the similarity of the five ambulacra, all of them level with the general surface; the subcircular form of the peristome; the narrow adoral margin of the labrum not expanded transversely, and protruding as in the higher Spatangidæ, — all these features combine to set forth the genus Urechinus — along with Cystechinus and Calymne — as a true living member of the group of the Meridosterni, by which the Spatangean type was first introduced, in the seas of the Mesozoic period, and which was long believed to be extinct. If Urechinus Naresianus — or, for what we know, a Cystechinus or a Calymne — had been found fossil in some Secondary or Tertiary stratum, any zoologist would have referred it, without hesitation and rightly, to the »Ananchytidæ«; — but at the same time one feature would have caught his attention as strikingly peculiar and distinctive, the total absence in the ambulacra of any trace of petaloid structure.

The recent Spatangidæ that live in the littoral belt, and the allied fossil forms of Prymnadetes and Prymnodesmians, all have, for a common character, the dorsal portions of their paired ambulacra, II and IV, I and V, transformed into more or less developed petala, within which the plates are crowded, shortened while transversely extended, and frequently more or less deeply sunk beneath the perisome, all this in order to afford as large a space as possible to the increased number of pedicels changed into triangular, compressed leaflets, evidently subservient to respiration. Now, it will have been remarked that in certain generic forms of Prymnadetes and Prymnodesmians found to inhabit the great depths, the petals, when compared with those of the properly littoral forms, are seen to be but feebly or not at all developed. In Homolampas their plates are but slightly shortened, and the minute perforations of their pores are placed diagonally, not transversely; — and Argopatagus and Palæotropus are entirely apetalous. The littoral forms of the Schizasters are provided with highly developed, deeply sunk petala, while their representatives in the great depths, Aceste and Aerope, in this point absolutely contrast with them, having the paired ambulacra wholly apetalous, narrowed in their dorsal portions, and level with the perisome. Thus, while in the littoral Spatangidæ a tendency universally prevails towards having their dorsal ambulacra with their pedicels modified for branchial functions, there seems to obtain, in the abyssal forms, within this part of their vital economy, a quiescence, that leaves these same ambulacral plates and pedicels in undifferentiated simplicity, — a peculiarity, the significance of which perhaps will be found, when the researches are brought to a close that are just begun, on the gases contained in the abyssal waters.

Urechinus, Cystechinus and Calymne, Abyssal, Ethmophract, Meridosternous, and true members of the ancient group of Adetes, are most decidedly apetalous. Are there, among the genera of that group, any forms extant that, from the structure of their dorsal ambulacra, may be put forth as the littoral or sub-littoral main stock, of which Urechinus and its living allies may be the deep-sea representatives? Anancites and Offaster had the paired ambulacra level with the perisome. On the flanks the pores have their perforations close together, rather diagonal, a little below the centre; in the dorsal portion the crowded plates, at least twice as broad as they are long, with the perforations transverse, larger, separated, nearer to the outer and the adoral margins, make very open and somewhat rudimentary petals, that evidently were the sites of branchial leaflets. Hemipneustes, combining with the ancient character of an exquisite zig-zag sternum an impressed III bearing peculiar peripodia, a produced and laterally expanding labrum, a madreporite widely spreading within the strictly ethmophract calyx[1]), has its paired ambulacra semi-petaloid, the pores of I a, V b, II a, IV b, being large, transverse, with the outer perforation a slit nearing the posterior margin, while the pores of I b, V a, II b, IV a decrease dorsally, as the former increase, and become very minute and sub-median, finally diagonal. Holaster, also, has the I, V, II, IV, semi-petaloid, but the pores of the anterior series not nearly so minute relatively, and diagonal only very near the calyx. In Cardiaster the petala are almost completely developed, the anterior pores somewhat less, but transverse and evidently branchial.

On the analogy thus clearly offered by the Prymnadete and Prymnodesmian Spatangi, the conclusion to be drawn from this difference, in the structure of their ambulacra, between the recent abyssal and those ancient Meridosterni, seems lawfully to be, that these latter, Anancites, Offaster, Hemipneustes, Cardiaster, and others, among which at least Anancites and Offaster lived in a polythalamian sediment comparable to that of the great depths of the actual seas, were not truly abyssal, but inhabitants of less deep, though oceanic parts of the Mesozoic sea. If they still survive in generically allied or altered forms, these are to be looked for on the sloping bottom between the littoral and continental shelves and the great depths. But whether extinct or still living, they once had or yet have, in Urechinus, Cystechinus, Calymne, or in ancestors of these, their representatives in the abysses of the ancient ocean, which are those also of our days.

It may be that the known species of the Pourtalesiadae, with apetalous ambulacra, are the abyssal representatives of other members of their family provided with developed petaloid branchial apparatus, and living nearer to the light and the air, in the littoral zone or in the vast regions interjacent between that and the great depths. In a fossil state such forms may possibly one day be met with, in Cretaceous layers enclosing Anancites and Echinothuria.

---

[1]) See woodcut p. 70.

PLATE I.

A

Plate I.

Pourtalesia Jeffreysi Wyv. Thoms.

The ambulacral system coloured.

Fig. 1. The skeleton, denuded; dorsal aspect.
Fig. 2. The same, ventral aspect.
Fig. 3. The same, side view.
Fig. 4. The periproct and the anal membrane.
Fig. 5. A pedicellar peripodium and tubercles.
Fig. 6. A lateral plate of an ambulacrum, with a pedicellar pore marked *.
Fig. 7. The same from the inside.
Fig. 8. The sub-labial area of another specimen.

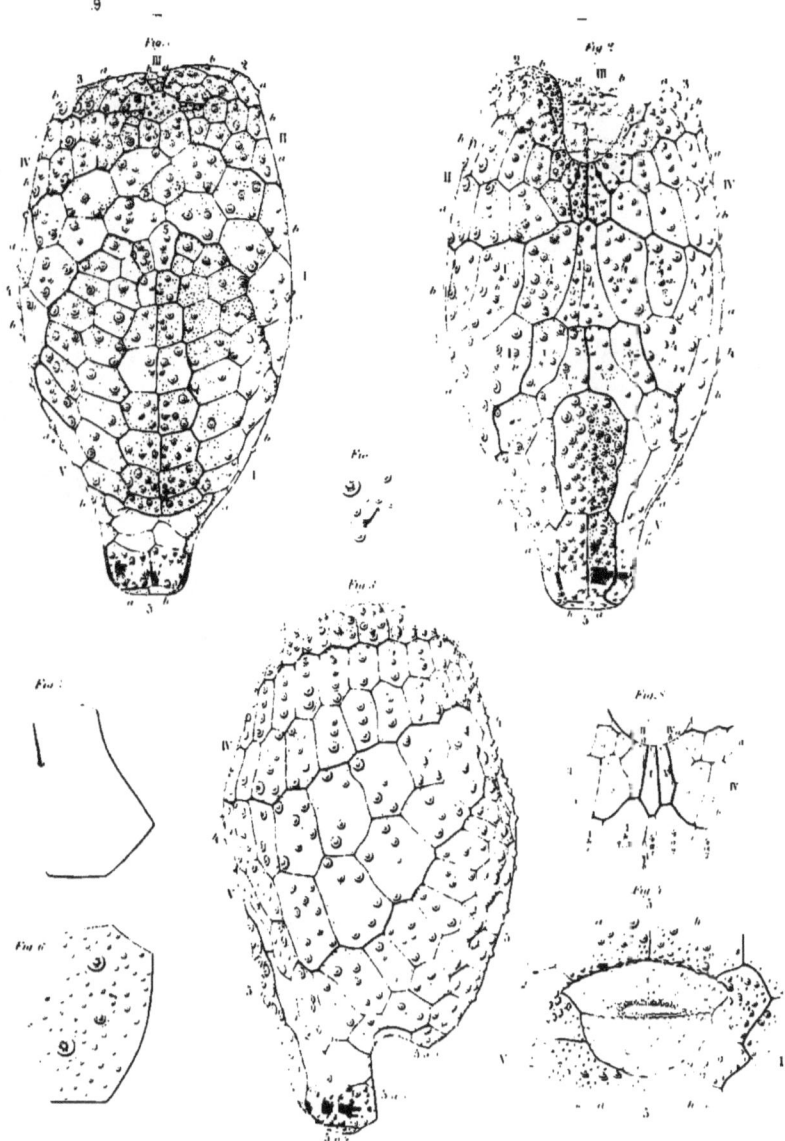

PLATE II.

PLATE II.

Pourtalesia Jeffreysi Wyv. Thoms.

The ambulacral system coloured.

Fig. 9. The skeleton, laid out. The plates 2 *b 1* and 3 *a 1* are necessarily foreshortened. The heteronomy of the interradials 1, *b 4* and 1, *b 3 + 2*, p. 14, as also the corresponding plates 4 *a 2*, 1 *a 3*, 4 *a 4*, are marked with arched, dotted lines.

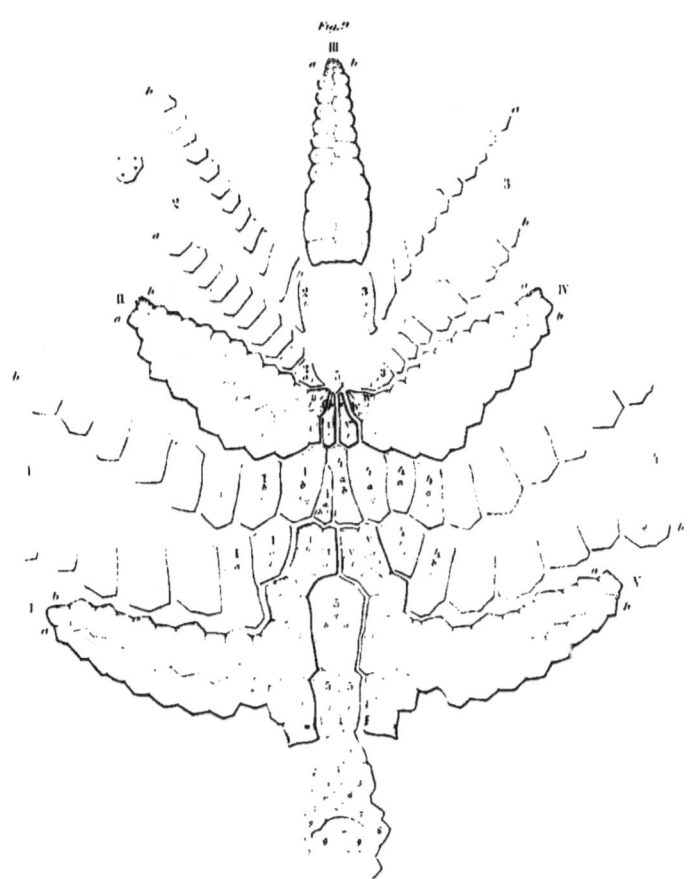

PLATE III.

Plate III.

Pourtalesia Jeffreysi Wyv. Thoms.

The ambulacral system coloured.

Fig. 10. The ventral half of the skeleton, seen from the inside. The heteronomy marked as in fig. 9.
Fig. 11. The dorsal half of the skeleton, seen from the inside.
Fig. 12. The infra-frontal recess seen from the peritoneal cavity, and from the left.
Fig. 13. Longitudinal section of the hindmost part of the skeleton, the caudal prolongation, the periproct, and the anal membrane; *am*.
Fig. 14. The dorsal termination of the ambulacrum V. from the inside.

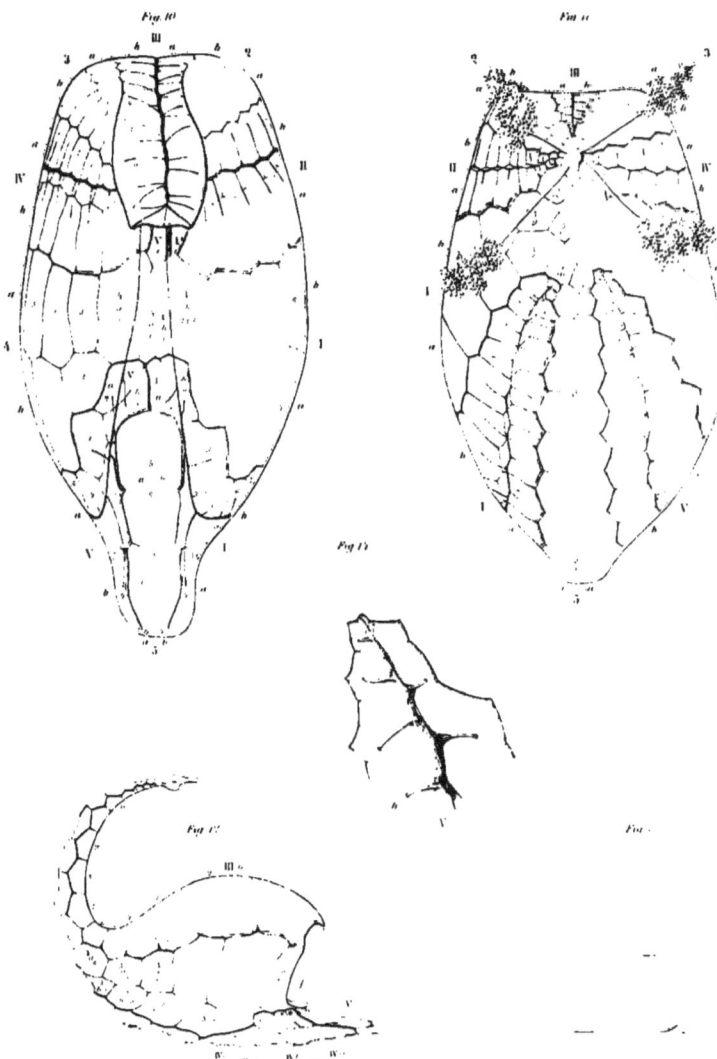

PLATE IV.

Plate IV.

Pourtalesia Jeffreysi Wyv. Thoms.

Fig. 15. The sub-labial region, from the outside, showing the ambulacrals I *l* and V *l*, II *a l* and *b l*, IV *a l* and *b l*, the four spherids, p. 40, and the four pedicellar peripodia.
Fig. 16. The same from the inside, showing the part bent in into the infra-frontal recess, the minute labrum, 5, and the four pedicels.
Fig. 17. Part of the same, placed so as to show the internal trabeculæ.
Fig. 18. The infra-frontal recess, p. 7. 28, seen from the peritoneal cavity, and from behind, showing the peristome with the buccal membrane and a part of the oesophagus, the neural collar (and vessel) and the main trunks proceeding from it.
Fig. 19. The same, from the left side.
Fig. 20. The buccal membrane, with the oesophageal opening, p. 29.
Fig. 21. The top of a sub-labial pedicel.
Fig. 22. The same, in a state of contraction.
Fig. 23. One of the sexual tubes.
Fig. 24. A part of the palate of the infra-frontal recess, showing its crowded tubercles and a minute pore.

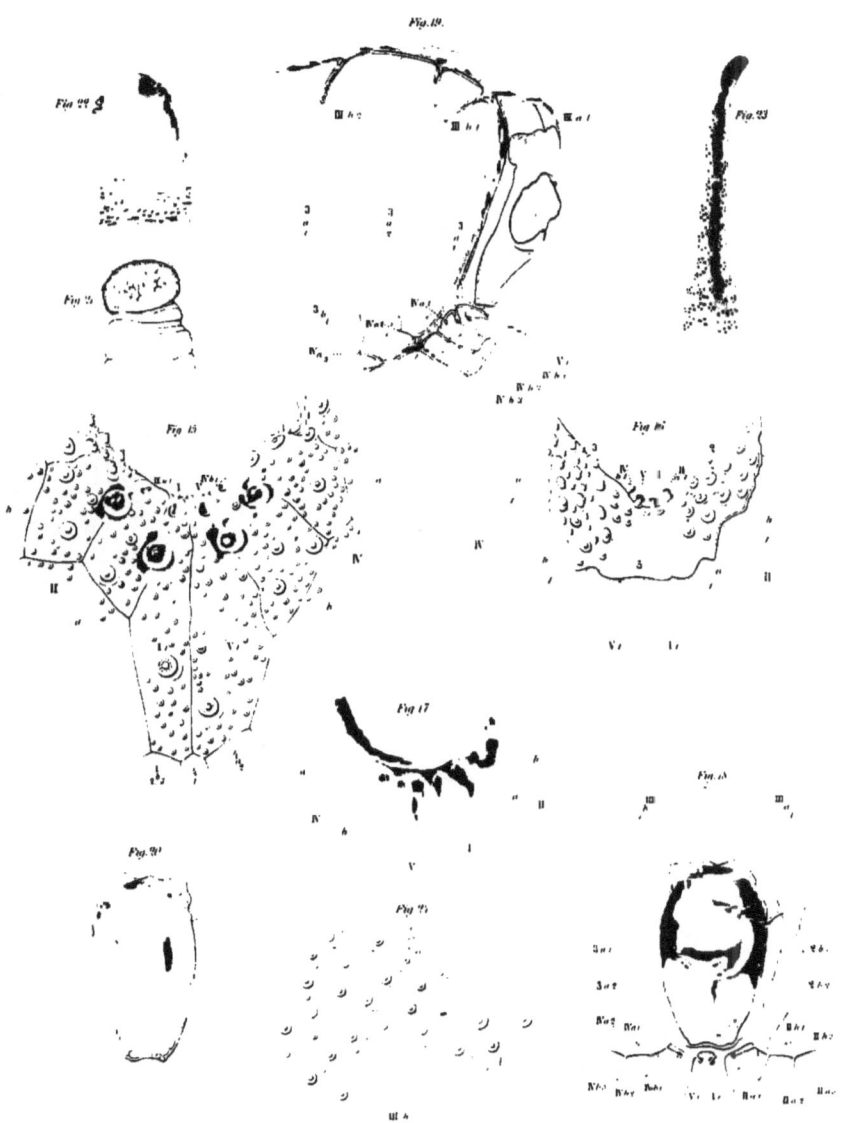

15 24 Pourtalesia Jeffreysi WYV THOMSON

PLATE V.

Plate V.

Pourtalesia Jeffreysi Wyv Thoms.

The ambulacral system coloured.

Fig. 25. The calycinal system and the surrounding area, p. 79.
Fig. 26. The same from the inside.
Fig. 27. The calycinal system and surrounding area, in another specimen.
Fig. 28. The same from the inside.
Fig. 29. The termination of the front ambulacrum.
Fig. 30. The articulating end of a spine. p. 24.
Fig. 31. The corresponding tubercle.
Fig. 32. The lower end of a spine.
Fig. 33. A calcareous fibre rising from the collar.
Fig. 34. A fibre with its processes, side view.
Fig. 35. Another fibre, front view.
Fig. 36. An oar-like spine; shortened.

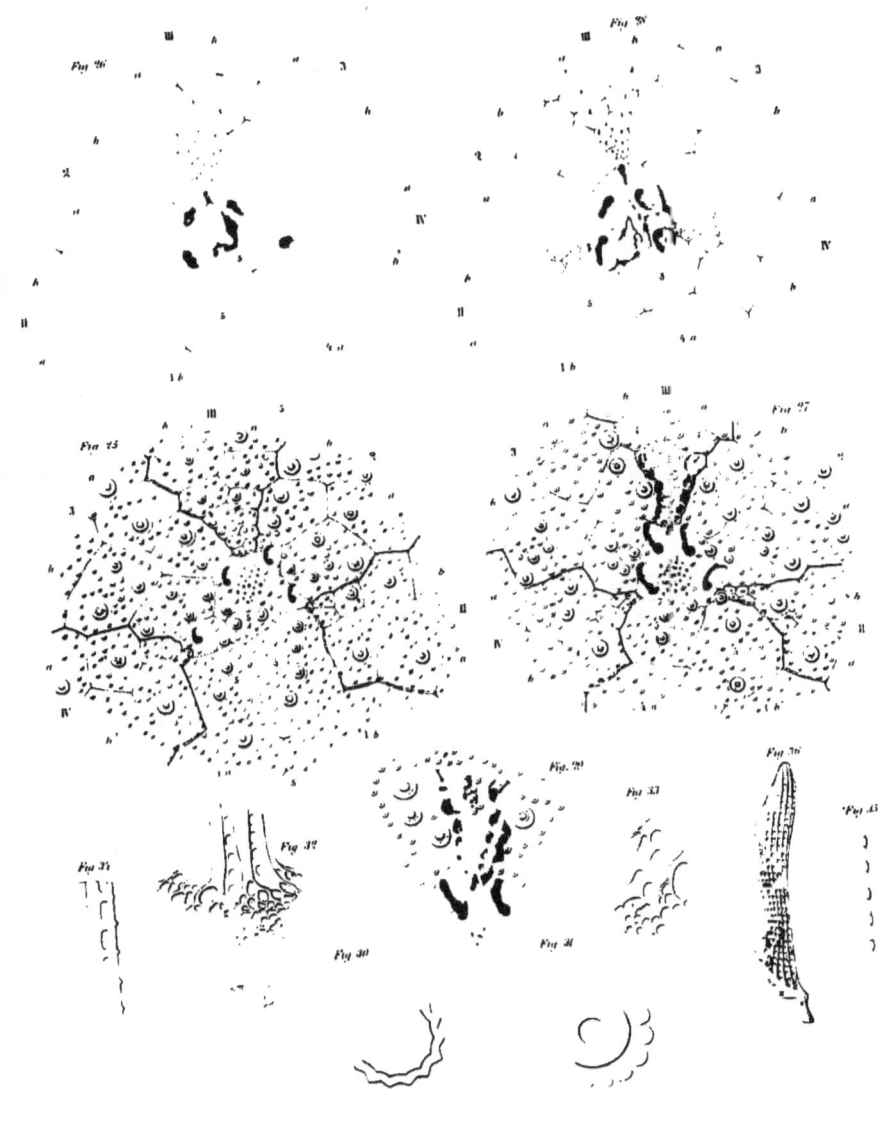

PLATE VI.

Plate VI.

Pourtalesia laguncula Al. Ag.   Pourtalesia carinata Al. Ag.

The ambulacral system coloured.

Fig. 37. The skeleton of P. laguncula, ventral view, p. 17.
Fig. 38. The skeleton of P. laguncula, another specimen, ventral view.
Fig. 39. The sub-oral region of the same.
Fig. 40. The sub-oral region of the specimen fig. 37.
Fig. 41. A peristomal pedicel and spherid, of the same.
Fig. 42. The sub-oral area of P. carinata.
Fig. 43. The same, from another specimen.
Fig. 44. Peristomal part of the same area, from the specimen fig. 42.
Fig. 45. The infra-frontal recess, seen from the peritoneal cavity; left view.
Fig. 46. The involuted part of the labial region.

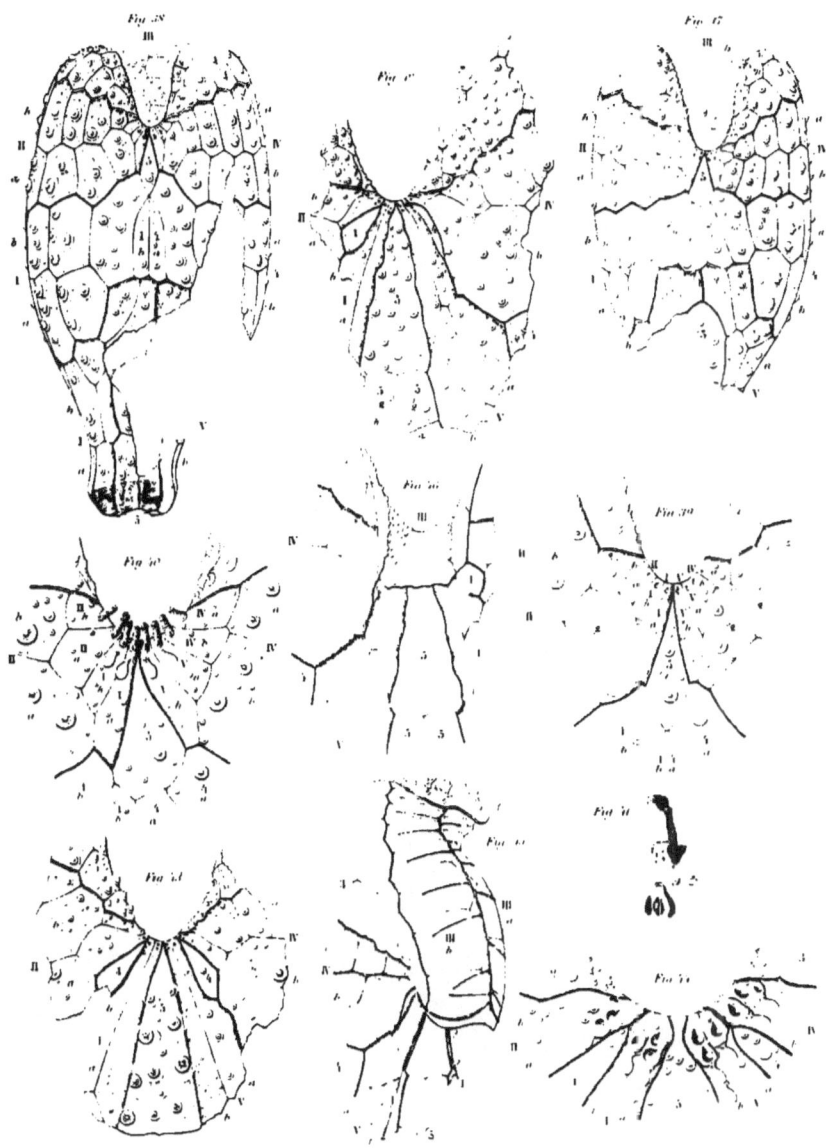

PLATE VII.

Plate VII.

Pourtalesia carinata Al. Ag.   **P. ceratopyga** Al. Ag.   **P. laguncula** Al. Ag.   **Echinocrepis cuneata** Al. Ag.

Fig. 47. Peripodia and sphæridia of the ambulacrals V a I and V b I in P. carinata.
Fig. 48. The sub-oral region of P. ceratopyga; ambulacrals coloured.
Fig. 49. A part of the same, in a different position.
Fig. 50. A part of the same with pedicels, spines, and sphærids.
Fig. 51. The calycinal system of the same, with the surrounding region. p. 80.
Fig. 52. The same parts in P. laguncula.
Fig. 53. The sub-oral region of Echinocrepis cuneata; ambulacrals coloured.
Fig. 54. The calycinal system and surrounding area in the same.

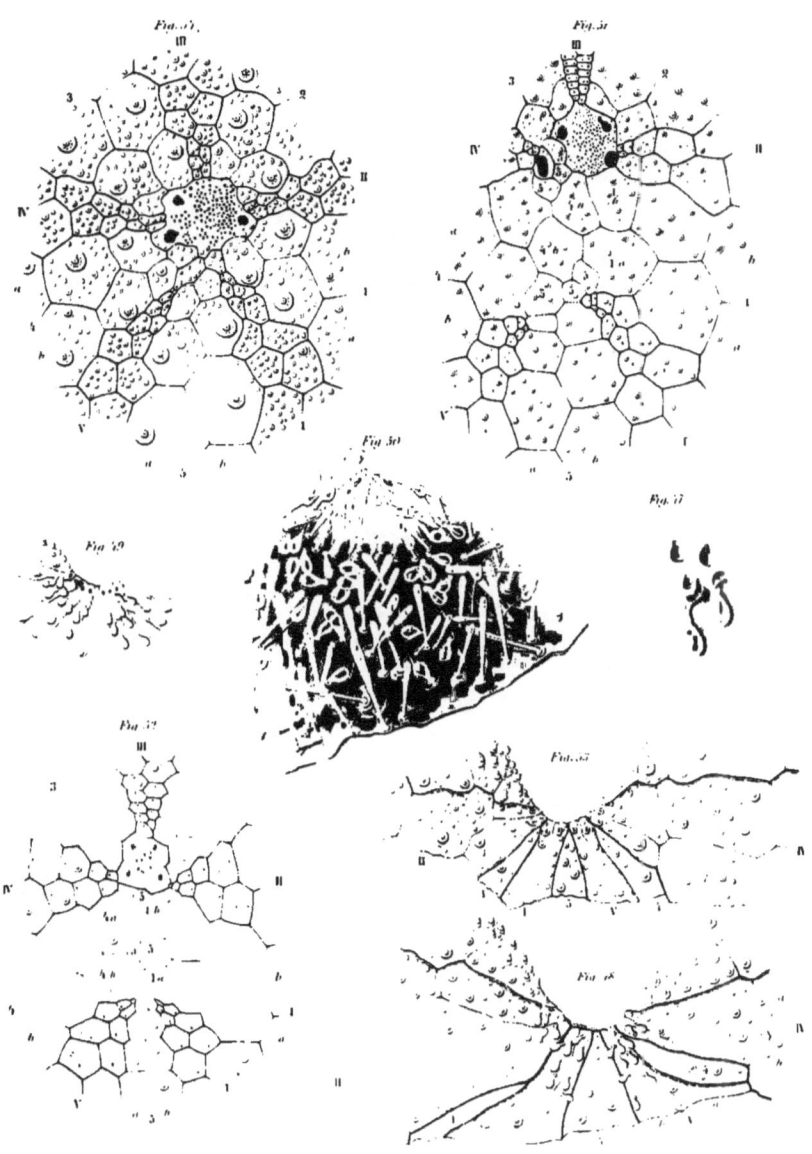

PLATE VIII.

Plate VIII.

Pedicels of Spalangidæ.

P. 45–56.

Fig. 55. A filament with its rod, from a phyllodean pedicel in Schizaster japonicus AL. AG.
Fig. 56. The same, in Urechinus naresianus AL. AG.
Fig. 57. The same, from a sub-anal pedicel in Echinocardium cordatum PENN.
Fig. 58. The same, from a phyllodean pedicel in the same species.
Fig. 59. The same, from a sub-anal pedicel in Lovenia elongata GRAY.
Fig. 60. The same, from a phyllodean pedicel in the same species.
Fig. 61. Tips of filaments from phyllodean pedicels in the same.
Fig. 62. The same, in Metalia maculosa GM.
Fig. 63. The basal part of the rod in a filament of a phyllodean pedicel in Abatus Philippii LOV.
Fig. 64. The circular disk of a phyllodean filament in Maretia planulata LAMCK. The filaments are only partially left entire, and cut down in the greater portion of the half.
Fig. 65. The disk of a subanal pedicel in Agassizia scrobiculata VAL.
Fig. 66. Monstrous bifurcation of a filament, from a sub-anal pedicel in Brissopsis lyrifera FORB.
Fig. 67. The disk of a phyllodean pedicel in Aceste bellidifera WYV. THOMS.
Fig. 68. The same, lateral view.
Fig. 69. The top of a ventral pedicel, V, in Meoma grandis GRAY.
Fig. 70. The terminal part of a frontal pedicel, III, in the same; side view.
Fig. 71. The same, from above.
Fig. 72. The disk of a phyllodean pedicel in Palæotropus Josephinæ LOV.
Fig. 73. The terminal part of a sub-anal pedicel in the same.
Fig. 74. The top of a sub-anal pedicel in Brissus compressus LAMCK, seen from the under side.
Fig. 75. The same, in Brissus mediator n., seen from the under side.
Fig. 76. A ring, psellion, from a sub-anal pedicel in Lovenia elongata GRAY.
Fig. 77. The same, in Abatus Philippii LOV.
Fig. 78. Laminæ from the phyllodean disk in Maretia planulata LAMCK.
Fig. 79. A sub-anal pedicel of the same, mutilated.

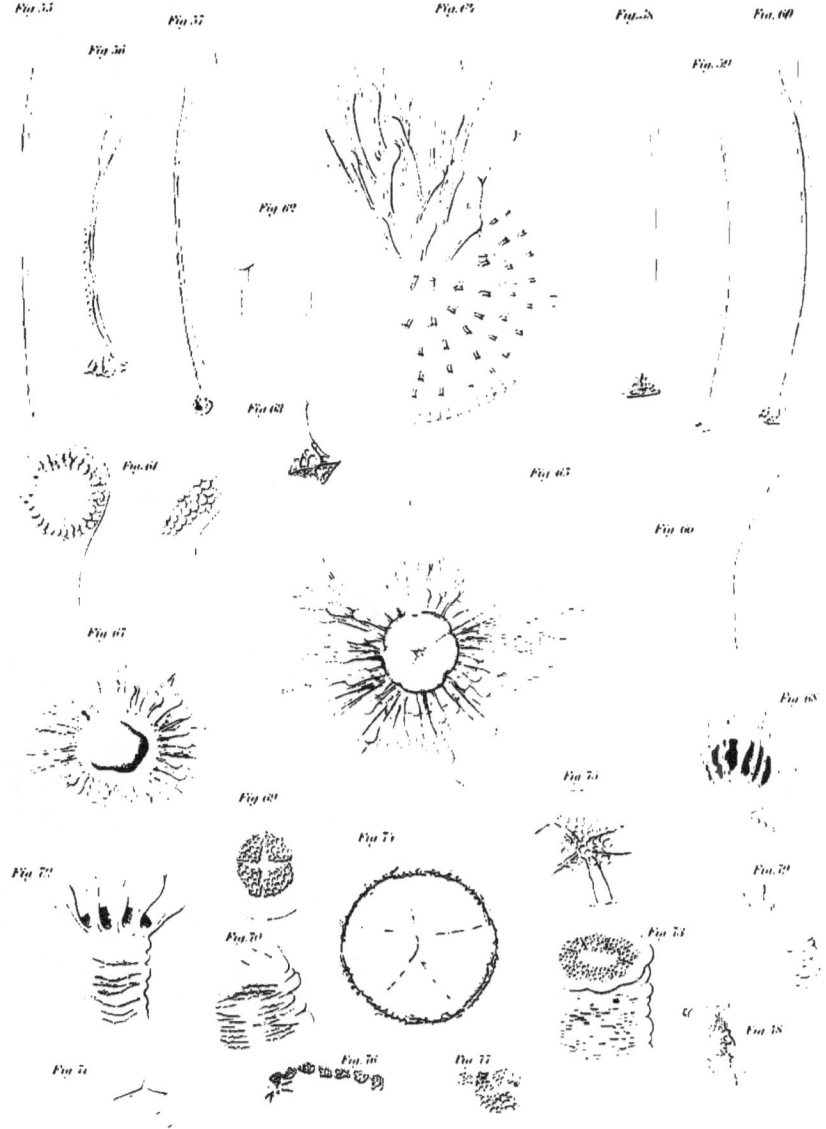

PLATE IX.

Plate IX.

Pedicels of Brissopsis lyrifera Forbes.

Fig. 80. The tip of a filament from a phyllodean pedicel, side view. p. 45.
Fig. 81. The same, end view, seen from above.
Fig. 82. Optical section of the same, highly magnified.
Fig. 83. Terminal part of a simple, ventral pedicel, p. 47.
Fig. 84. The same of another specimen.
Fig. 85. The top of a sub-anal pedicel, p. 48.
Fig. 86. The disk of a frontal pedicel, p. 54.
Fig. 87. Optical section of the margin of the same.
Fig. 88. Pigment-cells from the same.
Fig. 89. Optical section of an intra-lamellar part of the disk.
Fig. 90. Longitudinal section of the wall of the tube of a frontal pedicel. p. 55.

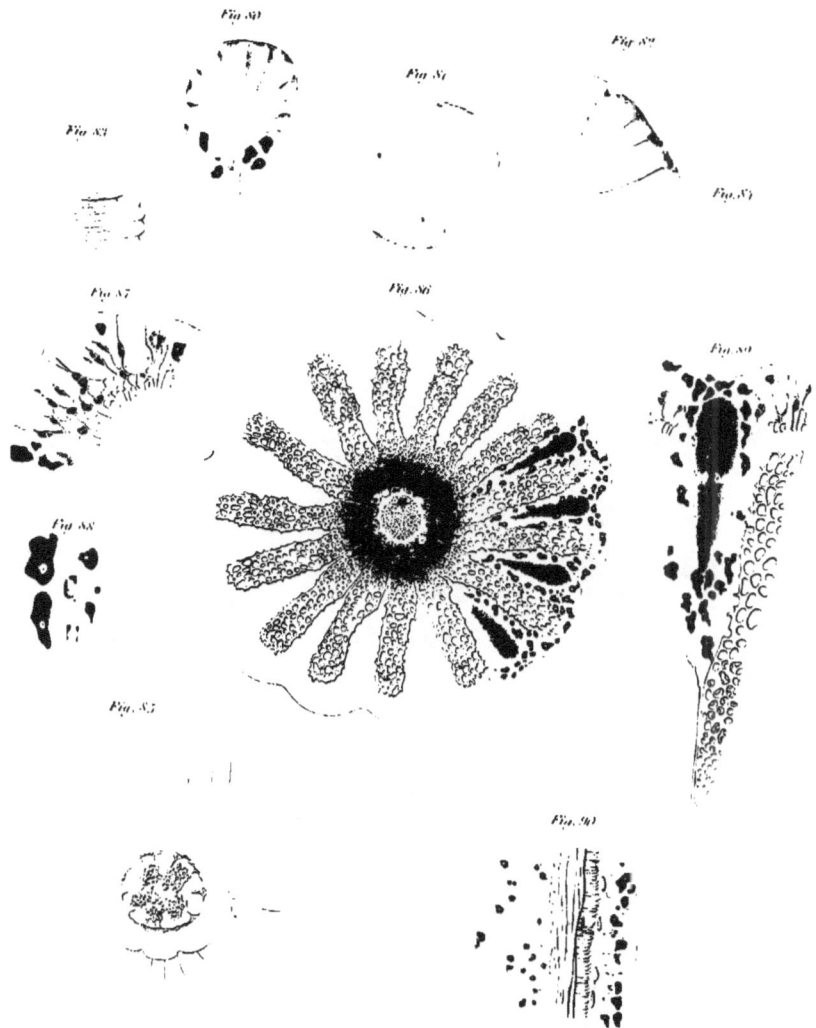

PLATE X.

Plate X.

Pedicels of Spatangidæ.

p. 52 56.

Fig. 91. The terminal part of a frontal pedicel in Abatus Philippii Lov.
Fig. 92. Half the disk of a frontal pedicel in Hemiaster expergitus Lov.
Fig. 93. The terminal part of a frontal pedicel in Agassizia scrobiculata Val.
Fig. 94. A quadrant of the disk of a frontal pedicel in Moira atropos Lamck.
Fig. 95. The basal part of one of its laminæ.
Fig. 96. A part of the disk of a frontal pedicel in Aceste bellidifera Wyv. Thoms.
Fig. 97. The basal part of one of its laminæ; side view.
Fig. 98. The same, seen from the under side.
Fig. 99. The basal part of a lamina from a frontal pedicel in Kleinia luzonica Gray, from the under side.
Fig. 100. A quadrant of the disk of a frontal pedicel in Schizaster fragilis Dub. & Kon.
Fig. 101. A part of the disk of a frontal pedicel in Schizaster japonicus Al. Ag.
Fig. 102. The basal part of one of its laminæ, from the under side.
Fig. 103. The same, from above.
Fig. 104. The tip of a simple frontal pedicel, in Maretia planulata Lamck.; side view.
Fig. 105. The same, in Metalia maculosa Gm.; side view.
Fig. 106. The top of a frontal pedicel in Metalia frontosa n.; seen from above.
Fig. 107. The same, from Lovenia elongata Gray; side view.
Fig. 108. The same; end view.
Fig. 109. The same, spicular framework, in Spatangus purpureus O. F. M.; side view.
Fig. 110. The tip of a simple, ventral pedicel, V, in Moira atropos Lamck.
Fig. 111. The same, in Schizaster japonicus Al. Ag.

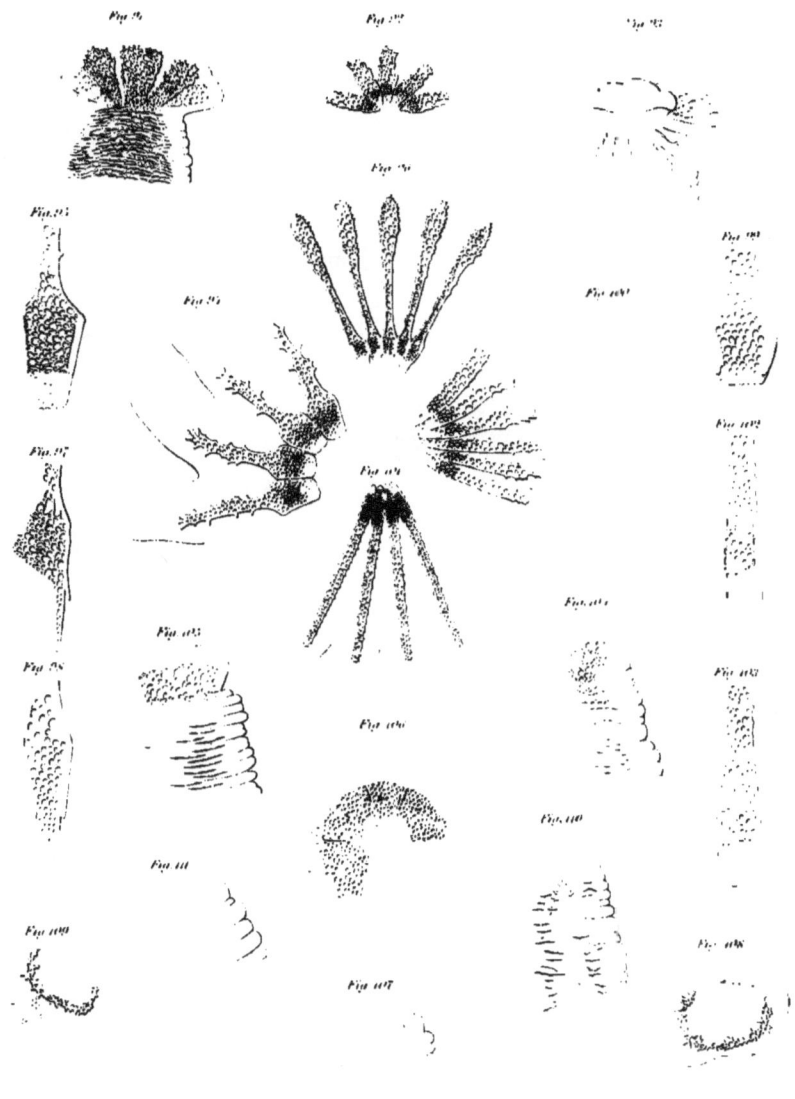

91 Abatus Philippii n. 92 Hem. esperettus n. 93 Agass scrobiculata VAL. 94 95 110 Moira atropos AMK 96 98 Aceste bellidifera
V. THOMS. 99 Kleinia luzonica GRAY. 100 Schiz fragilis D & K. 101 102 103 111 Schiz japonicus Al. A. 104 Maretia planulata LAMK
105 Metalia maculosa GM. 106 Met frontosa n. 107 108 Lov elongata GRAY 109 Spatangus purpureus O.F. M.

PLATE XI.

Plate XI.

Pedicels of Echinidæ, Echinoneidæ, Cassidulidæ and Spatangidæ.

P. 47, 49, 54.

Fig. 112. The disk of a pedicel in Toxopneustes droebachensis O. F. M., showing the laminæ and the converging muscular fibres; p. 49.
Fig. 113. The central circular space of the same, showing the angular depression and the plicatures of the surface.
Fig. 114. The same seen from the under side, showing the *psellion*.
Fig. 115. A part of the same more highly magnified.
Fig. 116. The disk of a pedicel in Echinoneus semilunaris Lamck., from above; p. 50.
Fig. 117. The same, from the under side, with the *psellion*.
Fig. 118. The terminal part of a pedicel in Rhynchopygus pacificus Al. Ag., p. 56.
Fig. 119. The same, in a different state.
Fig. 120. The disk of a frontal pedicel in Echinocardium cordatum Penn., with the enormously developed spicule; p. 56.
Fig. 121. A rod from one of the filaments of the same, somewhat shortened, with the basal circlet.
Fig. 122. Another form of the large spicule under the disk, in the same species.
Fig. 123. The same spicule, double.
Fig. 124. Another, spinous form of the large spicule.
Fig. 125. Another form of the same.
Fig. 126. Another smaller form of the same.
Fig. 127. The disk of one of the frontal pedicels in Echinocardium flavescens O. F. M.
Fig. 128. Two of its filaments with part of the ring, *psellion*.
Fig. 129. The rod from one of its filaments.
Fig. 130. Spicules from its ring.
Fig. 131. The terminal part of a frontal pedicel in Breynia Australasiæ Leach.

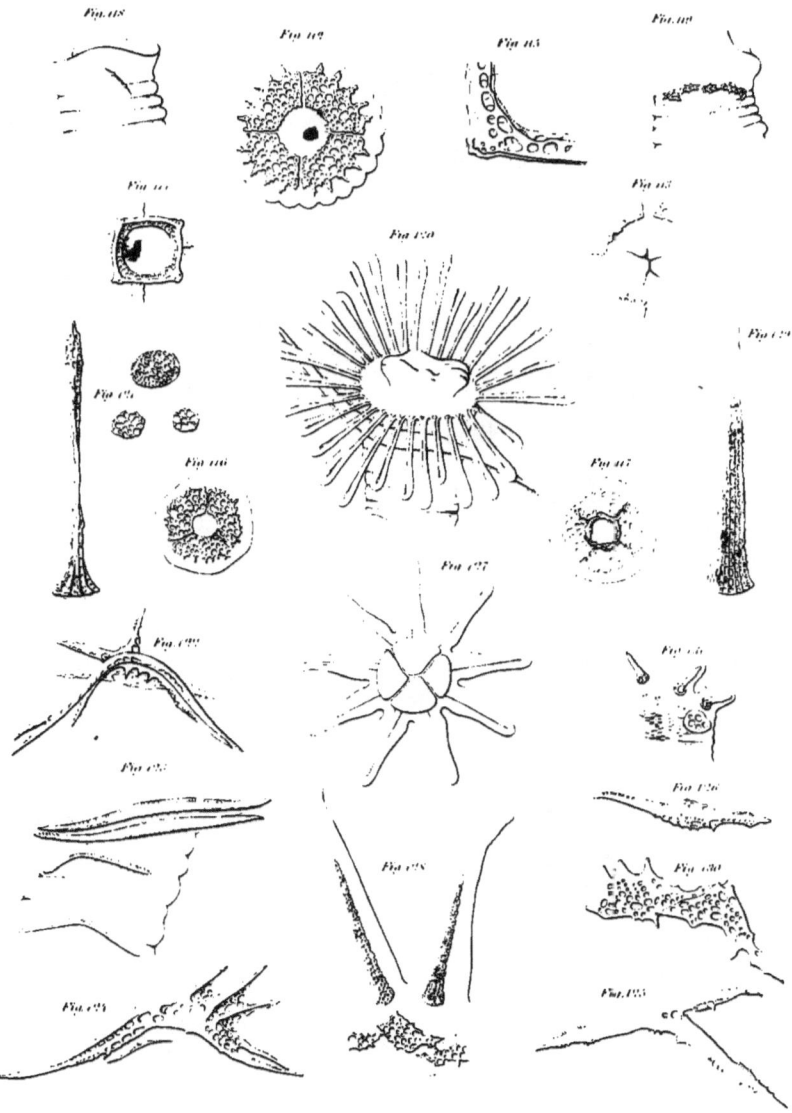

112–115. Tox. Drobachensis O.F.M. 116,117 Echinon semilunaris LAMK 118,119 Rhynchopygus pacificus AL. AG. 120–126 Echinocardium cordatum PENN. 127–130 Echinocardium flavescens O.F.M. 131 Breynia Australasiae LEACH.

PLATE XII.

Plate XII.

Peripodia of Neonomous Echinoids.
P. 56.

Echinoneidæ.
IV a 1; III a.
Fig. 132. Echinoneus semilunaris Lamck.

Cassidulidæ.
Phyll. IV a 1; Sub-an. V a, V b 22; Front. III a.
Fig. 133. Pygorhynchus pacificus Al. Ag.

Spatangidæ.
Phyll. IV a 1; Sub-an. V b, V a; Front. III a; Petal. II a.

Adeti.
Fig. 134. Holaster scaniensis Cotteau.
Fig. 135. Ananchites ovata Leske.
Fig. 136. Hemipneustes radiatus Gm.

Prymnadeti.
Fig. 137. Echinospatagus Ricordeanus Cotteau.
Fig. 138. Hemiaster Fourneli Cotteau.
Fig. 139. Palæostoma mirabile Gray.
Fig. 140. Schizaster japonicus Al. Ag.
Fig. 141. Agassizia scrobiculata Val.
Fig. 142. Faorina chinensis Gray.

Prymnodesmii.
Fig. 143. Brissopsis lyrifera Forb.
Fig. 144. Brissus Scillæ Lamck.
Fig. 145. Spatangus purpureus O. F. M.
Fig. 146. Lovenia elongata Gray.
Fig. 147. Maretia planulata Lamk.
Fig. 148. Echinocardium cordatum Penn.

Pourtalesindæ.
Fig. 149. Pourtalesia Jeffreysi Wyv. Th.

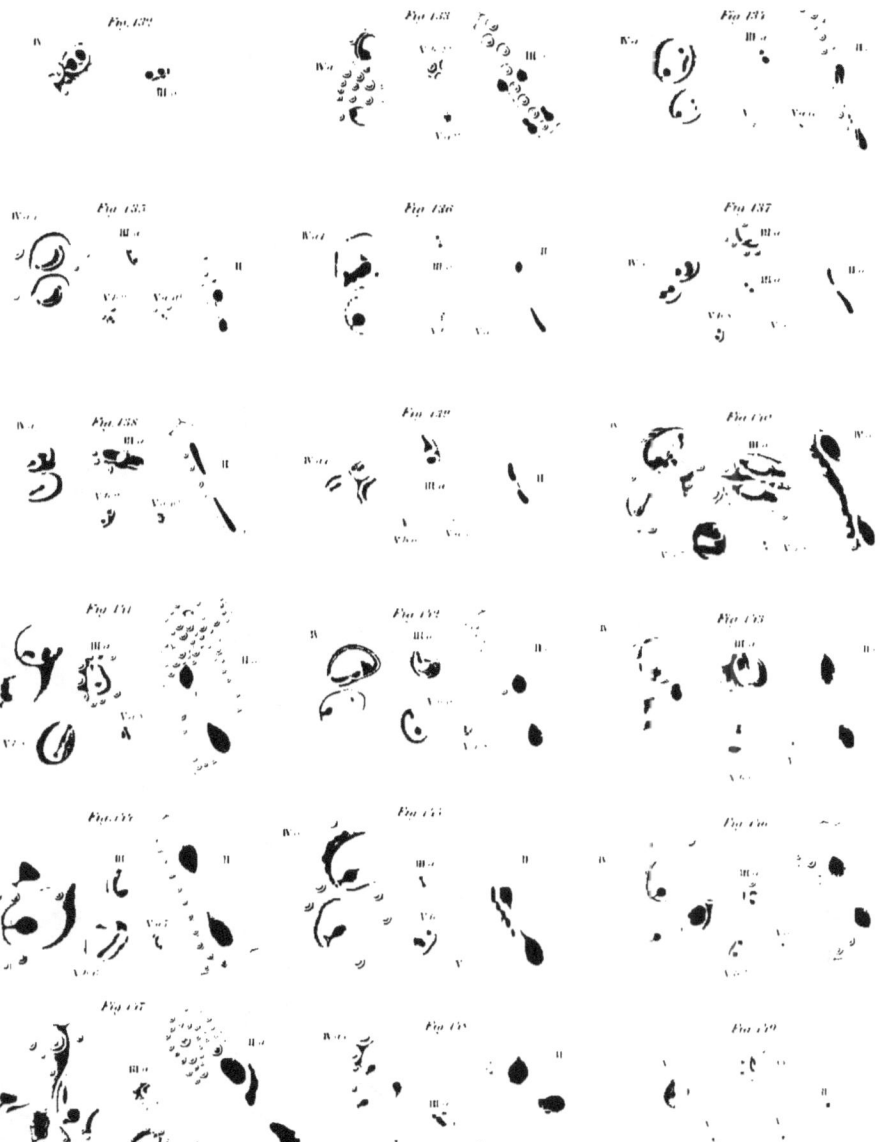

PLATE XIII.

Plate XIII.

Tiarechinus princeps Laube

P. II. 64.

Fig. 150. The specimen from the "K. K. Geologische Reichs-Anstalt", Vienna, dorsal view; magnified about nine times.
Fig. 151. The same, ventral view.
Fig. 152. The same, showing the plates.
Fig. 153. The same, side view.
Fig. 154. The same, showing the plates.
Fig. 155. The calyx of the same.
Fig. 156. One of the sexual? pores.
Fig. 157. Granulation of the interradia.
Fig. 158. The adoral part of an ambulacrum.
Fig. 159. The aboral part of the same.
Fig. 160. One of the large tubercles of the interradia.
Fig. 161. The specimen from the "K. K. Hof-Mineralien Cabinet" Vienna, ventral view.
Fig. 162. Another specimen, from the same collection, dorsal view.

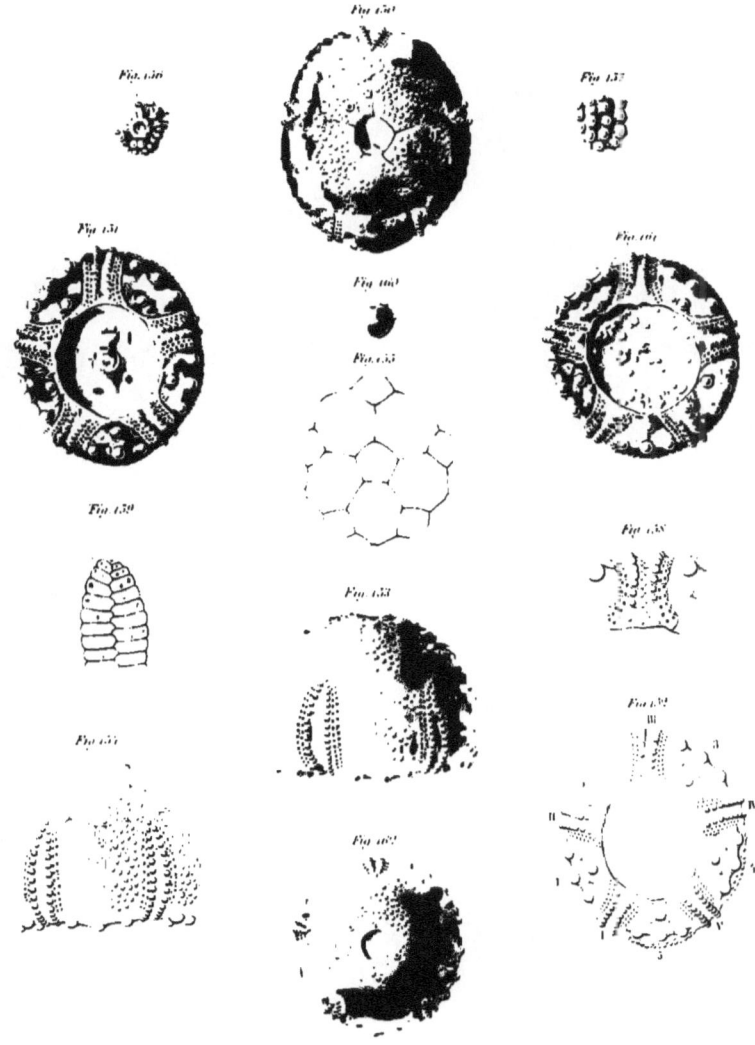

150 - 162 Tiarechinus princeps LAUBE.

PLATE XIV.

Plate XIV.

Abatus cavernosus Phil.

P. 20, 25, 46, 74.

Fig. 163. A young specimen, measuring 2,3 mm., taken out of one of the deepened petala by the late Professor Peters of Berlin. It is jejune, astomous, aproctic. Ventral view.
Fig. 164. The same, dorsal view.
Fig. 164, A. The calycinal region.
Fig. 165. The buccal membrane, entire, unpierced, the œsophageal end of the alimentary canal with its lumen appearing on its inside. To be compared with the woodcut p. 26, representing the same parts in a specimen a little more advanced, in which the oesophageal opening has pierced the buccal membrane centrally.
Fig. 166. The calycinal region from the inside, showing the blind excretory extremity of the intestine touching the closed membrane centrally.
Fig. 167. The peristomal region from the inside, showing the blind oesophagus resting against the buccal membrane.
Fig. 168. The blind excretory end of the intestine, suspended to the peritoneal lining.
Fig. 169. A spherid, optical section.
Fig. 170. A tubercle.
Fig. 171. A spine with the larval envelope.

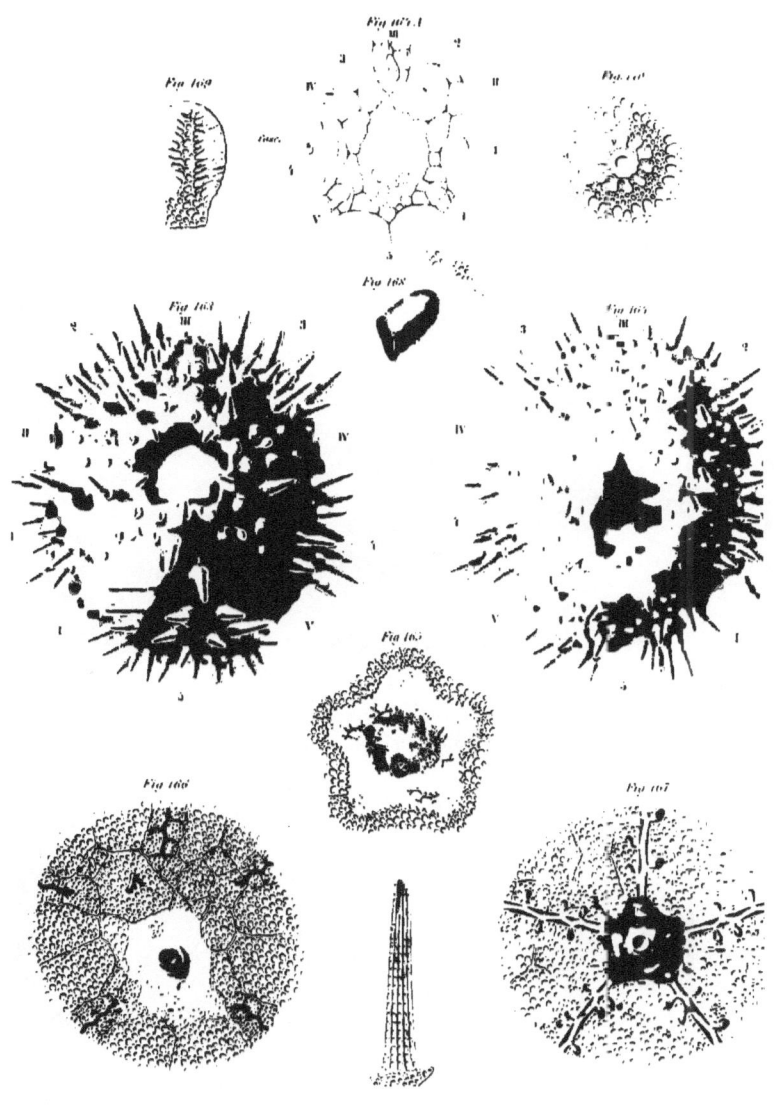

PLATE XV.

Plate XV.

Echinocardium flavescens O. F. M.

P. 26, 46.

Fig. 172. A young specimen, measuring 1,7 mm., denuded of its spines; ventral view. The oesophagus has already pierced the buccal membrane.
Fig. 173. The same; dorsal view. The periproct, just formed, high up on the back. The fasciolæ have begun to appear. In the frontal ambulacrum, III, a single pedicel, others being probably lost. The details of the calycinal system were obscured by some opaque substance contained in the intestine, and could not be made out properly.
Fig. 174. The peristomal region of a specimen measuring 3 mm.
Fig. 175. A part of the peristomal region of a specimen between fig. 173 and 174.
Fig. 176. The top of a phyllodean pedicel in the early state, fig. 172.
Fig. 177. Another with two rods beginning to form.
Fig. 178. The filaments with their rods a little more advanced.
Fig. 179. Another with the *psellion*.
Fig. 180. Another with the rudiments of three filaments.
Fig. 181. The disk of a phyllodean pedicel in a young specimen measuring 5,3 mm., with eight filaments in a circle and a ninth filament beginning an inner series.
Fig. 182. Spicules from its *psellion*.
Fig. 183. The peristomal part of an interradium from the inside, showing the transverse laminæ, p. 26.

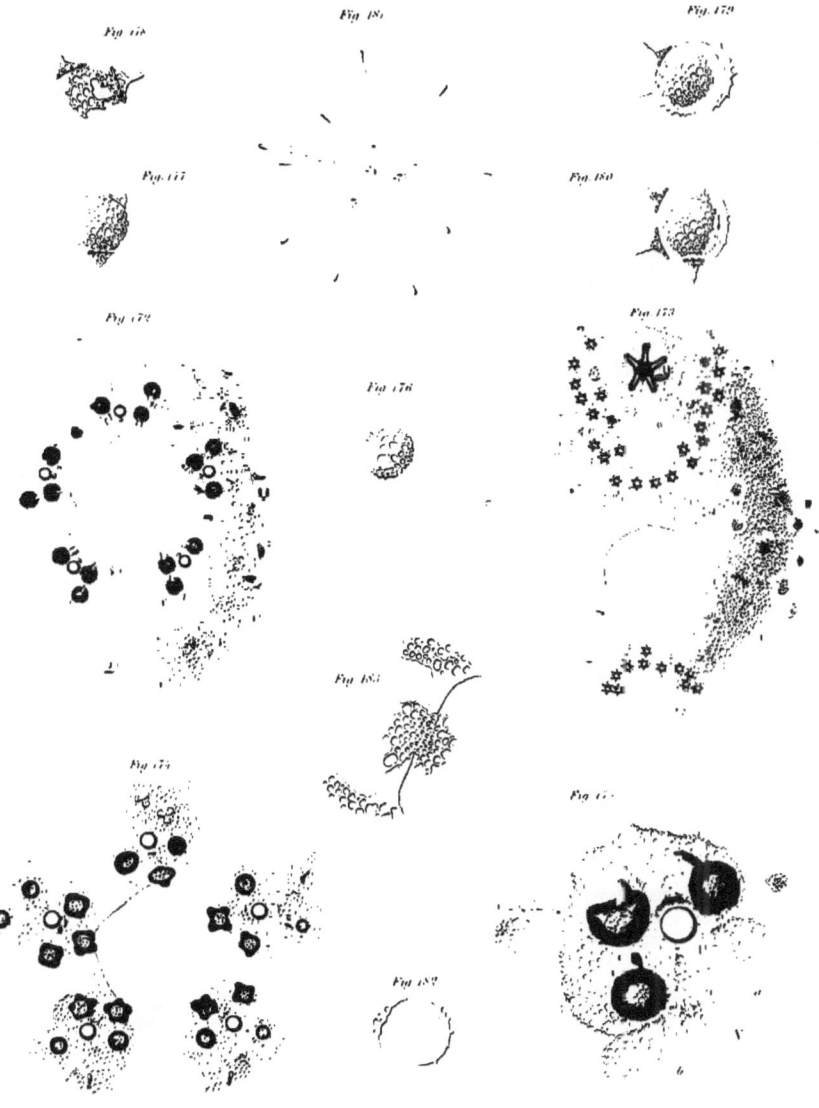

PLATE XVI.

Plate XVI.

Palæostoma mirabile Gray.

p. 27, 45, 53.

Fig. 184. A half-grown specimen, dorsal view.
Fig. 185. The same, ventral view.
Fig. 186. The same, side view.
Fig. 187. The peristomal region, with the pentangular stoma, the valves, the first spherids etc.
Fig. 188. The peristome, with the valves, from the inside.
Fig. 189. The valves, from the outside.
Fig. 190. The calyx with the two sexual pores.
Fig. 191. The excretory opening with its valves.
Fig. 192. A phyllodean pedicel.
Fig. 193. Another phyllodean pedicel, both showing what seems to be a central protuberance.
Fig. 194. The disk of a frontal pedicel, p. 53.
Fig. 195. Spicules from a pedicellar tube.
Fig. 196. A tubercle.

184—196. Palæostoma mirabile GRAY

PLATE XVII.

Plate XVII.

The Calycinal System of Spatangidæ.

p. 74

Fig. 197. The calyx of a specimen of Echinocardium flavescens O. F. M., measuring 3,5 : 3 mm
Fig. 198. The same, at 7 : 6 mm
Fig. 199. The same, at 8 : 6 mm.
Fig. 200. The same, at 9 : 7,5 mm.
Fig. 201. The same, at 9,5 : 8 mm.
Fig. 202. The same, at 10,5 : 9 mm.
Fig. 203. The same, at 10,5 : 9 mm.
Fig. 204. The same, at 12 : 10 mm.
Fig. 205. The same, at 14,5 : 12 mm.
Fig. 206. The same, at 30 : 26 mm.
Fig. 207. The same, at 36 : 32 mm.
Fig. 208. The calyx of Palæotropus Josephinæ Lov.

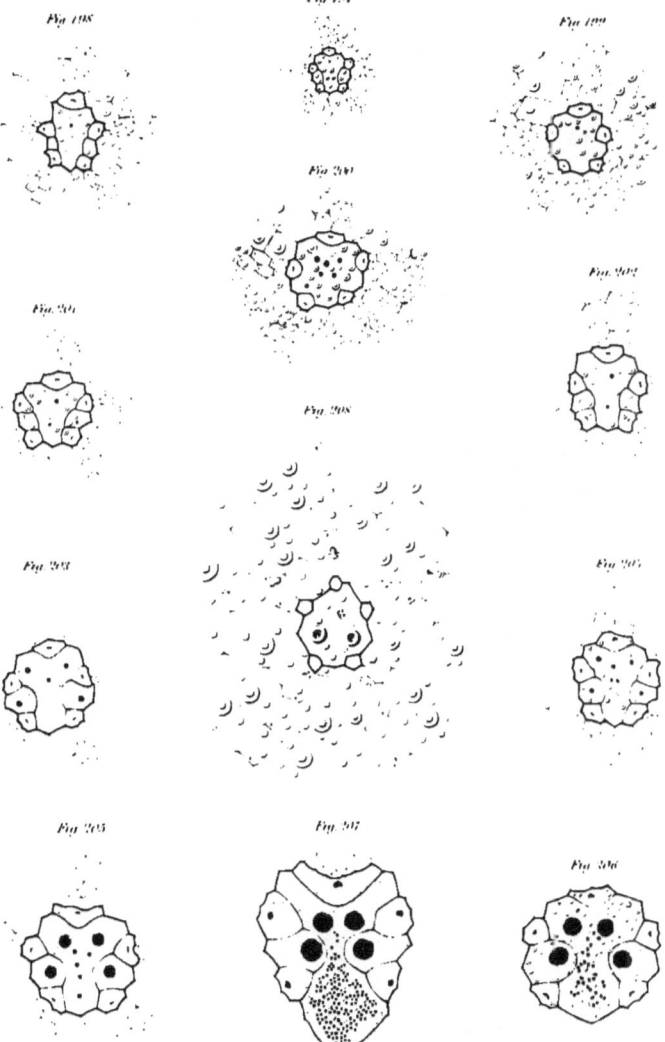

PLATE XVIII.

Plate XVIII.

The Calycinal System of Spatangidæ.

p. 74.

Fig. 209. The calyx of a specimen of Spatangus purpureus O. F. M., of 5 : 4 mm.
Fig. 210. The same, at 13,5 : 12 mm.
Fig. 211. The same, at 14 : 13 mm.
Fig. 212. The same, at 15 : 14 mm.
Fig. 213. The same, at 15 : 14 mm.
Fig. 214. The same, at 16 : 15 mm.
Fig. 215. The same, at 18 : 16 mm.
Fig. 216. The same, at 19 : 18 mm.
Fig. 217. The same, at 24 : 21 mm.
Fig. 218. The same, at 23 : 22 mm.
Fig. 219. The same, at 53 : 50 mm. A single madreporic pore, marked *, outside the calyx.
Fig. 220. The calyx of Abatus cavernosus Phil.
Fig. 221. The same of Hemiaster bufo Al. Brogn.
Fig. 222. The same of Hemiaster expergitus Lov.

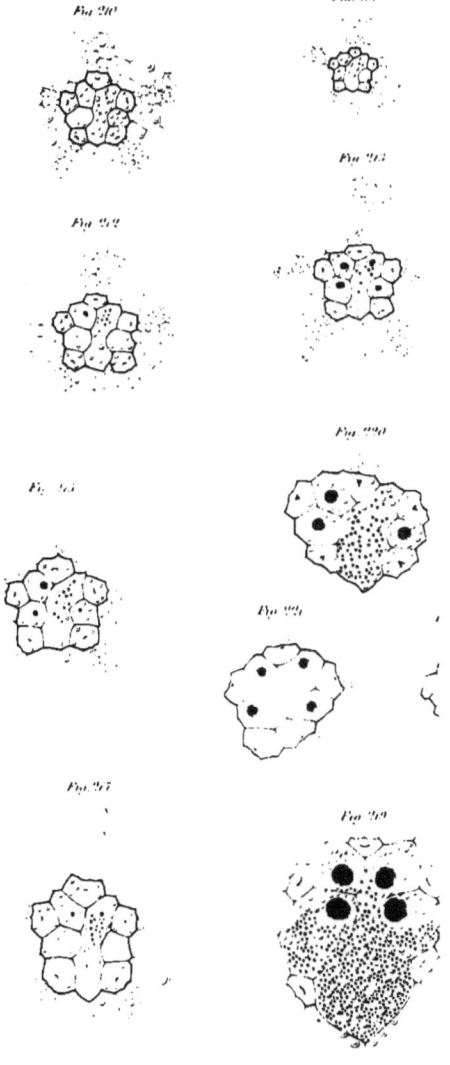

PLATE XIX.

PLATE XIX.

The Calycinal System of Brissopsis; young of Echinus.

P. 75.

Fig. 223. The calyx of a specimen of Brissopsis lyrifera Forb., of 9 : 7 mm.
Fig. 224. The same, at 11 : 9 mm.
Fig. 225. The same, at 15 : 12 mm.
Fig. 226. The same, at 15 : 13 mm.
Fig. 227. The same, at 16 : 13 mm.
Fig. 228. The same, at 38 : 35 mm., having a number of madreporic pores in the interradium 5.
Fig. 229. The same, at 42 : 38; the costal 2 without sexual pore.
Fig. 230. The same, at 44 : 40; the madreporite spreading outside the sexual pore in the costal 1.
Fig. 231. The same in a nearly full-grown specimen, with a larger number of madreporic pores in the interradium 5. and a few in the ambulacrum 1.
Fig. 232. Echinus sp. young, 0.6 mm., astomous, aproctic, jejune, same specimen as that described in Etudes p. 27, pl. XVII. fig. 149-152; dorsal view ; p. 25.
Fig. 233. The same, ventral view.

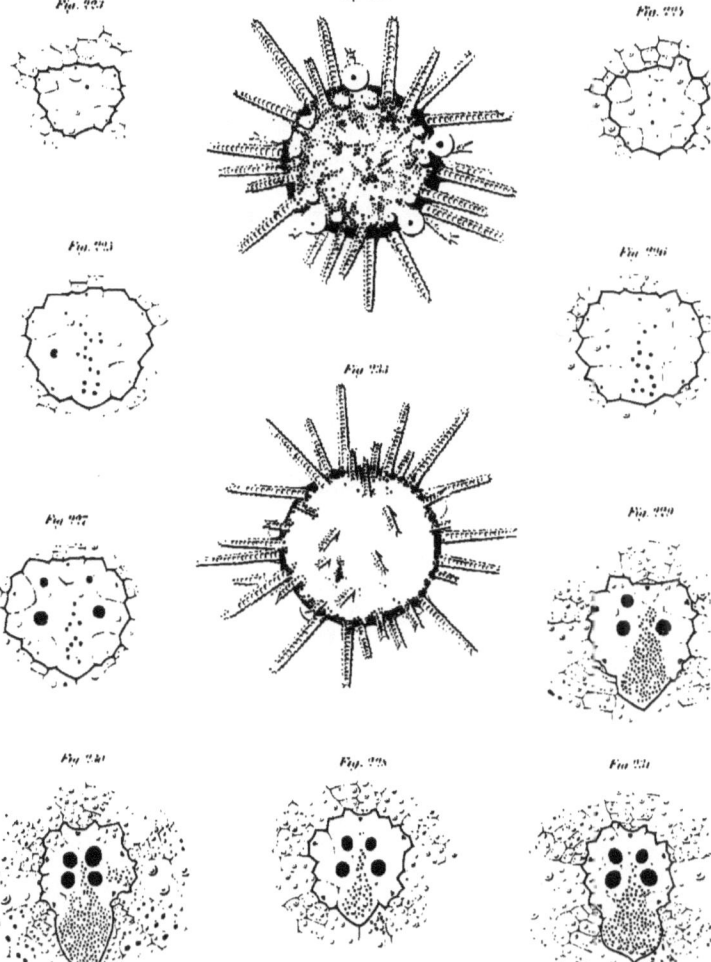

PLATE XX.

Plate XX.

Aceste bellidifera Wyv. Thoms. **Schizaster canaliferus** Lamck.

P. 188.

Fig. 234. The skeleton of Aceste bellidifera Wyv. Thoms., laid out
Fig. 235. The buccal membrane of the same.
Fig. 236. The anal membrane of the same.
Fig. 237. The calycinal system of the same.
Fig. 238. The calycinal system of Schizaster canaliferus Lamck.

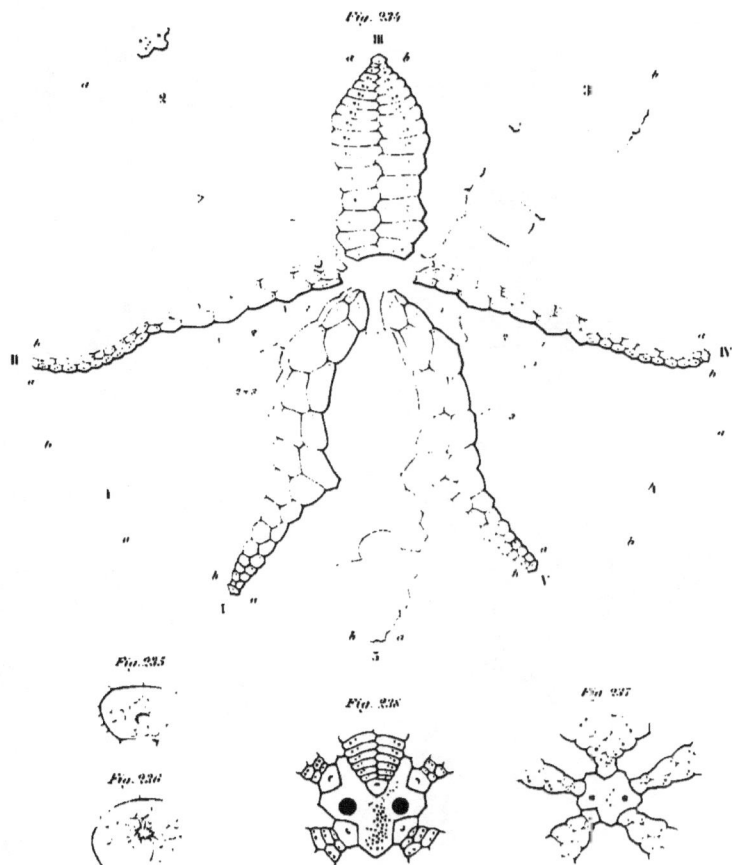

PLATE XXI.

Plate XXI.

Urechinus Naresianus Al. Ag.

P. 90.

Fig. 239. The skeleton of Urechinus Naresianus Al. Ag., laid out.
Fig. 240. The buccal membrane of the same.
Fig. 241. The anal membrane of the same.
Fig. 242. The calycinal system of the same.

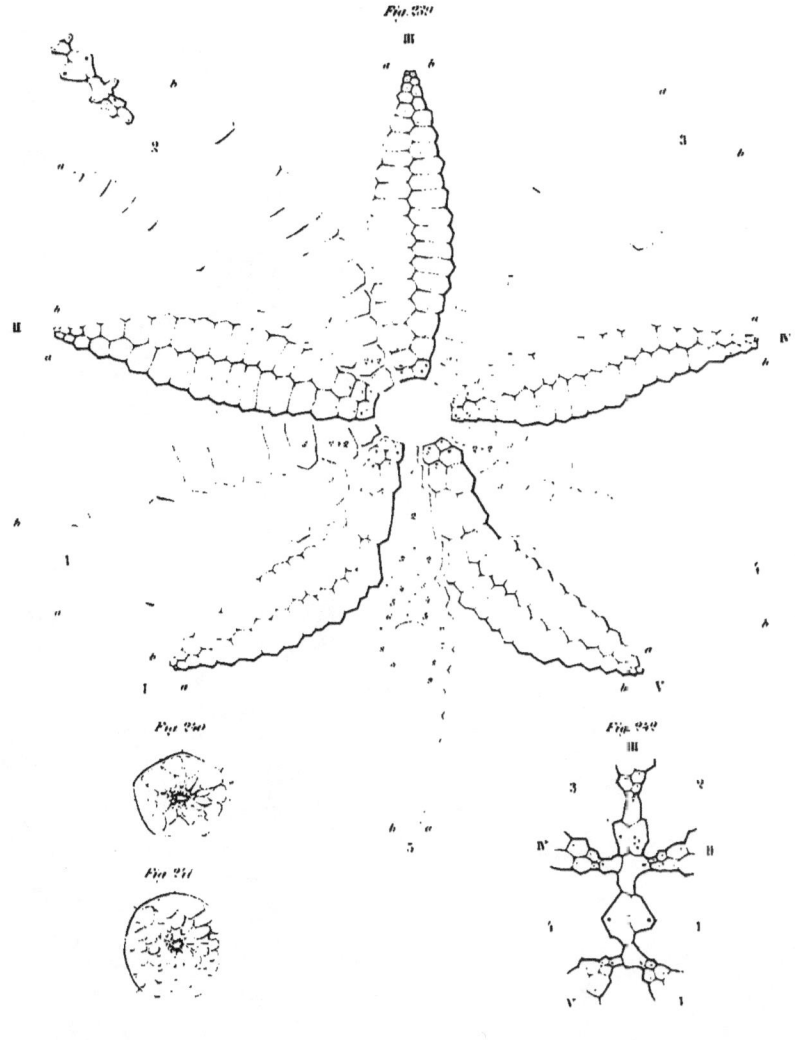

www.ingramcontent.com/pod-product-compliance
Lightning Source LLC
Chambersburg PA
CBHW032155160426
43197CB00008B/918